Therapy Talk

Therapy Talk

Conversation Analysis in Practice

Pamela E. Fitzgerald
School of Psychological Sciences, University of Manchester, UK

First published 2013 by
PALGRAVE MACMILLAN

Palgrave Macmillan in the UK is an imprint of Macmillan Publishers Limited, registered in England, company number 785998, of Houndmills, Basingstoke, Hampshire RG21 6XS.

Palgrave Macmillan in the US is a division of St Martin's Press LLC, 175 Fifth Avenue, New York, NY 10010.

Palgrave Macmillan is the global academic imprint of the above companies and has companies and representatives throughout the world.

Palgrave® and Macmillan® are registered trademarks in the United States, the United Kingdom, Europe and other countries.

ISBN: 978–1–137–32951–6   hardback
ISBN: 978–1–137–32952–3   paperback

This book is printed on paper suitable for recycling and made from fully managed and sustained forest sources. Logging, pulping and manufacturing processes are expected to conform to the environmental regulations of the country of origin.

A catalogue record for this book is available from the British Library.

A catalog record for this book is available from the Library of Congress.

To the memory of a great conversationalist and niece
Michelle with love

Contents

Foreword

There is a fair bit of argument about whether psychotherapies work and which of them do. One common technology of assessing differential effectiveness of psychotherapies uses randomized control trials. Such methodology, however, tests the effectiveness of therapeutic *practices* linked to particular theories (for example, Psychoanalysis) not the pertinence and validity of those theories themselves – practices are always richer than theories and linked theories and practices diverge, both generically and in individual therapists' ways of working. Moreover, the before–after technology treats therapeutic encounters as black boxes and does not throw light on how exactly therapies achieve their effects. This is why researchers on psychotherapy developed methods to investigate psychotherapy process and this is where conversation analysis (CA) comes to its own and helps. It examines the psychotherapy practice in minute detail, using methods and findings developed in studies of both 'everyday conversations' and the so-called 'institutional talk'. There is now a growing body of research on psychotherapy which uses conversation analysis and Dr Fitzgerald's is an excellent new contribution to the field. The particular strength of conversation analysis is in analysis and objective description of how talk is managed locally. Not surprisingly CA studies of psychotherapy already threw light on how sequences of talk in psychotherapy are locally managed – thanks to the CA investigations much is now known about how, for example, therapists use individual formulations and disclosures and present their interpretations. Clinical psychologists may use nonverbal techniques beyond common sense and specifically designed for their interventions but the common agreement is that psychotherapists and their clients together use just the devices available in everyday conversations, but use them *strategically* and *systematically* to create what looks like a preferred kind of psychotherapeutic encounter. (Discursive devices documented in CA studies are pigments that can be used to create very varied canvasses!) What this means is that the complete research requires understanding of psychotherapy not just as a mode of conversation but also as something that reflects therapists' strategic aims, training, academic paradigms and theories. For this reason the increasing number of conversation analytic investigations is carried out by teams that include practitioners of the therapy in the spotlight. Their inclusion allows closer understanding of therapeutic activities done through talk, which typically span stretches of talk wider than just adjacent sequences. Dr Fitzgerald is both a skilled applied conversation analyst and psychotherapist and her book reflects both strengths. Her training was in Rogerian therapy and cognitive-behavioural therapy with a specialty in solution-focused counselling. She examines 'her own kind of therapy' and does this not through introspection of her memories but through conversation analysis – she examines in minute detail transcripts of complete courses of actual therapies. She does not of course examine every aspect of her psychotherapeutic practice but focuses on three things: (1) how the therapist does formulations and what the client does with these; (2) how the therapist listens to the client *actively* and *expressively* and through such listening subtly guides the clients' thinking/talking through their problems; and (3) how the different devices – formulations, active listening and questions – work together to create extended patterns that look like CBT or like a genus of therapy Carl Rogers advocated. My impression is that her practice works like a Vygotskian zone of proximal development – she does not tell the client how to deal with their problems but empowers and equip them to deal with the problems of living through subtle guidance – her clients work towards dealing with the problems in sessions supported and guided by expressive listening, questions and formulations. (Other things of course happen or yet others notably do not.)

Intriguingly, Dr Fitzgerald's examination of her practice also documents the small ways in which it diverges and has to diverge from therapeutic paradigms she learned. This points to the second important use of conversation analysis indicated by the book. Not only can it document how psychotherapy works and indicate how it achieves psychological change; it can be, in addition, a valuable tool that brings psychotherapists closer to what they actually do and helps them to reflect on their practices. Conversation analysis helps Dr Fitzgerald to show that there are necessary limits to being 'non-directive' and this seems to be especially so in short-term therapy. As a reflection supporting tool, conversation analysis should help other therapists to deepen insight into their practices.

Professor Ivan Leudar

Acknowledgements

I would first and foremost like to express a sincere thank you to my advisor Professor Ivan Leudar, without whom this book could never have been completed. Second, I am very grateful for the help and support provided by my colleagues at the Employee Assistance Programmes firm INSITE-Interventions in Frankfurt: Dr. Hansjörg Becker, Dr. Matthias Conradt and the extremely competent EAP researcher, Jessica Keuthen. I am also very appreciative of the support I received from Dr. Stefan Leidig of EMU-Systeme in Berlin.

I would also like to thank all of my participants for allowing me to use our sessions for the purpose of this book. I am also grateful to my colleagues, Gerry Duffy, Pat Gregory, Deirdre Gallagher, Fiona Quigley and Gwen Clarke who gave helpful practical advice and inspiration. Special thanks go to Dr. Emily O'Brien for helping with the proofreading of this book. I would also like to thank the famous artist from Georgia, Mr Zurab Kereselidze for his inspiring ideas. I am also very grateful to my colleagues at the Donnybrook Centre in Dublin.

I would also like to give special thanks to all members of my family, especially my stepmother Maureen, my sisters Fiona and Linda, and my brothers David and Brian who continue to provide me with support and encouragement in all of my endeavours. I would especially like to thank my stepsons Thomas, Martin and Philip Bachert, my niece Sally McLoughlin and my nephews Robert Fitzgerald and James Mouatt for all their interest, encouragement and help.

My thoughts go to my dear friend Renate Bauer from Lindach in Bavaria, Germany during this time.

Finally, profound and heartfelt thanks go to my loving husband, Siegfried Bachert, whose support, patience, and encouragement provided me with the strength to bring this book to fruition.

Transcription Conventions

The transcription symbols used in this book are an attempt to capture something of the sound of the talk as it was originally spoken. There is some variety among contributors, both in the fine-grainedness of their transcription, and in the notation symbols they use. All symbols, however, are based on those developed by Gail Jefferson (see Atkinson and Heritage, 1984: ix–xvi).

(.)	The shortest hearable pause, less than about 0.2 of a second
(..)(...)	Approximately timed pauses: half a second and one second respectively
(0.3)(2 secs)	Examples of exactly timed pauses
.hh, hh	Speaker's in-breath and out-breath respectively
Wo(h)rd	(h) denotes 'laughter' within words
((shrugs shoulders))	A description enclosed in double brackets indicates a non-speech sound.
((3.0))	A number enclosed in brackets indicates the length of the sound of a continuer
cu-	A dash denotes a sharp cut-off of a prior word or sound
::	Colons show that the speaker has stretched the preceding letter or sound. The more colons the greater the extent of the stretching
(word)	Material within brackets represents the transcriber's guess at an unclear part of the tape
(syll syll)	Unclear speech or noise to which no approximation to number of syllables
(.)	Unclear speech or noise to which no approximation is made
run= = on	'Equals' signs link material that runs on

↑word	Arrows indicate the onset of a rising or falling intonational shift
↓word	
?	Indicates a rising tone
.	Indicates a nature ending
,	Indicates a comma-like pause
<u>under</u>	underlining indicates emphasis
CAPITALS	Capital letters indicate speech noticeably louder than that surrounding it
°soft°	Degree signs indicate speech spoken noticeably more quietly than the surrounding talk.
°°soft°°	Double degree signs indicate greater softness
>fast< and <slow>	'Greater than' and 'less than' signs indicate that the talk they encompass was produced noticeably quicker or slower than the surrounding talk
Over[lap	Square brackets between adjacent lines of concurrent speech denote the start of overlapping talk
[overlap	
→	Side arrow indicates point of special interest in the extract addressed in the text
[...]	Indicates that material has been left out of the extract
[high pitch]	Material in square brackets indicates transcriber's commentary

1
Introduction

Background to therapy talk

This book, like many others before it, focuses on the business of psycho-therapy and counselling which are known nowadays, in professional as well as lay circles, as 'the talking cure'. The invention of these practices is greatly associated with Breuer's work in the late nineteenth century with a patient of his, known as Anna O, who coined the phrase. Anna was diagnosed with hysteria and suffered many physical symptoms such as paralysis, aphasia, neuralgia and amnesia. In her case study she described how she experienced relief from her symptoms, distresses and concerns by verbalizing them and coming to understand their origins (see Freud and Breuer's *Studies on Hysteria*, 1991 [1895]). Since the time of Breuer, Freud and Anna O, several modifications have taken place within the field of psychotherapy. The past century has witnessed the evolvement of over four hundred different theories, clinical models and techniques, which encompass the field of psychotherapy today (Orlinsky and Howard, 1995; Norcross and Goldfried, 2005; Roth and Fonagy, 2005). These developments also include variants on the concepts, theories and techniques of the major psychotherapeutic approaches such as psychoa-nalysis, the humanistic therapies and cognitive-behavioural therapies. In fact, there seems to be so much diversity and so many subdivisions within each of the major psychotherapeutic systems that many schools have created new terminologies to highlight their differences (Bongar and Beutler, 1995). For example, Fromm-Reichmann abandoned the term libido in the 1930s in favour of the notion of self as a system comprising 'the good me', 'the bad me' and 'the not me' (Norcross and Goldfried, 2005). Kleinian therapists tend to think in terms of conflicts between the self and internalized objects rather than the id, ego and superego (ibid.). Roger's 'actualizing tendency' has been developed to include the term 'social mediation' which cushions the 'actualizing tendency' as it introduces a restraining force which helps the person maintain sufficient social contexts (Mearns and Thorne, 2007). Despite the growth in the number of new theories, approaches and terms, the idea of psychotherapy as 'the talking cure' has arguably changed much less; listening, reflecting back and questioning techniques remain, for the most part, the same and we are still in the dark about what exactly brings about healing. A fundamental question addressed in this book is: can talk be so powerful that it heals or at least changes a person? In the case of Anna O it was something in the way she talked about her difficulties and something in the way the therapist listened which moved her towards some inner healing process.

Nowadays, at least in the western world, the idea of 'the talking cure' is fairly embedded in medicine, psychology, education and the working world as a helpful service. Cushman (1995) argues that psychotherapy today provides a service which reflects the needs of our present-day society, and that throughout history the conclusions drawn concerning mental health requirements are a reflection of society's structure and the needs of the time. Whether those needs are real needs or fashionable trends is arguable. In any case, the multiplicity of psychotherapeutic models available today which offer a range of ways a therapist can talk to his or her client or patient reflects something of the mental health needs of today's individuals. The plethora of therapies on offer indicates that no one therapy can claim to have the 'clavis' to the absolute truth concerning the nature of human functioning. What we can say, however, is that all psychotherapeutic knowledge deals with knowledge of psychosocial change (Rogers, 1951, 1995; Miller and Rollnick, 2002; De Shazer, 1994; Streeck, 2008).

In today's working world, there is a growing trend for companies to provide psychological support to employees and their families. This support is largely offered through the services of an external Employee Assistant Programme (EAP). This programme is a managed care system, providing a service designed to help steer employees in the direction of psychological health and well-being, and is discussed in some detail in Chapter 8. It is an acceptable fact today that stress levels are intensifying, burnout is becoming a household term and disorders such as depression and anxiety are on the increase (WHO, 2007). Essentially, EAP providers facilitate clients by offering them psychotherapy and counselling for any distressing psychological issues that may be affecting their ability to perform at work. The goal is to help clients to take control of their own psychological health by providing them with short-term therapy lasting anywhere between four and eight sessions. In order to work in this field EAP therapists and counsellors need to be schooled in therapeutic orientations. The EAP therapist tends to combine the following models of therapy deemed useful for time-limited approaches. Firstly, the humanistic 'client-centred' or 'Rogerian' model which, focuses on the client's capacity for growth, choice and creativity, is paramount to this time-limited model. Secondly, the cognitive and/or cognitive-behavioural therapy (CBT) model developed by Aaron Beck, which focuses on maladaptive thinking, assumptions and core beliefs about self, others and the world, can be used to help clients learn to cope with psychological stress and disorders. Thirdly, the solution-focused approach developed by Steve De Shazer and Insoo Berg, which focuses on the client's inherent strengths, skills and resources, is a necessary prerequisite for any therapist hoping to provide therapy or counselling to EAP clients. All of these therapies stress the importance of the therapeutic alliance.

Furthermore, in recent times, reflective practices, practitioner based research, and continuing professional development programmes (CPD) have become important aspects of professional activity and training within a variety of settings ranging from psychotherapy, nursing and medicine to developmental trainings in the business world. Whilst different professional concerns have diverse roots, it seems that many combine in schemes which promote practice centred professional development. This book, which focuses mainly on psychotherapy, will help mental health practitioners, such as psychotherapists, counsellors, supervisors, doctors, nurses and so on, as well as human resource personnel and managers, to examine their work with the people who seek their services. Such specialists, who work mainly with patients, clients and employees who experience mental health difficulties can learn to appreciate and reflect on talk-in-interaction. The chapters in this book are concerned with examining actual lived practices as opposed to second order accounts of experiences.

The data and subsequent analyses in this book come from a single EAP therapist who came to understand and enhance her practice by using the tools of Conversation Analysis (henceforth CA) to examine the talk occurring between the therapist and the client. The focus is on how this practice is undertaken and examines how the therapist utilizes therapeutic interventions to generate understandings and insights to move the client in the direction of change. It would, however, be beyond the scope of this book to examine in detail all of the interactions occurring so the focus will remain on three basic therapist tools: listening, demonstrating understanding and encouraging long sequences of talk (Chapters 5, 6 and 7). Some extremely insightful processes were gleaned from a microscopic investigation of the data. In addition, I consider some issues which may shape the interactional processes and course of action occurring between therapists and their clients in Chapter 2 and I look at the previous literature done on CA and psychotherapy in Chapter 3. Chapter 4 then considers some other methods used to investigate the practice of psychotherapy and particularly how EAP therapy is at present being evaluated. At the end of each of the chapters I have included a therapists'/practitioners' corner. Here readers can partake in a guided tour through the devices and tools used by CA analysts when they marry their methods with those used by 'talking cure' specialists. There is a twist in the penultimate chapter when the focus turns to the EAP system and to the managers who adopt specific conversational approaches in an attempt to help employees by encouraging them to use the EAP service. A CA analysis of role-plays adopted in training programmes for managers yielded some very interesting findings and the practitioners' corner at the end of the chapter is designed with managers in mind.

Talk and psychotherapy

Talk is at the nucleus of psychotherapeutic practice. How a psychotherapist talks to a client or patient depends on the theory which influences that practice and the therapist's belief that their theory will work and they will bring about change. Most research to date on CA and psychotherapy has found that the same interactional practices involved in psychotherapy can be found in any social interaction (Peräkylä et al., 2008; Peräkylä, 2013). The art of listening, asking questions, providing comments, making interpretations and so on, are fundamental skills of verbal interaction which are necessary in all social worlds but what makes them unique in different schools is how and why they are used in particular ways. Psychodynamic therapy holds that if you use talk to engage with a client in a particular way, so that unconscious conflicts are made conscious, psychological changes will occur for that client. Cognitive-behavioural therapists (CBT) use talk to tackle a client's irrational thoughts and erroneous beliefs to bring about the same effect. CBT therapists also emphasize the importance of the therapeutic relationship. Rogerian therapy considers this relationship to be the essence of the change process (Rogers, 1957, 1995). The person-centred therapist adopts a non-directive approach and uses talk to convey the three core conditions of this therapy- empathy, congruence and unconditional positive regard so that the client can develop a sense of self which is congruent with experience and restore the 'organismic' valuing process[1] (Rogers, 1959). In solution-focused therapy, the therapist also adopts the three core conditions of Rogerian therapy but in addition, uses talk to help the client identify solutions that will help remove the barriers which block a client from achieving the life that they would like. Instead of going over past events and focusing on problems, the talk is future focused without today's problems (Hubble et al., 1999; De Shazer, 1994). While all talk therapies may have the same general goal in mind – to restore the psychological well-being of the client – the moves the therapist makes to achieve their objectives during the course of therapy depend on the therapist's conceptual model of psychotherapy (Norcross and Prochaska, 1983). An empirical investigation using CA can help ascertain if this is really the case. As the therapeutic relationship is a salient and determining factor in bringing about change, I suggest that this relationship can be investigated using CA because the nature of any relationship will be played out in the talk taking place between the participants.

The idea of change

In short-term work a therapist can hope that after a number of sessions a client will notice that they begin to change, hopefully for the better and that they now cope better with their environment. Such an assumption suggests that a therapist not only has the power to influence change within the sessions but also outside. Dreier (2008) followed up clients after therapy and found that, not surprisingly, there were many other influences in client's lives, apart from the one-hour weekly sessions, which influenced them to change. If therapists hope that a client changes mainly as a result of insights and understandings gained in the sessions then researchers may require a method of assessing change which would explain how people change within and between sessions. As change is a process which is accomplished over time, it is difficult to evaluate if or how these re-evaluations have brought about change in the client's life in general, as we do not know how people change after therapy ends (Prochaska, 1999; Dreier, 2008).

Despite these gaps which exist a trained therapist maintains certain assumptions. In the therapy examined here, it is generally assumed that when the client's level of consciousness has increased with respect to the problem they can then learn to assess how they think about themselves and the problem, express their experiences and feelings about the problem and the solution, and assess how the problem and the solution affects them in their social environment. It is also assumed, that in the sessions these understandings and insights are co-constructed by both parties in sequences of talk which hang together but are guided by the therapist's approach and theoretical orientation. By using CA to investigate the sequential order one can examine if the therapist is doing what he or she says they are doing (Peräkylä and Vehviläinen, 2003; Peräkyä et al., 2008). However, a therapist does not need to investigate every move made in order to evaluate his or her practice. I am suggesting that a focus on even the smallest of interventions will tell vast tales about how therapy is being conducted. In doing therapy a therapist invites a client to tell his or her story and the therapist is the co-constructivist who helps clients to change that story (Spence, 1984; Meichenbaum, 1995; Maione and Chenail, 1999). The central tenets of all of the therapies in this practice, and stipulated in training manuals, require that the therapist is able to adopt an empathic reflective listening style. This requires that the therapist will create a non-judgemental set of conditions in order to help clients tell their story at their own pace. To do this the therapist needs certain techniques to help the client relate to what happened or is happening in their lives. By investigating basic therapeutic skills, such as listening techniques and empathic interventions during the course of therapy one can quickly determine how this therapist enacts change in the client's story because the therapeutic relationship is developed by managing the talk. In this book the methods of CA are employed to do these investigations.

The empirical evidence

As already mentioned the investigation deals with the fine details of talk and the focus is on some specific actions which in CA's terms are called continuers, formulations and extended sequences of turns. Continuers are the *mms* and *ahs* and *uh huhs* and *yeahs* which a therapist might use to listen. Formulations are typical reflecting back techniques used in therapy when the therapist attempts to clarify what she assumes the client has just said. Sequences are longish snippets of extended talk where the client has the floor and the therapist listens, nudges, steers or even directs the client to keep talking. Using CA, this work seeks to explicate how these actions are performed by the therapist and how the client responds to them: what kind of structures are involved, what way the therapist aligns or misaligns when producing the actions and what one can determine about the therapist's focus and theoretical orientation by looking at the placement of these actions. Chapter 5 focuses on the therapist who uses continuers to support and pace the client as they tell their story. In Chapter 6 the focus is on the therapist who creates formulations which serve as 'first pair parts' and which urge the client to accept or reject them, thus creating 'second pair parts'. These two parts, therapists' comments and clients' responses form some of the basic sequential structures in the dialogue between the therapist and the client in this therapy. However, a sequence can be more than just two pair-parts (Frankel, 1984; ten Have, 1999). In this therapy the two pair-parts or what CA terms the 'adjacency pair' is the base structure from which a range of both brief and lengthy sequences can be built (Schegloff, 1968). In Chapter 7 the focus is on how formulations, continuers and questions come together to create extended sequences of talk.

In keeping with the CA paradigm, I examine how the actions of the therapist are examined in relation to the actions of the client and 'any action of the therapist – be it a question, a statement or something else – expresses an understanding of the patient's experience, and an understanding of how that experience can and possibly should be related to' (Peräkylä et al., 2008, 2013). The ideas presented should help practitioners to move their focus from therapeutic techniques and theoretical understandings of what one thinks should be happening, because of a particular intervention, to what is really happening. By explicating the details of how the therapist designs and uses these actions – and how they can come together in extended sequences – one can determine how a therapist informed by specific theories relates to the client to help him or her change their ways of coping with the problems which life throws at them.

CA can perform this task as it can be used to enter into dialogue with the theories and codes of conduct found in the manuals and texts which inform these practices (Peräkylä and Vehviläinen, 2003). By entering into dialogue with what Vehviläinen and Peräkylä (ibid.), following Schutz (1967) conceptualize as 'professional stocks of conversational knowledge' or SIKs, CA can correct or extend claims made by the therapists that they are bringing about change in their clients because they are doing therapy in a particular way, for example using interventions in a particular way. CA can therefore be used to help therapists reflect on their actions. Ideally therapists, informed by an empathic approach, will make use of their training and experience to talk about sensitive issues in an empathic and non-judgemental way and will not consciously try to get the client to solve his or her problem in the way the therapist sees fit. By applying the skills learnt in training, the therapist can help the client to make decisions about change and to assume responsibility for that change (Miller and Rollnick, 2002). However, this is the ideal and not every therapist applies these skills without imposing 'their own stuff' in the form of evaluations, judgments and defences. Sometimes therapists can be affected and constrained by pressures coming from the EAP organizations, whose company policies can determine the length of the therapy and what would be expected to be achieved in a certain space of time – thus putting pressure on the therapists. As CA can demonstrate how a task or activity performed in psychotherapy is carried out turn-by-turn it can explicate, at micro-level, the interactional dynamics of the devices employed by the therapist. CA can then be used to make a therapist's practice of their theory explicit as it avoids a focus on techniques and in doing so can highlight the fundamental vehicle of change – the therapeutic alliance.

In psychotherapy today it is expected that a client will be able to enter into a therapeutic relationship and introspect and reflect on their thoughts, feelings, behaviours and social relationships. Peräkylä et al. (2008) point out that the practices of introspection, reflection and self-monitoring are historically contingent and are relatively recent human conventions (cf. Foucault, 1985, ch. 9). Some studies have shown that the theoretical underpinnings of different psychotherapeutic schools cannot be studied in isolation from the social practices in which they are realized and the historical contexts in which they are practised (Cushman, 1995; Bongar and Beutler, 1995). In order therefore to be able to understand the generic practices which exist in the practice of modern day psychotherapy it is interesting to look at how these practices have evolved to where they are today.

Historical origins

Psychotherapy as a healing art, or as a method to effect change and relieve suffering, did not begin with the development of the practice of psychotherapy as it is known today through the work of Freud, Janet, Jung, Rogers, Beck, and so on. The practice of psychological and emotional healing has been around as far as history can trace. Healers such as the medicine man, the shaman and the priest, who were capable of performing a type of mental healing which centred around the restoration of the patient's lost soul or the expulsion of evil spirits and so on (Ellenberger, 1970), approached psychological healing from very different perspectives and approaches. Differing cultures performed rituals based on a particular disease theory which needed a particular treatment. However, the goal was always the same, that is, to cure a person of their illness or distress. Research in the field has shown that the development and growth of psychotherapy as a curative practice which helps people to understand and cope with their problems spans across all eras, ranging from the healing rituals from the dawn of time to the ongoing scientific research and findings of scientifically practised psychotherapy.

Ehrenwald (1976) traces the origins of magical healing to the Assyrian tablets dating back to 2500 BC where ceremonial rituals involving magical gestures, beat-drummers and dances were carried out in order to remove the disease object from a sufferer. The cleansing rituals carried out in the ancient world of the Mediterranean such as exorcism or the cures in the Asklepeia, mysteriously released souls from bondage and moved them in the direction of fate-determining stars (Dodds, 1965). The examples of the healing miracles described in the New Testament, such as the casting out of demons, are analogous to extraordinary magical cures. The Middle Ages saw priests and mystics engage in rituals and practices, such as witchcraft, exorcism, confession or hypnosis to help release people from sufferings induced by the material world (Weber, 1963). The Mesmerists of the eighteenth century, who expounded the magnetic-fluid-centred theoretical and scientific orientation of animal magnetism, believed they had developed a universal medical therapy and reported many psychological cures (Ellenberger, 1970). However, this quasi-scientific theory, which worked though the power of suggestion, was more connected to the healing magician than to the modern day psychotherapist (Ellenberger, 1970; Ehrenwald, 1976). A patient treated by mesmerism passively accepted a treatment from a healer similar to the way one may receive medical treatment for a physiological illness. The hypnotic trance states, altered states of consciousness or somnambulism described by the mesmerists such as Mesmer, Gassner and Puységur were employed to draw out forgotten memories or subconscious fixed ideas from the patient. These approaches have similarities with the healing rituals performed by many primitive cultures (Prince, 1975).

Magical healing practices which have psychotherapeutic effects can be found in all cultures and Ellenberger (1970) notes that, while these practices may seem ludicrous to the modern day psychotherapist the approaches often proved successful. However, the development of cures for psychological illness has witnessed the replacement of the principle of trial and error with experimentation, empirical observation and statistical results. While the practice of psychotherapy may have evolved to where it is today, with patients or clients attending a professional for hourly sessions once a week on average, the philosophy of healing upon which the art of western style psychotherapy is built has always been in existence. Also, the interactional tools a therapist needs to conduct 'the talking cure', such as listening, consoling, and encouraging another to tell his or her story are grounded in the practices of ordinary life. In addition, people who did not experience psychological distress were, and are still being, exposed to these practices in western cultures by clergymen in the confessionals. Helping relationships where one person listens, consoles, empathizes or encourages is a practice which became professionalized with the onset of the practice of psychotherapy. The main differences between modern day treatments and magical healing is that the former is more matter-of-fact and uses talk as its major tool while the latter is usually performed as a ceremony which could have involved the use of physical instruments or touching.

As far as the philosophy from which the practice of psychotherapy later emerged is concerned, Chessick (1977) traces its roots back to pre-Socratic times between approximately 600 BC and 400 BC and cites the Ionian city of Ephesus and the philosopher Heraclitus as being its earliest influence. In Ephesus at the time of Heraclitus, changes and flux in the city where no clear religion or philosophy of living had emerged led to a desire for permanence and stability. Chessick (1977) argues that Heraclitus of Ephesus developed this notion of the laws of change and the desire for permanence. A concept termed 'Logos' which according to Chessick 'implies something common to all existing things that could be accessible to men if it were not for their folly' (1977, p. 27) was developed by Heraclitus of Ephesus. This 'Logos' held the truth about the world but the majority of men failed to heed it. The occurrence of change and flux forced the mind to interpret the working of continuous change and even though the mind may seek stability, it is the stability which remains throughout the occurrence of change which is essential and which is overlooked by man. There is also 'the unity of forces' – the notion of tension and conflict which is necessary to produce harmony and is essential to life. In order to obtain harmony there must be struggle. The intellect struggles as it seeks unity and a system which is called stability, while the 'One', the whole according to Heraclitus as cited in Chessick (1977), can only be accessed by intuition. This would require one to look into oneself and it is only by understanding one's own inner self and one's inner processes that one can understand the human world.

The idea of self-reflection was later developed further by Socrates, who believed that man could only be himself if he was prepared to be guided by a something inside himself which held knowledge of that which was good and true (Chessick, 1977). Socrates believed in the advice of the 'daemon', a part of man's character, a voice, a divine sign or supernatural experience, which guided him from within. This daemon could be compared to Roger's 'actualizing or constructive tendency' (Rogers, 1980, p. 121) or the notion of 'the self' in some therapies or 'the spirit' in some religions. The 'daemon' allowed Socrates to control his passions through being guided by reason (Leudar and Thomas, 2000). As already mentioned, 'the restraining force' in Rogerian therapy helps the individual interact in the social context. Reason, according to Foucault (1988, p. 47) 'is the faculty that enables one to use, at the right time and in the right way, the other faculties ... it is this absolutely singular faculty that is capable of contemplating both itself and everything else'.[2] Whether one interacts with a daemon, spirit or one's self, communication is conducted through the medium of language and through the use of language a person can exercise control by choosing to heed its guidance or not. By exercising choice one has the freedom to control one's own life. Through the art of conversation – a method known as 'midwifery'[3] Socrates tried to get others to express true ideas from their minds as he believed knowledge of one's truth is necessary for control of one's life.

Socrates stated[4] that it was essential that men concern themselves with their souls and Foucault (1988) cites many examples from ancient Greek culture where the theme of 'care of the soul' was prevalent. Apuleius[5] is reported as having stated that the only way to live is by cultivating the soul. Epicurus[6] states that 'it is never too early nor too late to care for the well-being of the soul'. People were encouraged to study philosophy, not to do as the philosophers do, but to learn valuable principles by which one can live. Foucault (1988) argues that this 'cultivation of oneself' became a social practice, where one reflected on oneself, talked about it to others, either friends or a guide or counsellor and wrote about it. These social practices were conducted within communities or school-like structures. Similar to the practice of present day psychotherapy or counselling, one was encouraged to seek the help of another in one's efforts to care for oneself in ancient Greek culture. Also, things have not changed that much. Rogerian therapy encourages the client or patient to get in touch with their deeper selves. The Socratic questioning, used in CBT, is employed as a method to get clients to recognize and express their thoughts in order to counter negative patterns and straighten up their thinking. In CBT if one has control over the negative thinking processes one has control over the emotions.

However, this managing of one's spiritual direction was also an object of criticism as it took control of a person's existence in the same way as one may be against attending a physician if one is in good health. Foucault (1985) argues that a person's choice, and therefore his or her freedom, can be taken away from him or her as self-reflection can be enforced. These restrictions were especially prevalent if one were deemed psychologically unwell. Much later, at the asylum, Tuke and Pinel created a moral prison. In Tuke's home,[7] religious beliefs were used as a means of coercion to educate, induce guilt and impose external constraints in order to position the insane person within a moral component which would educe reason. His guilt was employed to draw out awareness of himself as an object and by acknowledging this guilt he would be restored as a responsible subject with reason. Patients had a minority status and were managed through fear, thus removing their right to autonomy. The institution was structured where the insane were subject to the authority of the man of reason – the adult dominant figure. This institution, through social rituals, imposed the drawing out of a silent social personality through observation. Pinel on the other hand was against religious segregation and replaced it with social segregation as Pinel believed that madness had social origins. Three moral syntheses' – silence, recognition by mirror (observation) and perpetual judgement – were used as a method of treatment. It was believed that the mind of the madman must contain a judge. Authority replaced repression and represented the reason which acts as judge. Nowadays, the judge has been replaced with a trust in the 'actualizing tendency', in person-centred therapy. In CBT the judge confronts negative thoughts and in solution-focused therapy the judge searches for positive strengths. Perhaps the judge in Pinel's time was a lot more negative that it is today. Foucault (1985) argues that psychoanalysis replaced the rituals of silent observation with language. The authority figure only had observation and later language to impose reason onto the mind of the insane. Freud brought an end to the asylum but not to the power of those in authority (Foucault, 1985). Freud instead bestowed all the collective powers in the asylum onto an individual therapist. When psychoanalysis appeared, it substituted for its silent powers of observation the power of language.

Society, culture, and the individual psychotherapist

As already mentioned, in order to understand psychotherapy it is not enough to examine it in terms of psychological theories (Cushman, 1995;

Orlinsky and Howard, 1995; Mahoney, 1995; Norcross and Goldfried, 2005; Wampold, 2001; Peräkylä et al., 2008; Peräkylä, 2013).

It is also necessary to look outside the consulting room and to the needs of the people within the culture in order to understand the forms of psychotherapy on offer. Ellenberger (1970) argues that a study of the history of dynamic psychotherapy and the movement of Freudian Psychoanalysis cannot be examined without taking the cultural, political and economic environments developing in Europe after the Franco–Prussian war (1870–1871) into account. Foucault (1980) argued that Freud's assumption that it was necessary for society to control sexuality and aggression was a history-bound concept prevalent in Victorian Europe. The idea that emotional problems were rooted in problems with sexuality was acceptable to the thinking prevalent in Europe in the 1880s and 1890s when psychoanalysis originated. Also, the notion of a person's self, emerging around the time of Freud, revealed a self less restricted by traditional and religious values and more geared towards the fulfilment of individual needs.

Foucault (1979, 1988) argued that the state needed to develop something which would control the less submissive and compliant individual. Over time the social institutions evolved in such a way as allowed a specific mode of scrutiny of the self and the realm of an individual's private psychological world. The scientific theory developing at the time of Freud seemed to construct a self, an individual's private world, which needed to be observed through inspection by entering into that world. However, the entering of that private world allowed it to be controlled (Foucault, 1979, 1988; Cushman, 1995). Cushman (ibid.) argues that a control of the self, described by Freud, was a reflection of the control exerted by the state where its citizens had to be protected from one another. For example, at the time women's natural feminine state was one of passivity and the control of women was implicitly entrenched in Freud's theory (Cushman). Freud's Oedipus complex has to be understood in terms of the era where the world was shaped by men for men; where a man's authority and control over his wife and children was undisputed (Ellenberger, 1970).

However, Freud did more than merely describe an era. Ellenberger (1970) argues that in addition to the cultural and societal aspects which witnessed the emergence of psychoanalysis it is also necessary to take the practitioners and their personalities into consideration. Ellenberger compares the psychotherapist to a writer or artist whose view of the world is based on his or her own aptitudes and sensitivities. For example, Ellenberger (1970) argues that Freud's childhood experiences influenced how he portrayed the Oedipus complex and Jung's experiences of religion in his childhood affected the system of psychology he developed. While it would be impossible to discern all of the sources of influence which led to the development of psychoanalytical thinking it could be fair to say that some of the sources came from outside and these were then fused with Freud's own contributions. Ellenberger divides Freud's sources and influences into three distinct categories. Firstly, his own masters, authors he read and thinkers, most notably Charcot, Janet, Nietzsche, Carus von Hartmann and Schopenhauer. Secondly, his own self-analysis taught him much about the working of the mind. Thirdly, his disciples and patients provided him with valuable insights and helped him develop his theories. It seems that psychoanalysis emerged though a combination of Freud's own self-analysis which blended with the analysis of his patients. These personal and professional experiences merged with his outside sources as well as with the thinking prevalent in psychiatric circles at the time. Around 1895 there were movements afoot which attempted to psychologize psychiatry[8] and develop new methods of psychotherapy. Freud's drive theory, with its emphasis on aggressive and libidinal wishes, was among many of the innovations emerging. However, Freud remarked on 14 August 1897 that 'the main patient who keeps me busy is myself' (cf. Ellenberger, 1970, p. 446). Freud's own self-analysis was more difficult for him to deal with than any of his other sources.

Ellenberger (1970) makes a distinction between schools of therapy which developed from scientific research and those which stemmed from the personal experiences of the theoretician. On the one hand there are the clinicians such as Adler and Pavlov who studied their own neuroses by means of self-analysis and obtained their results from clinical research. On the other hand, psychiatrists such as Freud and Jung suffered from what Ellenberger described as a 'creative illness' (ibid., p. 889). The 'creative illness' resulted in a long period of spiritual isolation, depression and exhaustion followed by an awakening to some spiritual truth. This 'creative illness', is similar to the descriptions given by James (1902) in his investigations of religious conversion. According to James, psychology cannot explain the forces which cause this conversion and neither observers nor the person themselves can explain how experiences can bring about such explosive change. He likens it to a sportsperson who awakens to the finer nuances of the game or to a musician who now experiences the music flowing through him.

Ellenberger (1970) hypothesized that those who experienced this 'creative illness', which preoccupied the sufferer in a quest for a certain truth, became pathfinders who went on to teach the theory as well as develop guidelines for others to follow by creating a model. The models developed by those who experienced the 'creative illness', like the beliefs and ideas of the religious converters, was premised on the belief that the sufferer had uncovered a universal truth about the nature of human psychological functioning and the tenet of this truth was located within the person. So, on the one hand there is the individual therapist whose life experiences influences their beliefs about their work, while on the other hand there is the social context and contemporary thinking which plays a part in how a therapist approaches their work. It seems fair to say that psychotherapy, as we know it today, took root and grew up in an era which seemed ripe for its development (Cushman, 1995; Vandenbos, Cummings and DeLeon, 1995).

Also, the techniques used by psychotherapy, such as the use of transference and free-association, devised to defeat the unconscious maliciousness of hysterics may be considered to be an alteration of the previous techniques employed by hypnotists. The use of transference is similar to the technique described by Mesmer which involves the development of crises in order to gradually bring them under control. Also relief from painful secrets by attending confession plays a role in psychoanalytic cures (Ellenberger, 1970). So, while the approach expounded by Freud may have grown into a psychological theory, which developed its own school, with an official doctrine – the psychoanalytical theory – the approach adopted had connections with many of the previous approaches designed to help people with their problems. Therefore the assimilation of the traditional indigenous form of magical healing into modern day psychotherapy and scientific practice can be traced to the transition from mesmerism and hypnosis to psychotherapy. The same can be said for the many different therapies that have developed since the birth of psychoanalysis.

Instead of competing for dominance and prestige in the psychotherapeutic world, much of the developing modern day theoretical approaches take something from the previously available approaches and transform them somewhat to create new integrative or 'ecletic' helping therapeutic approaches (Norcross and Goldfried, 2005). Eclecticism or integration is an approach which allows the therapist to select from a range of therapy techniques, based on what they believe will be helpful for a client. Much of the literature concurs with the thinking that the diversities and contradictions that exist within psychotherapy today have been shaped by the social and historical forces that have shaped modern day culture overall (Miell, 1997; Beutler and Bongar, 1995; McLeod, 2000; Norcross and Goldfried, 2005). Cushman argues 'that psychotherapy is somehow so accurately attuned to the 20th century cultural frame of reference that it has come to provide human services that are crucial, perhaps indispensable, to our current way of life' (1995, p. 24). It seems difficult to assume that modern day psychotherapy is more effective or veracious than the magical healing rituals which reported psychological cures since the dawn of time. However, its validity and relevance in today's society can be understood in terms of the culture and social context where it is practised because scientific practice and social organization combine to affect what people tend to be like. Psychotherapies can be created which are then relevant to the times in which they are practised.

Psychotherapy in contemporary society

It is beyond the scope of this book to examine today's culture and its effects on present day psychotherapy training and practises. Cushman's (1995) characterization of the psychotherapist as a 'the doctor of the interior' will be used, as such a definition places all therapies, regardless of era or historical difference, under the same umbrella. Nevertheless different definitions and descriptions do exist. Psychotherapy is defined in the Oxford English Dictionary as 'the treatment of disorders of the mind or personality by psychological or psychophysiological methods'. In the Wikipedia it is described as 'an interpersonal, relational intervention used by trained psychotherapists to aid clients in problems of living'. So, on the one hand it can be seen in a medical capacity where the term 'patient' is used, on the other hand it is seen as an aid to an individual's sense of well-being, to help them to cope with or alleviate distressing feelings and discomforts. As far as EAP short-term therapy is concerned Strupp's (1978, p. 3) definition which describes psychotherapy as 'an interpersonal process designed to bring about modifications of feelings, cognitions, attitudes and behaviours which have proved troublesome to the person seeking help from a trained psychotherapist' probably best fits the work investigated here.

However, the term 'psychotherapy' has different associations in different countries. Some mental health practitioners refer to themselves as psychotherapists while others who offer the same type of service call themselves counsellors. In the US, for example, the term 'psychotherapy' is associated with the provision of health care and is linked with those professionals who are connected to medicine through psychiatry or clinical psychology. In the UK and Ireland, however, psychotherapy is mostly associated with lay professionals.[9] In the US, while most psychoanalysts have a medical qualification, psychology graduates refer to themselves as either psychotherapists or counsellors. In Germany, the psychotherapist works in a *Heilberuf* – a healing profession, and is very much connected to the medical profession. A term such as *heilen* would in fact bestow psychotherapists with healing powers, such as those held by the medicine man, the shaman or even Jesus Christ. The term 'counselling', which developed in the second half of the twentieth century and was associated with Rogers is now associated with all areas of mental health and the term 'counselling psychology' is a common term (McLeod, 1998). EAP system providers in Europe work with both psychotherapists and counsellors but because of the distinctions in some countries many providers tend to use the terms EAP counselling even though the practices are the same. In the absence of a definitive distinction between the terms, and as counsellors and psychotherapists possess many of the same skills (McLeod, 2000) I will not distinguish between the two terms but use both terms interchangeably. In fact, it may simply be that counselling is an 'extension of psychotherapy, a way of "marketing" psychotherapy to new groups of consumers' (McLeod, 2000, p. 23).

In addition, the literature on which this work has drawn does not for the most part differentiate between the terms as there is very little literature on CA and psychotherapy which specifically investigates the practice of counselling as distinct from psychotherapy. Vehviläinen (2003b) mentions that counselling in Finland is mainly associated with education. Regardless of whether one calls oneself a counsellor or a psychotherapist, difficulties concerning cost-effectiveness and account-ability of both psychotherapists and counsellors are universal (Roth and Fonagy, 2005; Norcross and Goldfried, 2005). Although countries have developed divergent ways of providing for and funding the practice of psychotherapy or counselling through the health service or by allowing private practice, there have long been complaints that psychological therapies can charge what they like and that the service to the public is too vague (Beutler and Bongar, 1995; Norcross and Goldfried, 2005; Streeck, 2004). This undefined and blurred definition of what consti-tutes best practice has left the field open to a verifiable stampede to acquire knowledge of one's practice in an evidence-based fashion. It seems that 'evidence-based practice' has become today's buzzword in the therapy world. Duncan, Miller and Sparks (2004) argue that thera-pists will be left behind if they don't leap aboard the evidence-based train. However, since therapy includes the therapist's sources and beliefs developed through life experiences, personal therapy and training, a therapist, who want to investigate how therapy is conducted needs to do more than develop evidence by focusing on techniques.

Does psychotherapy work?

Judging from the growing number of psychotherapies and psychotherapists it appears to be accepted that psychotherapy works and is instrumental in providing cures. However, the issue regarding the efficacy of psychotherapy is far from settled. Eysenck (1952), who launched an attack on the field of psychoanalysis, argued that psychotherapy failed to show any better results than those which occurred through spontaneous remission. In his report, he argued that it is assumed that psychotherapy works and the client feels better afterwards. However, the unit of measurement is based on the therapist's opinion which is contained in their report at the end of therapy (Landis, 1938, cited in Eysenck, 1952). According to Eysenck one cannot assume that psychoanalytical therapy has a better improvement rate than no therapy at all if there is no conclusive evidence to show that it is therapeutically effective. For Eysenck, an advocate of the behavioural approach, psychoanalysis was too unscientific. However, although Eysenck was criticized for not using scientifically gathered data, as there was not much available at the time (Lambert and Bergin, 1994), the challenge which he posed led to the growth of empirical research on the effectiveness of psychotherapy and the numerous types of therapeutic interventions on offer.[10] These studies have indicated that clients who attended therapy were better off and had more positive results than those who did not attend.

Nevertheless these researchers have failed to address some areas of the efficacy debate adequately. Firstly, the 'deterioration' effect discovered by Bergin (1967, cf. Meares et al., 2002) has not been adequately tackled by psychoanalytical researchers or by researchers of behavioural therapies. The results of Bergin's study suggest that therapy can also do harm. In addition, Lambert and Bergin (1994) found that psychological treatments are in general beneficial but that not everyone benefits to an acceptable degree. Also, researchers have failed to demonstrate the superiority of any single major psychotherapeutic school of thought over another (Orlinsky and Howard, 1995; Wampold, 2001; Lambert, 2005, 2013) and the argument remains that the therapeutic alliance is still the determining factor as to whether therapy is successful or not. Despite differences in research methods a growing number of studies have shown that the different therapeutic models are about equal in terms of their effectiveness and the difference in the models have no major effect on the outcome (Lambert and Bergin, 1994; Roth and Fonagy, 2005; Elliot et al., 2013). Despite these finding adherents and researchers of cognitive-behavioural therapy have argued that CBT is curative (Hollon and Beck, 2013; Emmelkamp, 2013). In fact most of the recent efficacy studies have tended to focus on CBT and have found that it is effective in treating non-psychotic disorders. On the other hand, Lambert (2013) found that instances in most studies which showed mistakes made by the therapist also showed how these mistakes interfered with positive client outcomes. These studies did not however go into detail about how the therapist made the mistake and this information is important for the professional development of therapists working for managed care systems if the service is to be improved. As already mentioned and as Peräkylä (2011) suggests CA make these aspects of one's practice explicit and this can help therapists correct such mistakes.

The efficacy debate

It is beyond the range and scope of this book to examine all the studies which have been carried out on the efficacy of psychotherapy. Nevertheless, some of the general presenting problems and issues arising in EAP therapy and counselling will be looked in the light of present day research.

Cognitive-behavioural therapy

Despite the lack of evidence to support the effectiveness of specific types of therapy over others, the outcome of both qualitative and quantitative research on CBT pertaining to certain types of problems supports its efficacy (Dobson and Shaw, 1995; Roth and Fonagy, 2005; Lambert, Bergin and Garfield, 2005, 2013). Empirical evidence, based mainly on randomized controlled trials, is available to show that problems such as depression, generalized anxiety, panic attacks, post-traumatic stress disorder, social phobias, obsessive-compulsive disorders, eating disorders and personality disorders have been successfully treated by CBT methods (Meichenbaum, 1995; Roth and Fonagy, 2005; Hollon and Beck, 2005, 2013).[11] Also the controlled trials carried out by the American Psychological Association (Chambles et al., 1996) to determine the effectiveness of different forms of therapy for differently diagnosed categories of problems showed that CBT attained the highest success rates in meeting efficacy criteria. While factors such as researcher allegiance or the methods used to test and compare the results may have affected the outcomes it is generally accepted among the therapeutic community that CBT is effective with certain types of mental health problems. However, outcome studies (Roth and Fonagy, 2005; Hollon and Beck, 2005, 2013) also show that in dealing with the area of depression, CBT is at least as, if not more, effective, as other treatments such as interpersonal therapy or psychodynamic therapy. Distinctions have been made between those who suffer from acute depression and clients who suffer from depression in less intense forms. There have been numerous meta-analysis studies carried out which demonstrate that CBT is an effective treatment for major depression (Rush et al., 1977; Dobson, 1989; Robinson et al., 1990; Hoffman and Smits, 2008; Hopko and Johanson, 2010) and several studies have shown that treatment with CBT is better than no treatment or placebo (Dobson, 1989; Robinson et al., 1990; Gloaguen et al., 1998). However, while the research indicates that psychotherapy is highly effective Lambert (2013) argues that sometimes even a very small effect size is an indication of its efficacy.

In the area of generalized anxiety and panic attacks patients treated with CBT showed significant improvements after treatment with reasonable preservation of gains at the follow-up stage. Chambless and Gillis (1993) contrasted patients who received CBT against a control condition and found that the greatest effect sizes were for CBT treatments. Borkovec and Ruscio (2001) looked at patients who suffered from mixed anxiety disorder and panic disorder and found that those treated with CBT had advantages over those who only received placebo, psychodynamic therapy, supportive listening approaches and behavioural therapy alone. More recent studies also found that CBT is an effective treatment for anxiety disorders (Norton and Price, 2007; Stewart and Chambles, 2009; Craske, 2010). As far as eating disorders are concerned, it is also generally accepted that CBT is an effective method for treating binge-eating disorders, bulimia and anorexia nervosa.[12] However, most of the researched treatments occur in specialist centres with severely affected patients and as a result tend to make the conclusions, as far as efficacy is concerned, fairly tentative (Roth and Fonagy, 2005). Nevertheless, one can conclude from the research available that as far as depression and anxiety disorders and eating disorders are concerned CBT is highly effective and also as effective as other treatments (Dobson and Pusch, 1993; Chambless and Gillis, 1993; Hollon and Beck, 2013).

Person-centred therapy

Some of the earliest studies of psychotherapy outcome were carried out by Carl Rogers (Rogers and Dymond, 1954). His taped recordings of psychotherapy interviews were not only useful in the training of therapists but also provided empirical evidence which could be used for a thorough study of therapeutic procedures based upon objective data. For example, client responses can be categorized into meaningful categories, and the techniques applied can be classified as directive or non-directive. However, Roth and Fonagy (2005) argue that person-centred therapy is not a treatment therapy in the sense that medical therapies are, and is therefore not subject to the rigorous trials to determine efficacy. This experiential therapy is based on how one experiences the complexities of one's problem rather than on bodily symptoms, thoughts and emotions. While this therapy is conducted according to a model that guides the therapist's actions it represents the therapist's attitude concerning the personal growth process rather than the application of specific techniques or instruments. Therefore much of the outcome depends on the therapist's mind set as much as on the techniques. Nevertheless, evidence supporting or refuting the view concerning the therapist's contribution to the outcome is difficult to come by (Roth and Fonagy, 2005; van Kalmthout, 2007; Elliott, 2007; Elliot et al., 2013). Research designs with the therapist acting as the independent variable are scarce. Many of the studies indicate that there is some parallel between the therapist's level of competence and experience and effective outcomes, but the evidence is limited and no meaningful patterns have emerged (Roth and Fonagy, 2005). However trials investigating differences in outcomes for each therapist studied, found differences between individual therapists and rates of improvement (Luborsky et al., 1986). It was found that personal qualities of the therapist such as warmth, genuineness and the ability to develop a helping relationship had an effect on therapeutic outcomes (ibid.). Roth and Fonagy (2005) noted that the majority of studies carried out on the contribution of the therapist to outcomes confirm a fairly strong link between the therapist's ability to form a positive therapeutic alliance and positive outcomes.

Although many therapists and the public may be comforted by the idea that they are offering or receiving an empirically supported psychotherapy, the fact is that the success of treatment appears to be largely dependent on the client and the therapist and not on the use of proven empirically based treatments. Nevertheless due to economic pressure on mental health services in the US and Europe, as well as the need to improve and standardize training procedures across Europe, pressure has mounted to recognize certain therapeutic approaches as more effective than others (Lambert, 2013; Comer and Kendall, 2013). The report issued by Meyer, Richter, Grawe, von Schulenberg and Schulte (1991) put forward the argument that experiential therapies were ineffective. This report led to a series of meta-analytic reviews to prove the effectiveness of these therapies (Elliott, 1996; Greenberg et al., 1994). Elliott et al. (2004, 2013) conducted further reviews involving updates of the above mentioned studies and found that the results showed that experiential therapies are effective. So despite the assumptions held by many CBT therapists that CBT is a superior treatment to experiential therapies the results of these studies showed that in general there is little difference in terms of their effectiveness.

Experiential therapies have been found to be effective with depression, anxiety, trauma and interpersonal difficulties (Elliott et al., 2004, 2013; Elliott, 2001; Finke and Teusch, 2007). Elliott et al. (2004, 2013), who attempted to evaluate the status of empirically supported treatments for specific client problems found that clients with less severe or emotion-focused problems, for example depression, indicated greater improvement than those with cognitive or behavioural problems such as habit or personality disorders. The largest effects were found for relationship problems and the smallest for habit disorders. Little work has been carried out on the effectiveness of person-centred therapy in the treatment of eating disorders. There is limited evidence for the effects of experiential therapies and anorexia nervosa and where binge eating is concerned, there is small evidence from one trial in favour of experiential therapies (Roth and Fonagy, 2005). However, without follow-up data it is difficult to make interpretations.

Studies have found correlations between depth of clients experiencing and reduction in symptoms for clients suffering from depression (Watson and Greenberg, 1996; Goldman, Greenberg and Angus, 2006). Studies do suggest that person-centred therapy may be too non-directive for the sufferers of depression who require more direction to tackle their problems and this may be the same with anxiety disorders. Studies of pre-post effects have shown that client-centred therapies are an effective treatment for anxiety disorders (Teusch, Böhme and Gastpar, 1997; Teusch, Finke and Böhme, 1995).

Brief solution-focused therapy (BSFT).[13] In this book I interchange term solution-focused therapy for the acronym BFSF for easier reading)

There have been relatively few controlled trails carried out using BFST as it is usually used in combination with one of the major therapies such as client-centred therapy or CBT (Shiang and Bongar, 1995). Much of the investigations involved interviewing the participants after therapy. Metcalf and Thomas (1994) investigated the use of solution-focused therapy with couples, by interviewing the clients about what they found most helpful in therapy and the therapists about what they believed influenced change. The results showed that clients attributed positive results to the strength of the therapeutic alliance. Factors such as listening, highlighting strengths, praising, and questions which focused on what worked in client's lives had a positive influence. Therapists on the other hand attributed improvement to methods and techniques, for example punctuating the experience, validating and finding resources. Metcalf, Thomas, Duncan, Miller and Hubble (1996) compared the perceptions of both clients and therapists with six cases which were seen as successful. They found that therapists attributed the success to their techniques and the clients to the therapeutic relationship. This is an important finding for the future of therapy as most professional bodies expect therapists to keep improving their practice by learning new techniques and approaches. If this continues to be the case then the future of therapy is surely in trouble as it may be moving too much in the direction of the medical model and evidence-based treatments.

Duncan, Miller and Sparks (2004) suggest that all psychotherapies are effective if professionally administered and, where solution-focused therapy is concerned they focus the efficacy debate on client-directed outcome-informed therapy. They suggest using session rating scales, to rate the effectiveness of the therapeutic relationship and outcome-rating scales designed to assess areas of the client's life functioning which may be expected to change as a result of therapy. However, according to Duncan et al. these scales are clinical rather than research tools and they argue that 'gains in feasibility offset losses in reliability and validity' (2003, p. 10). These scales are designed to measure and monitor the therapeutic alliance as the main contributing factor to successful therapy. However, the alliance is a joint endeavour and while therapists may become aware of what they are doing wrong by examining the scale with the client they do not learn how and where they went wrong. These scales do not teach therapists anything about their style and why the approach they take is effective or not. As they mainly deal with the relationship they do not take into account what the other 70 per cent was which affected their client's improvement. Gale and Newfield (1992) used conversation analysis to investigate the techniques used by a solution-focused therapist and, when presenting their findings to the therapist, found that the therapist was totally unaware of how he was conducting the therapy. Therapist behaviours such as 'pursuing a response over many turns', 'modifying his assertion until he receives the response he is seeking' 'offering a candidate answer' or 'ignoring the recipients misunderstanding or rejection and continuing as if his assertion were accepted' opened the therapist's eyes to the possibility that he talks for clients, talks over the client's talk and ignores helpful things the client may say in order to get his point across.

Process research

While outcome research is fairly limited where person-centred therapy is concerned process research has been a feature of the person-centred tradition (Elliott, 2007). The area of process research is most relevant to this topic as it involves efforts to gain insight into what is happening in a psychotherapy session between the therapist and the client. By making tape-recordings of sessions the object of study, Rogers was able to investigate the moments of change and the moves surrounding them. His findings include examples of clients expressing their feelings from an 'internal locus of reflection' rather than an external one as well as moments when insight is attained (Rogers, 1951; Kirschenbaum and Henderson, 1989). This type of research into the process of psycho-therapy was continued and developed by Elliott and Greenberg, who also undertook 'post-session process recall research' with clients to investigate the helpfulness of the therapy offered (Elliott and Shapiro, 1988; Elliott, 2001; Elliott et al., 2004, 2013).

Sachse and Elliott (2002) looked at the relationship between therapeutic interventions and client processings.[14] This study used micro-process research methods to examine the immediate effect of therapeutic interventions on client processes as well as the effect the client processes had on the therapist's subsequent activities. Some process researchers take the view that therapists can influence clients by attending to particular aspects of the client's tellings which would help the client work through certain issues (Greenberg et al., 1994; Sachse, 1992). Sachse (1990, 1992) found that the relationship between the therapist's verbal interventions and the client's resulting verbal explications was based on the quality of the therapist's proposals and that the therapist's influence can have both positive as well as negative consequences. It was found that the therapist's actions were of decisive importance in terms of process characteristics and constructive outcomes. As far as active, process-directive actions by the therapist are concerned the therapist's focus should not only be on the content but should also be at the points where the client needs active assistance to help them manage the processing. However, Sachse's 1990s research findings have not been replicated by other researchers (Elliott, 2007). As far as the therapeutic interventions such as empathic responses and the therapist's listening techniques are concerned little research has been conducted into the effect these techniques have on client change (Elliott, 2007).

Elliott (2007) and van Kalmthout (2007) express concerns about the growth of Evidence Based Medicine (EBM; see, for example Wessely, 2001) which may satisfy insurance companies and funding agencies but which cannot do justice to the client's lived experience or their inner valuing processes. Elliott (2007) argues that the core conditions of empathy, non-judgemental warmth and congruence would be ignored by evidence-based medicine which seeks to provide evidence of validity and effectiveness by means of independently defined variables. Elliott (2007) calls on person-centred therapists to play a part in the research. This could be done by therapists contributing to dialogues on how to assess therapy, by examining their practices using basic research tools with their clients or in their training setting. Elliott (2007) and Van Kalmthout (2007) consider the situation critical and feel that something has to be done in order to prevent person-centred therapy from losing its status as a valid method of therapy in the future.

Concluding comments

As research findings have failed to demonstrate a consistent superiority of any one school of therapy over another, therapists who adhere to a particular paradigm have been forced to look at other approaches for solutions to certain problems (Norcross and Goldfried, 2005). Orlinsky and Howard (1995) noted that lack of evidence concerning the truth about man and his behaviour had resulted in ineffective guidance for clinical practice. Present day research has shown that no single research design can provide answers to all the questions related to the efficacy of psychotherapy (Comer and Kendall, 2013). In fact rigorous procedures are continually being updated in an attempt to provide the best service based on the best results. The consequences have been that psychotherapists themselves have taken to examining their own practice in an attempt to determine what works best for their clients and for them as therapists. In doing so they will invariably look at the helping relationship and how it is being played out through talk. This is where CA can be of use as it offers an objective description of the interactions in therapy and could be used as a tool in process research. While much of the focus in this book is on short-term counselling and therapy, the empirical findings can be used by any therapeutic practitioner to help them become their own researchers.

Therapists'/practitioners' corner

As far as CA is concerned, when practitioners interact with their clients or patients both parties orient and adjust to whatever rules and conventions of conversation operate at that time. Talk is a highly organized system of interaction that displays many structural elements which therapists and clients or patients will orient towards naturally in the 'doing' of their conversation. In the therapists' corner I explain some of the basic properties, analytic strategies, and terminologies used by conversation analysts and I will start here with the terms 'local', 'adjacency pairs' and 'turns'. An adjacency pair is an aspect of conversation which comes in two parts, spoken by two different speakers and these two parts appear in sequence or are sequentially organized, that is, one pair normally follows the other. For example, a greeting is likely to be followed by a greeting, a therapist's question to his or her client normally requires an answer and a therapist's reflecting back (formulation) or an interpretation normally requires a response. The term 'local' refers to the business of sorting out who has the current turn at talk; who might have the next turn, what you do if you want to interrupt and so on. CA demonstrates that talk is conducted 'locally', that is, on a 'turn-by-turn' basis and the organization and procedures of 'turn-taking' (pauses, overlaps, how turns are constructed and so on) are governed by a set of basic rules.

(1) a turn-constructional element, which can be a unit composed of a sentence, a word, a phrase or a sound such as 'mm' and

(2) a turn-allocation unit, composed of two sets of techniques: 1. those where a next turn is assigned by the current speaker who chooses the next speaker, for example, a therapist asks a question; 2. the next turn is assigned by the speaker self-selecting, for example, the client keeps talking and elaborating after the question has been answered.

So, during the in-session conversations the therapist or the client is assigned a 'turn-constructional' unit which designates him/her as the current speaker. At the end of this unit, which may be a one-word answer or a long sentence, speakers may change. This changeover point is known as a transition relevant place (TRP). In many instances in therapy the client tends to keep talking as they tell their story but even so many transition relevant places, where the therapist could intervene, appear as the talk proceeds. These TPR's normally occur when a sentence has been syntactically, pragmatically and grammatically complete, that is, a complete sentence has been uttered. Also, as the therapist nears the end of his or her question the pitch and stress of his or her voice will change. This pitch could become higher or lower but what is important to note is that there is a definite change, and this makes it clear to the client that the floor is now going to be handed over to them. In this way, the client as listener will know precisely when to 'come into' a conversation even if the therapist has not directly handed the 'floor' over by asking a question or by producing a formulation or interpretation.

Clients learn how to converse in therapy. They learn that questions require answers, reflecting back (formulations) and interpretations require responses, continuers (*mm hm* and *uh huh*) mean that they are expected to keep talking and silences mean that they should engage in reflections. Therapists ask most of the questions and clients provide answers. If however, a client ignores this convention by either remaining silent or replying with a further question then this will be seen as breaking or defying the rules which cover questions and answers. The therapist then may look for reasons why the client did not answer. The therapist may repeat the question believing that the client did not hear or, if they continue to remain silent, therapists may conclude that this client or case is complex. As far as CA is concerned conversational contexts are always lively, and in a certain sense 'confrontational'. It does not matter if the turn is insignificant or not, both parties are always accountable for their actions. Here is an example taken from the first session of therapy. I also include a short explanation of the transcription devices used in this CA analysis. The reader is however, encouraged to make themselves familiar with the transcription devices based on those devised by Gail Jefferson and described at the beginning of this book.

Transcription techniques

Using these transcription techniques we can come to examine the sounds people make in the places they are made. Normal punctuation is not included in CA transcripts; commas, capital letters and full stops mean something different in CA.

(.) small pauses, ↑↓ marked rise or fall in intonation, ::: marks stretching words or sounds, upper case letters indicate increased volume.

T = Therapist; C = Client

Session 1 Jane

1. T: o.k Jane (.) how do you think therap:y (.) can help you (3.5)
2. C: emm (4.4) I am not SURE really (6.5)
3. T: take your ↑time::: No ↑hurry↓ (3.3)
4. C: I feel depressed (2.5)
5. T: so you feel quite low at this time (1.5)
6. C: yeah::::

The therapist takes control of the conversation and fixes the topic with *ok* on line 1. The long silences (3.5) seconds on line 1 and (4.4) and 6.5) seconds on line 2, not only allow the client the time and space to answer, but display the expectation that the client needs to account for why they are in therapy by reflecting on the question posed. The problem was defined in therapeutic terms on line 4 and then the therapist intervenes in response to that definition. The therapist could have intervened and commented on the client's uncertainty on line 2 (marked by an increase in volume on *sure*) but instead choose to ignore this. The therapist accepts the problem on line 4, formulates what the client has said (line 5) and then gets a response to that re-formulation (line 6). Sacks (1992, LC1, p. 55) comments that the person asking the questions has control of the conversation. If we were to look at this in terms of control, the client controls the topic but the therapist controls the conversation, that is, how the topic is talked about.

2
Interaction Issues in Short-Term Psychotherapy

The interactional models of psychotherapy

As mentioned in the introduction, most therapeutic models empha-size the need for therapists to develop an empathic listening style with their clients and patients before any treatment can be administered. The caring aspect of therapy is demonstrated in and through this listening style. This suggests that the therapist's personality is a salient factor in the effectiveness of therapy. Some researchers go a step further and stress that the 'particular therapist delivering the treatment is absolutely crucial' (Wampold, 2001, p. 202). On the other hand, therapists who adhere to the medical model of psychotherapy assume that a client can be diagnosed and treated irrespective of the therapist's influence (Streeck, 2008). For example, therapists can employ specific techniques, such as use the Structured Clinical Interview (SCID 1 or 11) manuals to diagnose or they can focus on the problem in the here-and-now and ignore issues from the client's past or they can use the 'A-B-C model' or the 'downward arrow' technique in CBT. In BSFT therapists can bypass the problem and instead focus on the times when the client did not have the problem or they can use the 'miracle question' in the assess-ment or the treatment stage and so on. However, Rogers rejected these forms of interaction in therapy (cf. Finke and Teusch, 2007) and argued that the therapist should not be an observer but should behave as a partner who is a participant and co-constructor of the interaction. The emphasis should not be on recognizing some difficulty or cause or about applying a technique but on the communication occurring between the participants.

Balint's (1961) study, which focused on psychoanalysis and the prac-tice of psychotherapy in medicine, offers a way of investigating and challenging the assumption that psychoanalysis, or in fact any therapy is the 'pure gold' of psychotherapy. It challenges the privileged position occupied by psychoanalysts as mental health workers who have the answers to all psychological problems. The study exposed the limitations of psychoanalysis by examining the practice *in situ*. The conclusions reached illustrate that the practice of psychotherapy is affected by the setting in which it is conducted. The argument that each setting has its own limitations as well as possibilities opens up the way for psychotherapy to develop techniques and approaches which complement the setting. What matters then is that psychotherapy is not about imposing a set of techniques on to a client; it is about marrying the techniques with all aspects of the setting. That setting includes the therapeutic alliance; the type of clients presenting for therapy, for example, whether they have been diagnosed with psychological illness or not; the type of problem being dealt with; the time frame allotted to dealing with the problem; who is funding the therapy and so on. As previously mentioned it is accepted in the literature that the conceptual model practised by the therapist predetermines the moves made by the therapist during the sessions (Norcross and Prochaska, 1983; Norcross and Goldfried, 2005; Peräkylä et al., 2008). It is argued here that the way in which an individual therapist brings their theoretical orientation and training to the setting will have an effect on how they interact with their clients, and how the clients in turn interact with them. CA can investigate this by looking at how the above are talked into being.

Each therapeutic approach embodies a way of looking at people and those who have received specific training in the person-centred approach will see what it means to be a person from a humanistic perspective (Rice and Greenberg, 1995; Wampold, 2001; Mearns and Thorne, 2007). This means that the client will be invited to participate in an interaction which is led by the humanistic beliefs. At the heart of the person-centred approach is the belief in the uniqueness of human consciousness in general and this approach stresses the necessity for therapists to understand the client's perception of reality. This will affect how the client is viewed and handled. In the training of psychotherapists it is not enough that the therapist studies theories and learns how to apply techniques to different problems (Wampold, 2001). Neither is it enough for a therapist to use commonsense and sympathy or encouraging and reassuring words as a non-professional family member may do. It is also not enough that a therapist provides a treatment designed to relieve the client of the symptoms of distress. What is important is that the therapist is aware of what they are doing, how they are doing it and how this is bringing about change or not, as the case may be. Therapists need to be able to stand over their own style or brand of therapy.

If, in the clinical field, most of the new developments in psychotherapy are coming from reports from clinical practice, then CA can be used as a tool to investigate at a microscopic level how both participants – the therapist and the client – interact in the consulting room. For example, person-centred therapy is supposed to be non-directive but studies have shown that it would be impossible for one person in the relationship not to influence the other even if only slightly in some way (Truax, 1966; Truax and Carkhuff, 1967). That influence is much more obvious in an asymmetrical relationship where one person, in this case the therapist, is much more informed than the other. As argued by Balint (1961) and Streeck (2008) the therapist is not dealing with symptoms or experiences which are completely separate from the therapist's influence. By examining the communication between the participants from the 'interactional, social model of psychotherapy' approach (Streeck, 2008, p. 296) interactions which occur in the sessions would be seen as integral parts of the interactive process. According to this model the relationship between therapist and client and the resulting interaction constitutes the centre upon which all therapy is based. By examining the practice from this perspective, psychotherapists could then begin to see how they do their therapy and by examining the finer details of the interactions they could also be able to account for their approach – to themselves, their clients and any managed care system they work with.

The responsibility of the therapist

Despite the therapist's best efforts to be as transparent as possible a therapist may try to impose a certain approach or solution onto a client without taking the client's individual character into account. If one looks at therapy from an interactional approach then it could very well be, that the manner in which a psychotherapist has satisfactorily dealt with their own personal conflicts will affect how they conduct therapy with someone whose presenting problem is similar to their own. This can be more obvious if a therapist purports to employ more than one psychotherapeutic model. Corey's (1996) suggestion of the need for therapists to adopt an 'eclectic' approach to therapy may not always work as the therapist's own solution to a problem may predominate, that is, a therapist may try to treat particular problems with specific theoretical approaches if they found they worked for them. If that is the case the way a therapist conducts therapy is something peculiar to the therapist's way of handling problems and not something imitable to the clients. What is clear from the literature, however, (Beutler and Bongar, 1995; Norcross and Goldfried, 2005) is that a therapist will conduct therapy the way they think best based on their training, their personal therapy and their life experiences.

However, becoming a therapist it is not as straightforward as learning a new skill and we cannot assume that one or two approaches will work when applied to all persons with similar presenting issues. This is because we do know exactly how 'the talking cure' brings about healing but we do know some things about the therapist's influence. In psychotherapy the therapist's emotions play a vital role (Rogers, 1995; Finke and Teusch, 2007). Rogers emphasizes the dangers of emotional involvement and sees it as 'the major barrier to interpersonal communication' (1995, p. 331). Balint repeatedly argues that 'if the doctor feels anything while treating a patient, he must stop and examine his feelings as a possible symptom of the patient's illness but on no account to act upon them' (1961, p. 81). Rogers (1957, 1995) also talks about the effects the therapist's emotions can have on the interaction as these can lead to evaluation or judgement of the client's statement. Despite the fact that accrediting bodies, for example the BACP, BABCP or UKCP in the UK, expect a therapist to have undergone their own personal therapy – usually between fifty and one hundred hours, which has to be carried out before the practicing certificate is awarded – the question which needs to be answered is: can one ever be a hundred per cent free of the influences in one's own life? Surely, if therapists, such as Freud and Rogers acknowledged these influences in their own style of therapy then all therapists need to do the same. A therapist may talk about these influences in supervision but only if they, or the supervisor recognizes them. What therapists need is to see how these influences are at work and if they are affecting the clients in negative or positive ways. There are external features which make up the setting which need to be considered as they can impact on the interaction. The following sections will examine this work in the light of some of these features: institutional interactions, asymmetrical relationships and the client as owner of experience.

Institutional interaction

CA has been used to look at typical and routine talk in institutions (Drew and Heritage, 1992). One can look at the 'talking cure' as simply a way of conversing which is organized as an institutional interaction.

The differences between talk in psychotherapy and ordinary conversation become evident when one examines what is excluded from one speech-exchange system and included in the other and also how given resources are used in therapy by the participants. This means that certain types of actions or range of options normally found in ordinary conversation may be excluded from talk in therapy while activities, sequences or forms of listening not found in mundane talk will appear in a therapist's repertoire. For example, in ordinary conversation both parties can engage in activities such as offering sympathy, second storytelling (Sacks, 1992, LC2) or self-disclosure while the symmetrical distribution of questions, answers and interpretations and so on, remove constraints and restrictions found in institutional talk (Drew and Heritage, 1992; ten Have, 1999). In therapy, on the other hand, therapists follow certain guidelines, such as time constraints, restraints on advice-giving or restraints on talking at length. These strategies guide therapists to talk to their clients in a particular way. In addition the very nature of institutional action constitutes the institutional identities and settings (Heritage, 1984a; ten Have, 1999). In therapy, the therapists marry some of their stronger policies, such as the beliefs about the therapy they are practising, with their identity as a person and a therapist and then create a way of talking in line with the 'policies' unique to their person. As well as this a short-term EAP therapist has to take the length of therapy and what they are expected to achieve in that time frame into consideration. This differs from other institutional settings such as the classroom or courtroom where the teacher and barrister follow pre-defined procedures as well as pre-established systems of turn-allocation (Drew and Heritage, 1992). On the other hand, a therapist, like a teacher or barrister, must accomplish institutionally ascribed tasks which are goal-oriented.

Peräkylä (1995) argues that counselling takes place in an informal institutional setting or involves quasi-informal institutional talk (Arminen, 2005) as the participants orient to turn-taking rules different from what one may find in either ordinary conversation or formal institutional settings where the rules are pre-allocated, for example classroom, courtroom or job interview. In psychotherapy there can be a mixture between ordinary conversation and therapeutic talk-in-interaction (Arminen, 2005). Although the psychotherapy sessions examined here differ slightly from the format involved in the Aids counselling sessions described by Peräkylä, which permits advice-giving practices, the turn-taking procedures are similar – they are carried out through the strategic use of turn-taking rules. The client is encouraged to speak and tell their story while the therapist listens or prompts further talk with continuers, questions, reflecting back techniques (formulations) or interpretations. Psychotherapy does not seem to use a specific turn-taking system such as one might find in doctor–patient interactions where the doctor does most of the asking and the patient listens and waits for an expert diagnosis (ten Have, 1991). It found here that clients do not self-select but their turns are in response to questions or formulations and their long turns are created through strategic use of continuers.

Talk in institutional settings will entail formal or officially based activities (Heritage and Greatbatch, 1991). Clients come to therapy requesting assistance which necessitates that the therapist obtains background or additional information before they can proceed. The gathering of information carried out by a doctor in doctor–patient interactions helps a doctor piece together the information to make a diagnosis. Therapists also need background information before they can make an interpretation or offer a formulation. However, a therapist does require a client to talk and at times to talk at length. Also in psychotherapy the therapist is bound by a code of ethics and procedures[1] which outline how a therapist is expected to behave and inhibits them from performing activities such as advice-giving. Drew and Heritage (1992) argue that institutional talk is characterized by a decrease in the range of options and opportunities available in ordinary talk. The question then is whether all properties of institutional talk can be accounted for in terms of constraints. Drew and Heritage (ibid.) do not support the possibility that there are additional specialized activities involved in institutional talk. However, there are unique moves specific to psychotherapy which do not involve restrictions, for example, visualization techniques, systematic desensitization or mindfulness, and these are partly conversational and embedded in conversation, that is, they are conducted with the help of talk. While activities are done in and through the talk one needs knowledge of the relevant practice to understand these activities. Not only does institutional talk differ from ordinary conversation but each institution has its own 'unique fingerprint' (Heritage, 1984b) for each type of institutional interaction. Although, EAP organizations offer the same type of therapy to all clients each approach can actually be unique in its delivery.

The necessity of background information

The investigations in this book use the turn-taking rules involved in conversation (Sacks, Schegloff and Jefferson, 1974) to explicate how a psychotherapist and a client carry out their business but it also argues that background information is necessary when analyzing psychotherapy.

Some CA analysts have argued that the provision of information (other than a transcription of the talk in the sessions using CA's transcription methods) is not necessary as the relevance of context is only of importance if it is consequential in the talk itself by the participant's adherence to that context (Schegloff, 1997; Pomerantz, 1998; Wetherell, 1998). More recently Leudar et al. (2008a, 2008b and Antaki, 2011) have taken a more ethnomethodological stance that unless an analyst has some understanding of the specific therapy being conducted he or she may miss out on the meaning the talk holds for the participants. Also, certain therapeutic procedures such as 'unobtrusive leading' performed by the therapist may go unnoticed if the analyst adopts a purely 'unmotivated looking approach'. I suggest, like Mooerman (1998) and Leudar et al. (2008a, 2008b), that without taking into account the broader social context a conversational analyst's work overlooks what it is in the talk that makes it meaningful for the participants. I suggest that if a researcher does not have any understanding of the approach adopted by the therapist a researcher could see the therapist's approach as incomprehensible, for example, in EAP type therapy a researcher could believe that the therapist is totally ignoring the client's problem. How much background information is to be revealed can be left to the therapist and the analyst to decide. Strictly speaking, the extracts from the sessions presented in this book have been analyzed using a CA/ethno approach as the type of therapy being conducted is taken into consideration. However, for ease of reading I mainly use the term CA.

Asymmetrical relationships

According to McLeod (2011) matters of power and powerlessness are issues which are always present in any psychotherapeutic encounter. While all of the major therapies talk about empowering the client (Bongar and Beutler, 1995; Miell and Croghan, 1998) they also accept that in the caring professions professional relationships cannot be considered equal mainly because the professional is the expert. In a counselling encounter asymmetry always exists between the participants (Foppa, 1995; Drew, 1991). The therapist always assumes the role of expert or the one with more experience regarding how the client could resolve their problem. The client is coming for help with their problem. There is generally never a crossover of roles. Foppa (1995) examines advice giving in counselling encounters and argues that it is difficult to determine whether or not the client has comprehended the counsellor's recommendations or the adequacy of the counsellor's advice when we do not know how accurately the therapist understood the client's problem to begin with. In this type of therapy we – both analysts and therapists – are also in the dark concerning whether or not mutual understandings exist between the interlocutors. In this therapy the therapist is neither concerned with whether the client complies with the therapist's recommendations nor is the counsellor supposed to give advice. The only way of determining this mutual understanding is by examining whether the client comes to talk differently about their problem or not.

Ten Have (1991) in his investigation of asymmetry in doctor–patient interactions notes that the participant roles differ as the doctor assumes the role of leader and the patient that of follower. However, the asymmetrical allocation of questions, comments or interventions involved in a psychotherapeutic encounter is not something which has been distributed beforehand but is shaped by the task in which the participants are engaged (ten Have, 1991; Drew, 1991). Instead it is argued here, like ten Have, that asymmetry is an accomplishment and we need to examine how it is produced in various ways by the participants. Although the institutional structure places constraints on the different roles, that is the client goes to the therapist's office and waits to be questioned about their difficulty for example 'how can therapy help you?', it is expected that there will be a mutually agreed goal – the client comes for help (Käsermann, 1991; Proctor, 2002). Peräkylä and Silverman (1991) point out that a counsellor will demonstrate professionalism by asking questions and in doing so invite the recipient to take on the role of client. This pattern contrasts with the question–answer sequence involved in ordinary conversation and the moral matter[2] involved when a person responds to an invitation to speak. The patterns involved in therapist/client question–answer adjacency pairs are uniform according to Peräkylä (1995) with therapist asking questions, commenting or interpreting and clients supplying answers or elaborations to the therapist's questions and interventions.

Nevertheless, the professional can assume the dominant role (ten Have, 1991; Käsermann, 1991) as they have more access to knowledge and resources (Drew, 1991). Ten Have (1991) found that the doctor dominated the interaction while the patient submitted answers and accepted and complied with suggestions. As already mentioned in Chapter 1, Sacks points out 'as long as one is doing the questions, then in part one has control of the conversation' (1992, LC 1, p. 55). If that is the case the psychotherapist who does most of the asking has most of the control and as a result can decide much of the content and direction of the conversation. Also clients do not know the reasoning process that guides the therapist's interventions and clients' answers become framed by the therapist's interventions. For example, a question that the therapist here might ask, such as: 'what stops you from putting yourself first?' encloses the topic in a controlled way as the client is forced to reflect on the therapist's interpretation of the client's behaviour.

However, one would not expect an empathic therapist to dominate, control or direct the client. Proctor (2002), who is a non-directive therapist, argues that the very ethics of therapy is one of equality of both parties who are equal in worth. In fact EAP therapists would be expected to do as much as possible to avoid controlling or constraining the client's account in any way. They would also not expect a client to be in any way compliant and, while clients provide answers they may not always fully accept what the therapist has said in a formulation or an interpretation. However, sometimes the therapist may not fully embrace the power bestowed upon them by virtue of their role and may underestimate the effect that any structural power and authority has on the client's life in their attempts to stress the client's agency (Proctor, 2002).

Proctor (2002) notes that the person-centred therapist's concept of power focuses on the notion of 'power-from-within'. It emphasizes the individual power of the clients. Therefore to avoid using power or control over their clients a therapist needs to ensure that their own personal power is strong (Proctor, ibid.). That however is the ideal expounded by all therapists but the reality may be that the therapist could be oblivious to the power they actually exert over their clients as this balance is also affected by the client's own history of power and control. For example, therapists can use continuers such as mm, or yeah or even silences to assert interactional dominance. Käsermann (1991) is of the view that therapists could intentionally obstruct therapy by remaining silent or using continuers instead of intervening. A CA examination of sessions can help correct such views. As the therapist has access to resources which would help the client, it is hoped that the therapist would interject with some supportive remark – such as a formulation as an empathic response or an interpretation which the client could accept or reject. They could also allow extended sequences to develop and use continuers to direct the client to continue on even though the client may be finished. By not intervening and using continuers to prompt the client to keep talking the therapist exercises his or her interactional control. As far as formulations are concerned the therapist expects agreement or disagreement. While according to the CA literature agreement is preferred (Pomerantz, 1989), the therapist must also accept what the client has said as being correct (Käsermann, 1991) and cannot offer a comment such as 'I don't believe you'. A therapist cannot reject the truth as the client sees it. However, a therapist's rejection can be evident if he or she utters, for example, mm or right in a doubtful voice as this still amounts to a rejection.

In a psychotherapeutic setting the experts can be empowered to impose their own definition of client's needs (Käsermann, 1991). This can often happen in medical encounters or in psychiatric interviews. Drew and Heritage noted that 'institutional representatives may strategically direct the talk through such means as their capacity to change topics and their selective formulations, in their next questions of the salient points in the prior answers' (1992, p. 49). In psychotherapy the therapist can interrupt the talk, halt the topic and re-direct it by using interactional devices such as formulations (Antaki, 2008) or questions (McMartin, 2008) which can lead the talk in the way the therapist wishes it to go. In this therapy, questions lead to answers which can then lead to formulations. By using what McMartin calls 'positive questioning devices' solution-focused therapists can direct the client's thinking so that clients are forced to recall positive experiences. Also therapists can perform actions which can have an effect on the outcome. Clients do not have the same 'know-how' as the therapist about the protocols involved in the psychotherapy sessions. The client may also be unaware of the agenda the therapist is working from, for example, a solution-focused therapist can get the client to talk about the times when they did not have the problem without the client knowing what purpose this would serve. This could cause confusion for the client, especially if they want to talk at length about their problem.

Also some studies have found (Schegloff, 1968; ten Have, 1991; Heritage and Greatbatch, 1991) that access to the first position, for example, a question or a formulation privileges the speaker as they not only have control over the second pair part but also have a right to speak again after the answer has been provided. This provides them with the opportunity to take another turn with a further question, a formulation or a continuer. Furthermore, therapists can decide to withhold information about themselves, and in doing so can avoid giving their opinion which could reinforce their expert role not only on psychological issues but on matters of living and problem solving. (The idea of self-disclosure is discussed later in Chapter 3). Peyrot (1987) found that some therapists use what he calls 'oblique proposals' to guide or nudge the client towards a particular solution by providing information to the client about how another person solved the same problem. However, by using expressions such as '*another client I had did…*' or '*I knew someone who did such and such and it worked'*, the therapist can convince the client in a circumspect way that they should try to engage in some behaviour as it would be beneficial to them. Finally, professionals have more rights 'to know' than clients (Heritage, 1997), which in psychotherapy may cause a client to hold back on knowledge they have concerning solutions to the issue at hand. This holding back, if exercised in psychotherapy, may serve to dis-empower the client rather than empower them. Whether the therapist's influence is positive or negative cannot be determined by talking it through in supervision or with peers alone, as a professional can sometimes have blind spots in terms of how they professionally affect clients. A good way of solving this is for therapists or managed care systems to look at how these ideas are developed in the therapeutic relationship which, I argue is continually being practised and repro-duced in the conversation between the participants.

Client as owner of experience

While the therapist may have power in the form of knowledge, skills, protocol, professional title and so on, the client has the power over the content and what they choose to disclose to the therapist. Studies have shown that in the social world people have epistemic privileges with respect to privately acquired experiences. In therapy, research has shown that the client is the expert as they come to therapy owning an experience to which they alone have complete access (Peräkylä and Silverman, 1991; Peräkylä, 1995; Anderson and Goolishian, 1992). However, in order to work on that experience it needs to be shared. One could argue that when it is shared it no longer belongs just to the client. It is possible that sharing thoughts duplicates them rather than removes them from the original person who has experienced them; during the sharing process the experience also becomes transformed. Rogers (1992) talks about the client owning their experience and emphasizes that it is necessary for the therapist to try to understand the client's experience from the client's point of view. The primary task of the therapist is to listen to what the client says and make space for what the client has not yet said. According to Anderson and Goolishian (1992) the therapist should take a not-knowing stance in this dialogic process. However, by using what Rogers (1995) calls 'accurate empathy' a therapist would be expected to be able to empathize to such a degree with a client that they come to share the feelings related to that experience with the client. Therapy is not about learning to own the experience of another, it is about listening to such a degree that the therapist comes to share the client's feelings so that the client feels understood. To do this a therapist needs to be able to build a genuine therapeutic relationship; one that effects beneficial change in the client or patient.

However, Peräkylä and Silverman argue that 'the knowledge that the owner of the experience has about his or her mind is systematically treated as belonging to a different kind of category than the knowledge that others may have about it' (1991, p. 449) and as a result the description of a client's feeling which a therapist may provide is tentative in comparison to how the client would describe that same experience. On the other hand however, Vehviläinen (2003) who examined interpretative sequences in psychoanalytical psychotherapy found that the interpretations provided by the therapist can be in contrast to what the client knows to be true but can be the truth or contain elements of the truth. 'The analyst is seen as able to interpret the meaning of the patient's talk before and even beyond the patient's awareness of it, and thus eventually also able to help the patient reach a new awareness of her or his mental experience' (ibid., p. 575). In therapy the client's experience is made public so that it can be examined and may then be transformed in the therapy as both therapist and client begin to work on it. Further then to what Peräkylä and Silverman (1991) and Peräkylä (1995) found, the interactional devices of interpreting in psychoanalysis and formulating in person-centred therapy can provide new avenues of mental experiences of which the client was unaware before beginning therapy. It is the business of therapy to transform the experiences which the client brings so that they perceive and interpret those experiences differently. This is done through the relationship which is made visible in the talk.

Concluding comments

In psychotherapy, talk is used as a discursive resource to guide reflections and understandings and various linguistic forms can be drawn on by both participants to achieve its aims. The therapeutic relationship differs then on the point of power which is tied to the therapist's 'therapeutic policy' (Antaki et al., 2005), institutional defence and know how about what will work. The institution is the therapist's protection and the theoretical orientation is their defence. The therapist's discursive role becomes evident in the relationship through their theoretical orientation delivered through the medium of language. Freud suggested that 'by words one person can make another blissfully happy or drive him to despair' (cf. de Shazer, 1994, p. 3). For therapists their belief about how what is psychological health is developed through their training, their personal therapy, their life experiences and their personal and professional philosophy. In the empirical chapters I look at how the therapist's beliefs can be observable as powerful by looking at how they are instantiated in the talk. And CA is a fitting method for examining this.

Therapists'/practitioners' corner

In this corner I will look at overlapping talk and interruptions which in CA terms can indicate that the listener is very attentive, or on the other hand there may be a jostling for interactional power. A close analysis will draw one's attention to subtle and sophisticated aspects of the 'talk-in-interaction' that in ordinary conversation we never notice, or at least never pay attention to. According to the turn-taking rules only one speaker talks at a time and speaker change normally occurs with relative ease (Sacks et al., 1974). However, overlaps and interruptions do occur and in such cases practitioners need to take note of any features or behaviours which go against this rule by asking themselves questions such as: why that now? Sometimes overlaps can occur at the very end of TPRs (Transition Relevant Places) and this is an indication of how ordered and fine-grained conversation can be (Sidnell, 2010). Sometimes therapists may find that they come in and take a turn at talk just before the client's talk has come to completion. These types of overlap indicate that the therapist is closely monitoring the client's talk and is marking the action or topic embodied in the talk. In this example, the therapist hears that the client is nearing the end of her turn.

Session 1 Jackie
1. T: so:: Jackie how ca- can therapy help ↑you.
2. C: where I'm::: concerned what I'd love to work on is (0.8) my (0.7) se:lf-
3.   esteem self-confidence and fi:n:ding a >sense of self< because I:: it sto:pped
4.   me doing so many things up till ↑no[w::,
5. T: [o.k] and how how does that ah (0.5) ma
6. manifest itself like how do you how are you aw:a:r:e that it's self-esteem
7. that's blocking you

The continuing intonation indicated by the comma on line 4 suggest that the client did not intend stopping but the therapist hears the rise in pitch on the first part of *now* and may have projected stopping. The therapist has also heard and accepted the problem, described on lines 2–4 and attempts to take control using *ok* (line 5) and move the client to think along the lines of awareness.

[ ] overlap, > < the talk is noticeably faster, a full-stop indicates a closing or stopping intonation while a comma means continuing intonation.

In this extract the therapist clearly interrupts the client

Session 4 Jane
1. C: and that's why I cry when I tell people that i::::: and not to mention my
2.   family and my [clo:::s-]
3. T: [so it's] not, it's not the people, it's the way you're ... your
4.   reacting to it, isn't it↑ they way you are thinking::::: about it and then reacting↑

The overlapping talk (lines 2 and 3) displays a clear interruption by the therapist. The client had not finished her turn, there was no pause or TRP but the therapist interrupted and the client quickly dropped out. The therapist here is steering the conversation away from talk about others and moving it back to the client's reactions.

Underlining is used when the speaker places emphasis on a word or sound.

In this extract however, it is the therapist who is clearly interrupted and drops out.

Session 3 Liz
1. T: °greenpeace° an all that [is it↑
2. C: [yeah
3. T: ↓°right° (0.6) ↑right (.) and er (1.0) [eh so::
4. C: [but I ne]ver thought that I'd be able to
5.   live like that I thought I'd have to (0.3) you know (0.8) recyc::le everything
6.   an >bring it down to the bank every weekend but live in the city because it
7.   wouldn't be practical in the country an-< .hh (0.3) but I can see now that
8.   that's the way I'd really be comfortable liv↑ing (0.3)
9. T: °°mm°° (0.3)

The therapist attempts to come in on line 3 after the question had been answered by the client on line 2. However, she is forced out of the turn by the client's intention to go on, which is marked by yeah ... *but* (lines 2 and 4). The overlap on line 4 does not occur at the completion of the therapist's turn but in the middle and can indicate competing activities. The therapist did have something to add here but the client also had something further to say and needed to continue. What is interesting to note here is that control of the topic can be with the client but control of the direction the conversation takes is more often with the therapist and this will become evident as the reader works through the empirical chapters.

°word° when a piece of talk is noticeably quieter than the surrounding talk, °°word°° the talk is quieter again.

3
Conversation Analysis and Psychotherapy

Introduction – a brief look at the literature on CA and doctor–patient interactions

As Conversation Analysis (CA) is an approach which is slowly beginning to be used as a method of research for psychotherapy, I also looked at some research involving doctor–patient interactions and made some comparisons (Schegloff, 1963; ten Have, 1991; Mellinger, 1995; Garafanga and Britten, 2004; Heritage and Maynard, 2006; Antaki, 2011; Heritage and Robinson, 2011; Gill and Roberts, 2013). Doctor–patient consultations, such as might be found in a G.P. surgery or psychiatric unit are analogous to psychotherapist–client interactions as both are of an institutional nature where the trained professional offers a helping service to a patient or client in need. Most of the research carried out using CA on doctor–patient consultations found that both participants orient themselves to a specific structure or expectation about how the consultation will proceed. As would be expected in a professional–client consultation the asymmetrical relationship affects the turn-taking procedures, which are designed in a particular format where the doctor asks the questions and the patient answers until a diagnosis is reached. However, using doctor–patient interviews as a basis for studying psychotherapist–client interviews may not do justice to the practice of psychotherapy as some of the more intimate and powerful aspects of therapy may be overlooked. Hak and de Boer (1996) found that in a medical first encounter interview, formulations were non-existent. The question–answer format, coupled with the notable absence of formulations (reflecting back techniques) provided an indication of how the doctor is able to impose a particular type of order on to the conversation, that is reflecting back techniques were absent (ibid.). In a doctor–patient psychiatric interview only *gist* formulations, which summarize what the client has said and as described by Heritage and Watson (1979), were used and were employed as devices for checking on information so that professional assessments could be conducted (1979). Hak and de Boer (1996) concluded that the absence of *upshot* formulations, where the professional draws out some relevant implication from what the patient/client says (adding something to the reflecting back technique) forms the main difference between a doctor–patient psychiatric interview and a psychotherapeutic one.

What one can say however is that all practitioners adopt a specific agenda and use this agenda with all patients and clients. Patients and clients on the other hand adjust their talk to those agendas (Antaki, 2011).

Mellinger (1995) investigates talk-in-interaction in a psychiatric interview where the patient is being assessed concerning their suitability for psychotherapy. However, the interaction is examined from the point of view of dominance which may be too strong a word in the psychotherapeutic encounter. Mellinger (1995) sees the power relationship in the interaction as very asymmetrical and sees the psychiatrist's talk, where all the questions asked are indications of control with the patient offering little resistance. Heritage and Robinson (2011) suggest that patients may sometimes withhold concerns if they are secondary to what they see as their main concern unless the practitioner pins a patient down with specific questions, for example, 'is there anything else we need to take care of today' (p., 11). Garafanga and Britten (2004), who see the doctor–patient relationship pointing more towards mutuality, found that patients in a medical consultation did resist suggestions made by the doctor and did not just accept the doctor's preferences. Ten Have (1991), who looked at how doctors and patients achieve asymmetry through the details of their situated interactions, found that the participants choose to act in accordance with what is expected of them by the institution and that both participants could try to influence the course of conversation. As doctor–patient interactions work mainly around a diagnosis and how the patient can be treated, the elements of influence followed by client resistance are much less subtle than one would find in psychotherapy – at least in short-term therapy where one expects to be helped in a short space of time.

Conversation analysis and psychotherapy

Much of the literature to date on CA and psychotherapy focuses on a thorough description of how psychotherapists accomplish their tasks through talk. CA examines structures of talk (Drew and Heritage, 1992; ten Have, 2001; Antaki, 2011) and can be used to examine the structures of therapeutic talk – how the talk is constructed by the therapist and client. CA can also provide a detailed elaboration about therapists' 'stocks of interactional knowledge' (SIKS) – the member's theories concerning their interactional practices as therapists (Peräkylä and Vehviläinen, 2003) and 'can enter into dialogue with SIKS – extending, specifying or correcting the picture of interaction given by them' (Peräkylä et al., 2008, p. 23). As CA does not commit to pre-existing theories and instead adopts an open-minded approach to the exploration of interaction, it can uncover practices and discover patterns of interaction of which therapists may be unaware (Peräkylä, 2011, 2013). Therapists may be sure about the theoretical approach they take with their clients, the specific agenda they employ and the moves they make to influence change. However, they may not be fully aware of how they as participants are interacting to bring about these changes. As most therapists work alone with their clients the finer details of their practice may be hidden from view so much that the therapist may be oblivious to the fact that he or she uses language to carry his or her theoretical orientation and assumptions to enact change. CA aims to 'fill in the gaps in psychotherapy theory by conceptualizing and describing the moment-by-moment exchange between therapist and client' (Stiles, 2008, p. 1). CA can explicate the finer details of the talk to make visible how a therapist uses interactional devices which are either aspects of the SIK, not part of the therapist's SIKs, or are mismatches between the SIK and the therapist's interactional practice. CA provides concrete empirical research of actual social action and it is an assumption of CA that all aspects of social action and interaction exhibit organized patterns of stable, recurrent structural features to which the participants are oriented. A therapist's action is not independent of the action of their client but is patterned in relationship to their client. According to CA meanings are created in psychotherapy by the contextual interactions occurring between the therapist and the client and can be understood by examining the patterns of interaction.

CA does not assume that language represents the world in either true or false fashion – different descriptions and formulations can present different versions of events. A speaker's communicative action is context-shaped as well as context-renewing (Heritage, 1984). This means that an utterance achieves its meaning in relation to its immediate context. For example, take a client's statement such as, 'If I had one wish it would be not to be alive'. This statement achieves its meaning by examining the therapist's prior question, 'What goes through your mind when you are in a depressed state'? Also such a statement uttered by the client, helps shape a new context as it leads to a new question or formulation by the therapist. According to CA, understanding language means 'understanding actions – utterances – which are constructively interpreted in relation to their contexts' (Heritage, 1984, p. 139). One of the basic assumptions of CA is that 'no order of detail can be dismissed, a priori, as disorderly, accidental or irrelevant' (Heritage, 1984, p. 241). As the details of conversation analysis can be extremely precise – taking micro-pauses and in-breaths into account, the finest detail of the talk can be investigated to help therapists see and understand how they use language to achieve particular results with their clients. CA can look at why these details and utterances exist in the talk and it does this by examining the talk in terms of the theory (Stiles, 2008). The research is about linking CA's rich descriptive language of possibilities to therapy theory and practice. CA can therefore help therapists to reflect on how they do their therapy by describing how their theoretical orientations are realized in practice.

Much of the work to date, however, such as Davis (1986); Buttny (1995); Madill et al., (2001); Peräkylä (1995); Antaki et al., (2004, 2005a); Antaki (2008); Hutchby (2005); Rae (2008); Muntigl and Zabala (2008); Voutilainen et al., (2010); Peräkylä (2013) examines the interactional moves and processes of psychotherapeutic interaction without placing much emphasis on the therapeutic orientation of the therapists. Most of the researchers make reference to the therapeutic orientation, but the analyses are carried out without taking the therapeutic orientation into account. This type of approach to research into psychotherapy is in keeping with the CA tradition that pre-existing knowledge of context is not necessary to do good CA and may even blur the specific features of the activities under examination (Sacks, Schegloff and Jefferson, 1974; Heritage, 1984; Schegloff, 1991). The mechanics of the talk occurring between a therapist and client simply involve a reduction of and a restraint on the conversational practices used in ordinary conversation as well as a more concentrated focus on particular procedures found in ordinary conversation (Heritage, 1984; Drew and Heritage, 1992). For example, the practice of troubles-telling as well as listening, questioning, interpreting and even formulating what the teller has said can also be found in conversations among friends or family members.

However, in psychotherapy the participants adopt specific discourse identities, such as listener or speaker to engage in the sequential activities as well as manage role-specific activities (Madill et al., 2001). These identities become ratified by the participants and remain more or less constant throughout the sessions.[1] In this therapy the discourse identity of the therapist is mainly that of listener, story recipient, questioner, interpreter, formulator, encourager and facilitator. The therapist's more or less fixed identity projects a converse identity for the client so that the client then assumes the identity of speaker, story-teller and answerer. However, these discourse identities are not equal in all therapies. In CBT a therapist may also assume the identity of story-teller by engaging in self-disclosure or may act as advice-giver, educator or skills trainer (Proctor, 2008b). In psychoanalysis and psychodynamic therapies the therapist will never act as advisor and rarely assumes the identity of questioner but will instead act as listener, interpreter, establisher of links between patterns in current and early relationships, or elaborator (Peräkylä, 2004, 2005). In solution-focused therapy the therapist overwhelmingly assumes the identity of listener, questioner, facilitator and encourager. In person-centred therapy the therapist normally acts as questioner, formulator (of empathic reflecting back responses) and facilitator.

The problem which may arise for analysts who examine the practice of psychotherapy is that unlike institutional settings such as a courtroom, classroom or interview, the discourse identity of the therapist can vary greatly between the different therapeutic approaches and also in the way the identities are played out. For example in solution-focused therapy the therapist's questioning can appear forceful (McMartin, 2008) whereas such styles of questioning would be the antithesis of the person-centred or the psychoanalytical approach. In CBT the therapist may continually aim to keep the client focused on the agenda (Antaki and Jahoda, 2010) whereas the approach of psychoanalysis is free association. Therefore it would do the practitioners of psychotherapy an injustice if CA were to generalize about psychotherapy and analyse all therapies in the same way. It is argued here, as in Leudar et al., 2008a, 2008b; Peräkylä et al., 2008; and Antaki, 2011, that CA must take into consideration the very different assumptions and theories within each model of therapy if CA is to do justice to the practice of psychotherapy. If CA is to enter into dialogue with these theories and elaborate on them, then the CA analyst must appreciate these theories and how the therapists understand their work in terms of these theories.

As far as person-centred therapy is concerned, 'stocks of conversational knowledge' (Peräkylä and Vehviläinen, 2003) can assist in the unpacking of the idea of a 'frame of reference' (Stiles, 2008) by explicating possible distinguishing factors between a therapist's frame of reference and a client's. Antaki et al. (2005a) and Antaki (2008) found that some formulations can delete and select certain aspects of the client's story in order to push through a tendentious reading of the client's account in order to move ahead with some therapeutic or institutional agenda. This suggests that therapy is also about advancing the therapist's needs. These therapist interpretations or implications can sneak into the client's frame of reference with or without their consent (Stiles, 2008; Antaki, 2008). This suggests that the therapist enacts institutional power, not only through the knowledge they have but also through dishonest techniques. Schegloff (1963) also demonstrated that a therapist's task is to help patients become capable of using psychiatric theory in order to help them understand themselves. The patient comes to use this theory – its language, narratives and so on – properly when they can talk about the causes and cures of their own illness and demonstrate how they can apply the theory to themselves. In addition in solution-focused therapy McMartin (2008) found that certain types of WH questions containing 'optimistic presuppositions' can move the client's action contained in the telling into the therapist's frame of reference so much so that the client is restrained to talk about their strengths, skills and resources which could mean complying with the therapist's frame of reference. In cognitive therapy Bercelli et al. (2008) has shown how clients can resist therapist proposals and how therapists can then exploit the client's response by encouraging extended responses. It is during this expansion that the client may come to change their perspectives. This can be carried out if the therapist keeps control of the expansion by ignoring some aspects and intervening at points where the therapist wishes to direct the talk to some therapeutic end. Many of the studies so far have explicated that a therapist's job is to get the client to think like them.

Much of the findings then seem to be about explicating how much power and control a therapist exercises with their clients. This however provides a negative view of psychotherapy and therapists and resonates with opinions put forward by some researchers who believe that the client is completely powerless (see Proctor, 2008a, chapter 2) and that the therapist has the potential to misuse and abuse their power through their assumptions and values about what works best for clients. In fact Rowe (1989; cf. Proctor, 2002, p. 12) suggests that 'the most dangerous people in the world are those who believe they know what is best for others', while others equate the asymmetrical relationship in therapy with oppression and abuse. Masson (1989; cf. Proctor, 2008a, p. 11) argues that 'the therapeutic relationship involves an imbalance of power.... only one person is thought to be an "expert" in human relations and feelings. Only one person is thought to be in trouble'. Drew (1991) also suggests that unequal participants in talk in psychotherapy may result from moves which position one participant as an 'expert' in relation to the other. Madill et al. (2001) argues that the therapist's discourse identities or role-specific activities 'are the means through which asymmetries in status are realized' (p. 415) and Buttny (1996) notes that a therapist's control can be empirically displayed by investigating the interactional asymmetries between the therapist and the client. Conversational control (Schegloff, 1968) can become evident by identifying various practices such as therapeutic 'reframings' which a therapist uses to move a client's account into a therapist's one (Buttny, 1996; Davis, 1986). The solution then is to investigate how these asymmetries are managed on particular occasions because if there is systematic abuse it will show.

Drew (1991) and Antaki (2011) also argue that an unequal distribution of knowledge may be found in most institutional settings. This suggests that there is an imbalance of power to be discovered in almost all institutional talk. In psychotherapy this is true for certain therapies more than others (Proctor, 2008a). For example, from a Foucaultian perspective, CBT is rife with 'regimes of truth', normalising principles on which the 'right' or 'helpful' way to think are based (Proctor, 2008a, p. 67). As the CBT model, which gets the client to try out some new behaviour, can call on science to convince clients what is best for them, therapists need to be vigilant about not imposing their own needs onto the client by ensuring that they remain neutral. Psychoanalysts on the other hand can also use their knowledge of their theory to display imbalances of power and this is mostly evident when a client displays resistance. If a client resists insights provided by a therapist's interpretation or resists the therapist who provides this, this can then be interpreted as a client's resistance to uncovering repressed material and can be used by the therapist as a means to present further interpretations of the client's unconscious. 'The analyst is seen as able to interpret the meaning of the client's talk before and beyond the client's awareness of it, and eventually to help the client reach a new awareness of her or his experience' (Vehviläinen, 2008). The practice of focusing on the client's prior action and interpreting it in relation to the theory of psychoanalysis helps to ensure that asymmetry is maintained throughout the sessions. Rogers, on the other hand (cf. Proctor, 2008) attempted to eliminate the therapist's power through the therapist's unrelenting use of the core conditions: empathy, congruence and unconditional positive regard.

A therapist's judgmental attitude, evaluations or interpretations are seen as threatening for the client (Rogers, 1995). The person-centred approach is supposed to eradicate or, at the very least, reduce the power which others have over clients by increasing the client's own personal power. Solution-focused therapists are expected to use their power of knowledge but in a positive way – to empower their clients to become aware of their ability to find resolution. Therefore, as each of the major schools of therapy tackles this issue of power and empowerment from different perspectives it is necessary that CA takes these different perspectives into account before deciding that a therapist is using institutional power and conversational control through the asymmetrical relationship in a negative way.

A brief look at the treatment of research to date

Much of the research to date has focused on: psychoanalytical therapy (Vehviläinen, 2003a, 2008; Peräkylä, 2004, 2005, 2008, 2011, 2013; Streeck, 2008); psychodynamic, interpersonal psychotherapy (Madill et al., 2001); group psychoanalytical psychotherapy (Halonen, 2008); cognitive and cognitive-behavioural approaches (Antaki et al., 2004; Antaki et al., 2005; Bercelli et al., 2008; Antaki and Jahoda, 2010; Voutilainen et al., 2011) and group work using psychoanalytical approaches (Leudar et al., 2008). Peräkylä (2004), Vehviläinen (2003a) and Peräkylä (2008) examine interpretations in psychoanalysis and how interpretations link aspects of the client's talk together to produce a creative act. Peräkylä (2004) and Vehviläinen (2003a) argue that what is created by the therapist is a new perspective on the way the patient sees their problem and this is accomplished through the act of interpreting. In fact Peräkylä (2008) notes that the act of interpreting the client's talk is the therapist's most valuable tool in influencing the client to change. Both Peräkylä (2004) and Vehviläinen (2003a) investigated how interpretations are constructed. It was found that events leading up to an interpretation engage the analyst in a specialized task and so the act of interpreting spans longer turns. The analyst listens and tries to help by establishing links between past and present relationships, unconscious conflicts and motives and the known and the unknown parts of the self, and the analyst is very aware that they are doing this. The objective is to help the client understand their experiences in a new way. Change will occur when the client has developed new insights (Peräkylä, 2008). Vehviläinen (2003a) argues that interpretations are built up step by step in what is known as 'the interpretative trajectory'.

This trajectory is seen as more than an interactional achievement as the process involves linking together unconscious and conscious revelations and their underlying reasons and conveying these to the patient when appropriate. These interpretations are made by joining something in the patient's present talk with something which was revealed in their prior account. Further to the traditional CA findings, preparation for this is not just a local matter but takes place over many turns.

Vehviläinen (2003a) suggests that psychoanalysis 'has methods for listening and interpreting another person's talk that are not found anywhere else' (p. 574). This suggests that these processes are in some way exclusive and tailored to the needs of psychoanalysis. Vehviläinen (ibid.) notes that topics expressed by the client are linked together by the analyst as unconscious associations of other mentioned topics, for example narrations of dreams are linked to topics. Certainly where a psychoanalyst puts their focus, that is what they listen out for and what they gather from the client's account to develop unconscious associations and create interpretations is different from other therapies, for example cognitive-behavioural therapists do not focus on the past and solution-focused therapists do not focus on the problem – despite the client's attempts to do so. However, there are so many different theories and branches of psychoanalysis available today, for example, object-relations theory, self-psychology, ego-psychology, and so on, that it would be a mistake to place all listening and interpreting approaches in the same category.[2]

Nevertheless, psychoanalytic therapy and psychodynamic therapies in general have a unique feature: transference. Transference is defined as 'a phenomenon wherein patients relive experiences, feelings and memories from the past as if they were occurring in the present' (Bertram et al., 1995, p. 27). Counter-transference occurs when therapists have feelings towards their clients indicating something unresolved in the mind of the therapist. The importance of the therapeutic relationship is common to all therapies, but the transference and counter-transference relationship, where the relationship is used in a pre-planned way to bring about change is not an issue in person-centred and solution-focused therapies. Transference has of yet not been examined as an element in its own right by CA analysts although it is an important element for a large number of therapists. However, for analysts it could only be examined in the psychodynamic therapies where it is used. This indicates the importance of examining each approach to therapy as an independent type of therapeutic practice.

Formulations are also used in psychoanalysis but their function is different from the person-centred approach. In psychoanalysis formulations are used 'in order to highlight and clarify particular issues or details' (Vehviläinen, 2003a, p. 584). In this study (see Chapter 6) formulations are also used to clarify issues or details – *gist* formulations – but they are also used to make implications concerning what the client has been saying – *upshot* formulations (Hertitage and Watson, 1979). Antaki, who examined various different types of therapies, found that formulations are a form of interpreting. He also noted that 'interpretation is a core feature of much therapy' (2008, p. 34). To suggest that psychoanalysis has different methods of listening and interpreting from other therapeutic approaches may be an overgeneralization which has not been established empirically. While it is true that person-centred, CBT and solution-focused approaches may not focus on, for example, dream-work or unconscious conflicts they do make links between what was mentioned in the client's prior talk and their present utterances. Psychoanalysts do not seem to have different methods of listening and interpreting from time-limited short term therapies; they simply focus on different aspects of the client's account and interpret the expressions differently. What interpretations do in psychoanalysis, *upshot* formulations do in person-centred therapy and Socratic questioning does in CBT, that is 'unobtrusively lead' the client in the direction of change by leading them towards fresh insights.

The notion of resistance

Antaki et al. (2005a) and Antaki (2008) found that formulations can act as vehicles to get across a tendentious, formulation-type description of the client's experience. Similarly Buttny (2001) found that *upshot* formulations (reflecting back techniques containing some implications) channelled the client to talk about themselves in a way appropriate to the therapist's talk. This channelling could be enacted over a series of turns which could indicate that the therapist is being persistent or may be persuasive. However, while *upshot* formulations may 'tell the clients things about themselves' (Bergmann, 1992) they tend to do so in an attempt to get the client to think about themselves in the way appropriate to the theory. In that way these formulations attempt to channel the client to think about their problem in a particular way – in the way they have been trained to do – and therefore may not be as controlling or negative as Antaki (2008) suggests. Also some formulations, such as the question-formats ones, project a variety of responses, not all of which are yes/no but are used by the therapist to channel the client to talk in a particular way about a topic and not to think about themselves in a particular way. Also not all interpretations have to be accepted; and Vehviläinen (2008) examines how clients may exhibit resistance to the insights offered by the therapist's interpretations. According to Antaki et al. (2005a) and Davis (1986) a positive response to the therapist's interventions, whether they are formulations or interpretations, is preferred in order for the business of therapy to proceed towards the accomplishment of its goal. Both Antaki (2003) and Davis (1986) also suggest that a negative response may be interpreted as resistance. However, there is a difference between resistance and mere disagreement.

Different therapies approach resistance in different ways. Some solution-focused therapists see resistance as an indication of a problem in the relationship between therapist and client (Miller and Rollnick, 2002) while other therapists see it as something which only exists in the minds of therapists (de Shazer, 1994, 1988). Rogers (1942) wrote about the concept of resistance in person-centred therapy and hypothesized that 'resistance to counselling and to the counsellor is not an inevitable part of psychotherapy, nor a desirable part but it grows primarily out of poor techniques of handling the client's expression of his problems and feelings ... out of unwise attempts on the part of the counsellor to short-cut the therapeutic process by bringing into discussion emotionalized attitudes which the client is not yet ready to face' (p. 151). Insight, on the other hand, according to Rogers 'is an experience which is achieved, not an experience which can be imposed' (1942, p. 196). Resistance in CBT needs to be dealt with through elicitation, discussion, psycho-education and a focus on psychological problems and not just on practical problems (Leahy, 2003, 2010). While there are many reasons a client may resist interventions, homework, and behavioural experiments therapists who overlook the fact that schemas and core beliefs are self-preserving may employ too many practical techniques and fail to engage with the client's apprehensions and fears. An EAP therapist needs to be aware of client resistance, and client disagreement as resistance can be seen as negative and therapists, in conjunction with the advice from the case manager, may suggest to break-off therapy until the client is ready whereas disagreement indicates that insight has not yet been achieved.

Vehviläinen (2008) explicated this dichotomy in her analysis of client resistance and put forward an argument similar to that adopted by Rogers. Vehviläinen sees the client's responses to the analyst's confrontations as a product of the interaction. Confronting a client is a legitimate activity in all therapies. The CA studies have not explicated what the therapist does as being right or wrong as that would mean that CA analysts take on board and criticize theoretical orientations and their applications. However, CA analysts can demonstrate that psychotherapists do not do what they say they do and criticize a therapist's way of working in this way. Antaki (2008) for instance found that a therapist's way of confronting a client can at times appear like a 'combative approach'. McMartin (2008) found that the therapist's 'optimistic questions' on solution-focused therapy can be attempts to force the client to think positively. Vehviläinen (2008) examined a psychoanalyst's approach to a client's resistance when confronted and concluded that the therapist could also be held accountable for the resulting problem. Antaki et al. (2004) found that therapist's dealt with the client's resistance by turning it into a universal or self-evident matter. In fact some of the CA literature finds fault with the therapist's approach in this sense and it seems that the work so far has highlighted ways of making therapists more accountable by explicating how the therapist tries to psychologize the client's problem and in doing so impose the therapist's version on to the client (Davis, 1986; Buttny, 1996; Antaki et al., 2004, 2005a; Antaki, 2008). If therapists use CA's findings to help them to reflect on their work and become accountable for their work the therapeutic maxims and also the therapist's own interpretations of the interactions need to be taken into account and the client's resistance needs to be taken seriously.

Therapeutic policies

Drawing on the work carried out by Leudar et al. (2006, 2008a) one can determine whether a 'therapeutic policy' is active in an episode of therapeutic interaction. A 'therapeutic policy' encompasses all areas of the therapist's practice: the referral agencies, are they EAP clients, is the therapy time-limited, are they health system referrals, self-referrals, and so on; the theoretical orientation, the therapist's beliefs about how their therapy works and anything else that may influence how the therapy is conducted. However, in addition to having information about the therapeutic orientation, mentioned in Chapter 2, one has to know something about these policies. Leudar et al. (2008a) found that it is not enough simply to look for examples of a particular theory in action; what matters is how this is accomplished in the interaction. The theoretical orientation revealed itself in the study through the therapist's focus on the client's emotional reactions and how interpretations were made about these emotions. This in some way contrasts with cognitive-behavioural therapists who focus more on the thought processes and how these affect emotions. As mentioned above the therapist may know what they are doing and how they are using the theory but this may not be evident to others since therapists may not formulate to themselves what they are doing, and they do not explain each therapeutic move to their clients. If the CA analyst is not aware of the approach the therapist is taking, analysts may explicate something negative in one therapy. For example, the directiveness of 'optimistic questions' in solution-focused therapies may appear far too directive for a humanistic psychotherapist. Also, the 'miracle question' used in many EAPs: 'if the problem disappeared overnight, by magic, what would your next day be like?' is one of the main goal-setting questions but totally by-passes the problem, its causes or cures. A humanistic therapist may say, 'and this problem is something you have battled with all your life'. What may be alien to one therapist may be an integral part of the change process in another therapy.

Other studies which have been conducted using CA investigate different forms of counselling practices (Peräkylä, 1995; Vehviläinen, 2003b). These studies provide insights into interactional procedures, such as listening and asking questions. However, the institutional setting where counsellors have clearly defined tasks ensures that the therapeutic relationships have different meanings from those found in psychotherapy. Vehviläinen (2003b) examines the idea of self-directedness in educational contexts where the institutional expectations affect how the client behaves in the sessions. The client expects the counsellor to offer advice and as a result the client takes on the role of questioner in many of the examples provided. The counsellor refrains from giving advice until the student has demonstrated that they have some ability to self-direct. If this is evident the counsellor will proceed to provide information to the client on where they could look for work. In addition, in order to help the client to use self-directedness the counsellor may adopt a didactic role.

The same problem was found in Peräkylä's study of Aids counselling. Psychotherapists who use reflective listening and active listening procedures, which according to Miller and Rollnick (2002) involve being non-directive, need to avoid what they refer to as 'roadblocks'. Miller and Rollnick (2002) argue that roadblocks such as directing, giving advice, agreeing, approving or praising, interpreting or making suggestions are blocks to the change process. In addition Peräkylä's (1995) study looks at the procedures involved in circular questioning in sessions involving more than one individual. The answering format will be different here from that found in a one-to-one encounter where different members of the group will occupy different positions to the questions posed by the counsellor as they may hear the questions differently (Peräkylä, 1995). In the data collected here all questions are directed at one individual.

Some of the research to date on CA and psychotherapy has been extremely critical of therapists and the way they perform therapy without taking the 'therapeutic policies' into account. Davis' work on formulations, or re-formulations has had a lot of influence on CA analysts and the way they approach psychotherapy (Peräkylä, 2008). According to Davis (1986) a therapist in the course of a psychotherapeutic interview will make use of formulations as a transformational device. In doing formulating a therapist is attempting to get the client to agree to a problem definition as defined by the therapist. If the client does not comply it is termed resistance. Davis's study is focused on the client's problem and the way the therapist works with the problem. Davis (1986) argues that the re-formulation of the client's problem during the initial interview is the first step in treatment. As soon as the presenting difficulty is transformed into a problem which the therapist can treat, then the succeeding sessions of therapy have a focus and a goal. This is true at the assessment stage of this therapy where EAP clients are assessed for their suitability for short-term therapy before they are sent to the therapist. During the first session the therapist examines or re-formulates the problem in terms of the theory. According to Davis, if the client co-operates, collaboration can occur and therapy has a purpose and a realizable goal, and the same is true for this therapy.

Davis argues that the problem definition becomes a construction. It is the job of the therapist to achieve collaboration with the client in the process. Davis however suggests that the therapists typically manipulate the situation. Firstly, successful therapy is seen as a victory for the therapist as there can be no problem to work on if the client does not agree and secondly, when the therapist has successfully managed to get agreement from the client, the client can expect an understanding of their distress. Davis argues that therapists are not necessarily doing what an onlooker will see or hear and will steer the interaction to where they want it to go. This may be true if the interactions in therapy are examined as asymmetrical relationships only. If one examines the therapeutic encounter using a conversational device such as formulating then one will almost certainly see subtle forms of control emerging. The client's problem is defined by the theory, for example in person-centred therapy the client is in a state of incongruence (Sanders, 2007). A researcher needs to know something about how this problem gets defined this way and not another way, and why a therapist intends to adopt the approach he or she does in a particular situation with a particular client. The therapist's intentions are informed by their therapeutic practices and policies and therefore the theories held by the practitioners are a valid aspect of their work. We cannot ignore the 'therapeutic policies' employed by the therapist when examining the interactive process.

CA, the relationship and self-disclosure

Almost all therapies stress the importance of the therapeutic relationship[3] (Rogers, 1995; Halgin and Murphy, 1995; Orlinsky and Howard, 1986, 1995; Miller and Rollnick, 2002; De Shazer, 1994; Hubble et al., 1999; Leahy, 2003, 2010; Proctor, 2008a; among others). Most psychotherapy researchers as well as clinicians consider the therapeutic relationship to be the foundation upon which all therapeutic activities are constructed (Halgin and Murphy, 1995; Norcross, 2002). We take the view that therapeutic relationships can be investigated using CA because the nature of any relationship will be played out in the talk taking place between the participants. However, there are certain activities which are inherent in ordinary conversation but notably absent in forms of psychotherapeutic interactions. According to Schegloff (1963) a distinctive quality of the therapeutic relationship, which distinguishes it from a conversation, is that it can be seen as acceptable to speak and act unacceptably. However, there are different rules for both participants. The client is encouraged to abandon inhibitions and to speak and act in ways one would not normally do when they free-associate in psychoanalysis. In EAP the client is expected to spend some of the session reflecting on the problem but also on their thoughts, feelings and behaviours during times when they did not have the problem. The therapist, on the other hand, guided by their therapeutic orientation is also required to speak and act in less spontaneous ways and to follow a format which is different from normal conversation. For example, continually 'reflecting back' to the client what they said by using formulations or using Socratic questioning techniques which may be seen as overload in ordinary talk.

A particular feature which marks out psychotherapy as being different from ordinary conversation is the area of therapist self-disclosure (Antaki et al, 2005b; Leudar et al., 2006). Practitioners' opinions differ on whether or not to self-disclose. McLeod (2011) argues that all psychodynamic and humanistic therapies require that the therapist keeps self-disclosure of their own life experiences out of the consulting room whereas self-disclosure would be a norm of conversation. On the other hand, cognitive-behavioural therapists can see self-disclosure as a valuable tool. In cognitive-behavioural therapy self-disclosure is used to normalize some problems of living or to teach the client how a problem could be dealt with effectively (Goldfried et al., 2003; Leudar et al., 2006). The therapist's training will provide an indication of what the therapist will focus on in the sessions as well as the value-specific interventions such as self-disclosure for that therapy (Farber, 2003; Leudar et al., 2006). Certain training schools, which refer to their approach as 'eclectic', encourage self-disclosure if the therapist feels it would be of help to the client. So some training schools view self-disclosure as negative and others as positive even though there is no conclusive evidence that either one is correct.

CA research into the area of self-disclosure does not concern itself with whether therapist's self-disclosure is desirable or not but whether the act of self-disclosure has an effect on the therapeutic relationship. This according to Antaki et al. (2005b) can only be investigated by examining the practice *in situ*. What is important is how self-disclosure is done and 'how the circumstances of its bringing-off will colour what it does in the interaction' (Antaki et al., 2005b, p. 183). According to McNamee and Gergen (1994) there is a level of reflection occurring throughout the therapeutic interaction and that reflection will involve ways of solving the client's problem. These reflections contain the therapist's philosophy of what works in therapy and what therapy is about and will invariably guide the sessions. Schegoff (1963) details what works in therapy from a psychoanalytical perspective and the management of therapy as seen through that narrative only. In psychoanalysis the therapist will work with the transference and will make sure to eliminate accounting features, such as feelings and values, which may affect that transference. Antaki et al. (2005b) looked at examples from CBT and humanistic therapies and found that self-disclosure could be helpful especially if it was done though the therapist's use of second stories. Second stories according to Sacks (1992, LC2) can help a speaker feel understood and this is a better means of displaying understanding with the speaker's talk than claiming to understand what was said by using devices such as formulations.

However the necessity of self-disclosure can be contingent on the setting and the clients. Constantine and Kwong-Liem (2003) argue that self-revelations in some therapeutic situations such as cross-cultural therapy may help to convince clients that the therapist is real and genuine in their understanding of certain personal concerns such as feelings of discrimination. Gains (2003) suggests that therapist self-disclosure can show sensitivity by the therapist and this can help put adolescents at ease so that they are able to feel safe and understood in the relationship. Farber (2006) examines the client's ability to self-disclose and argues that a therapist's ability to relate to a client can help the client to disclose more. This would correlate with Gains' (2003) work with children and adolescents. Farber (2006) also suggests that a client's self-disclosure depends a lot on the client's ability to self-disclose as well as on whether an issue is important enough to warrant revelation.

Goldfried et al. (2003) found that self-disclosure emerges as a natural part of the human interaction and relationships are supposed to be as real as possible. A technique such as therapist self-disclosure can sometimes strengthen the therapeutic bond and this can also be said about the therapist's supportive listening techniques or positive assessments. However, it is important to keep in mind what the therapist is trying to achieve and how they are trying to do this. If the therapist chooses to reveal something of themselves through self-disclosure or in the way they listen then CA can reveal how and with what consequences this is done (Antaki et al., 2005b; Leudar et al., 2006). If a therapist breaks with protocol because they see this as beneficial to their client, CA can help the individual to examine if and how this utterance or intervention has been beneficial.

It is accepted here that much self-disclosure is tacit and as it is a natural part of human interaction for participants to express feelings and opinions about social situations between each other then this aspect of interacting cannot be avoided in therapy. As a therapist is part of a social world it is impossible to switch off all opinions, feelings and values, regardless of how the therapist is trained so these elements of the therapist's humanness will seep out somewhere in the sessions. One way these elements become visible is in how the therapist listens and where they take turns without necessarily interrupting the talk or where they attempt to come in and take the floor.

Concluding comments

The literature to date suggests that even though the theoretical approaches expect that the therapist will remain free from assuming what might be good for a client and free also of the need to give directions or impose anything on to the client, CA analysts have found that the therapist can nevertheless try and coax the client to approach their problem from the therapist's frame of reference. On the other hand, the therapist is supposed to work and explore within the client's world. Certainly more work needs to be done on this area. The literature to date suggests that CA can show therapists of particular theoretical orientations what they are doing either correctly or incorrectly. I take this a step further and argue that CA can best help individual therapists to investigate their own style of practice if CA has a good knowledge of what the therapist is supposed to be doing, not just locally but over several turns.

Finally, suggestions made by Peräkylä and Vehviläinen (2003) that CA could engage in dialogue with the therapist's SIKS need to be extended to include the therapist's beliefs and assumptions about what they believe they are doing and what the institution, such as an EAP expects them to do. If the practice is constrained by institutional restrictions such as EAPs, where a therapist is expected to perform and get results within a time framework, CA could help clarify, falsify and correct not only what a therapist does and thinks they do but also if such changes are being achieved in the way the institutions like to believe they are.

Therapists'/practitioners' corner

By examining how therapists' and client's together do the business of talk-in-interaction practitioners will come to understand how both parties make sense of their work together. In this corner I look at how transcribing and analysing one's work using CA can help practitioners understand their work better. By doing transcriptions therapists can come to engage in critical reflexive procedures and this can help them become aware of details of the interaction that would normally escape their attention. CA can help therapists to look at what might be hidden from both therapist and client and this is different from other methods where the therapist may be expected to look for categories and themes. For example, therapists encourage clients to reflect on how they think and feel. Clients may give an account of what the feelings and thoughts are and the therapist may pick up on what these thoughts and feelings are like rather than what they are. Therapists do not have access to their client's thoughts and feelings and the only thing they can access is the shared world. A CA analyst will understand that therapists can come to understand that clients will design their story with an awareness that will make them accountable (to themselves and to the therapist) for the thoughts, feelings and behaviours expressed in their story. They own the story and now choose to share it. A close analysis will help therapists work out exactly what things are like for the client. This is done by looking at how something is expressed and not what it is *like* for the client when translated into a therapist's world.

Session 1 Jane
1. T: o.k Jane (.) how do you think therap:y, (.) can help you
2. C: emm (0.4) where I'm: concerned what I'd love to work on is (0.8) my (0.7)
3.   se:lf-esteem self-confidence and fi:n:ding a >sense of self< because I it
4.   sto:pped me doing so many things up till ↑[now::,
5. T: [o.k] and how
                                                how does that ah
6.   (0.5) ma manifest itself like how do you how are you aw:a:r:e that it's self-
7.   esteem that's blocking you.
8. C: be:cause em (0.8) because e:very single problem that I have in any
9.   relationship that I h:ave is down to (0.5) having no self-con-fidence and no
10.   being incredibly insecure and thinking other people are e:verybody else is
11.   better than me (0.4) essentially

The client answers the therapist's initial question about therapy with a description of a problem rather than saying what the problem is. The problem is instantiated in the talk although she does not say it outright. *It* (line 3) the problem stops her from doing mundane things – *so many things*. In describing the problem the client's focus on *it* removes herself from the description as she talks about self-esteem as if it were a separate entity, separate from herself. The therapist accepts the client's description but re-formulates it in terms of something that is blocking her. The therapist accepts her terms, that is, self-esteem, self-confidence but then moves her away from her explanations about her problem and asks her to account for her difficulty in an ordinary way like telling a story. So, does the therapist's intervention work? Well not quite, as the client does not answer the question *how are you aware* (line 6). She instead provides a causal answer indicated by the use of *because*, used twice on line 8 to provide a further description of the problem instead of again saying what the problem is *thinking other people ... are better that me* (lines 10–11). In CBT a therapist would take the problem and look at what feelings and behaviours this type of thinking is causing. A person-centred therapist might allow the client to work this out for herself. A solution-focused therapist might look for relationships where the client does not have the problem. In the above the client tells a story while the therapist attempts to formulate a problem by directing the conversation.

4
A Note on Methodology

As already mentioned I take the view in this book that CA can highlight key aspects of psychotherapeutic talk that are not usually noticed by participants. I believe that if EAP providers wish to research the effects and efficacy of EAP counselling then the fine details of how the service is helping or not helping cannot be ignored. In addition, students of psychotherapy, who are receiving supervision, and wish to develop and fine tune the way they practice 'the talking cure' will need to look at the minute details occurring in the psychotherapy interaction between they as trainee therapists and their clients. If practising psychotherapists wish to examine, either in supervision or continuing professional development (CPD) courses, how they conduct their own style of therapy, which they have developed through clinical practise and further training, they would do well to examine the moment-by-moment unfolding of the psychotherapeutic interaction.

CA and the various psychotherapy modalities

CA concerns itself with structures of interaction and focuses on how content is being dealt with by the participants. It purposefully ignores broader contextual features such as the location, the speaker's social identities, and the purpose of the interaction. As far as investigations into the practice of psychotherapy are concerned CA analysts would consciously ignore the therapist's identity as well as the setting. As CA ties its observations to sequential structures of interaction in an attempt to uncover the recurrent properties and practices of talk in psychotherapy it essentially ignores exophoric information in the analysis unless that information can be shown to be consequential to the participants (Schegloff, 1972, 1991; Antaki, 2011). Studies on institutional talk have nevertheless shown that the concepts and methods of CA can be used to show how ordinary talk differs from institutional talk in systematic ways (Drew and Heritage, 1992; Rapley, 2002; Arminen, 2005; Antaki, 2011). As already mentioned in Chapter 2, as far as psychotherapy is concerned, these differences can be evidenced by more reduced and constrained ways of talking than one would find in ordinary conversation as well as additional types of activities, for example, the use of visualization or mindfulness techniques. According to Drew and Heritage 'the ensemble of these variations from conversational practice may contribute to a unique "fingerprint" for each institutional form of interaction – the fingerprint being comprised of a set of interactional practices differentiating each form both from other institutional forms and from the base-line of mundane conversational interaction itself' (1992a, p. 26). As mentioned in Chapter 3, a CA analysis needs to be mindful of the distinctive and identifiable formal structures each therapeutic approach and context offers. In this way an analyst can come to understand what work is being done through the sequential structures, that is, the work that the turns are doing.

In psychotherapy actions such as summarizing what the client was saying or making interpretations can be recognized based on a common sense appreciation of how a therapist conducts therapy (Leudar et al., 2008b). An analyst does not need to become competent at performing a particular brand of therapy in order to fully grasp utterances and turn types occurring between the participants. After all, therapists use ordinary language structures to conduct the business of 'the talking cure'. However, one does need exophoric information if one wants to investigate what is going on therapeutically – what therapeutic actions participants do in and through talking. How much external information one needs to have is questionable. I suggest that it is sufficient to know something about the tools employed by a therapeutic orientation and this is especially necessary if the practice adopts an eclectic approach. Since what is going on therapeutically is external for much of the session analysts who have any knowledge of one therapy or of therapy in general may overlook the meaning a particular brand of therapy has for the participants. In the Gale and Newfield study (1992), which investigated a single session of solution-focused marital therapy using CA, therapists who practised other orientations such as psychodynamic or person-centred therapy and who had no knowledge of CA's methods may have considered some of the interactional approaches as instances of therapeutic incompetence (McLeod, 2002).

If CA is to be used as a method to study the fine-grained talk-in-interactions occurring in therapy it needs to appeal to the psychotherapeutic community as a worthwhile method of investigation (Peräkylä and Vehviläinen, 2003). Several of the interaction strategies found in a model used in short-term therapy, such as the solution-focused or CBT approaches may conflict with therapists schooled in psychodynamic approaches. As a result, psychodynamic therapists may consider EAP counselling as superficial, not deep enough or maybe even ineffective. In fact there may be so many conflicting aspects which would be accepted by one group of therapists and dismissed by another that analyzing therapy using CA could become a futile endeavour as therapists would merely argue against it using knowledge of their practice and approach to justify their interventions to an analyst.

Approaches to psychotherapy research

This work seeks to fill in some of the gaps within the approaches to research in psychotherapy and counselling, which occur when researchers omit the importance of the individuality of therapists who, despite being schooled in specific orientations, and despite working as an affiliate for a managed care system, nevertheless develop their own style. When the therapist experiences the working of the theory in their lives, both professionally and personally, and adopt its tenets, they then marry that theory to the setting and their individual beliefs concerning the nature of human psychological functioning. What emerges in the sessions is a particular style of working. That style consists of three layers: the basic theoretical orientation informing the practice, as well as any continuing professional training workshops undertaken, from which the therapist has integrated certain approaches; the therapist's beliefs concerning the nature of human psychological functioning; whether it is a private practice or it is time-limited and under the control of a managed care system and if the EAP therapist also carries out long-term work with patients suffering from a psychopathology. That style of each therapist is expressed through language and language is their greatest tool. A therapist relies on the use of language to bring about psychological change as it is within conversation that new understandings, insights and increased awareness are engendered and conveyed between them and their clients. Even though therapy is the 'talking cure' most research studies, which investigate the words uttered by the parties, have not examined the words uttered by the participants as elements of interest in their own right (McLeod, 2011). Instead research has tended to treat the expressions as signals of something, such as unconscious processes, resistances, new insights or expressions of depth of feeling. From a constructivist viewpoint, therapists do things with words (Peräkylä, 2008, 2011). The activities which take place in a therapist's office can become visible to the outside world by providing samples of the talk. The empirical chapters in this book aim to show how a therapy gets 'talked into being'.

Research in EAP practice

As mentioned in Chapter 1 most research studies carried out into the practice of psychotherapy are based on either outcome studies or process research studies. Outcome studies are driven by the effectiveness debate. Policy makers and health service company managers as well as individual consumers are all concerned with how therapy works and in what way it can make a difference. The providers of the EAP service EAP are focused on making a difference in the shortest time span at the best price. The psychotherapists, while remaining independent and operating out of their own private practice, have chosen to work as affiliate counsellors for these providers so that case managers are permitted to call the therapists and ask them to take referrals. However, the providers do not generally provide additional training or appraisal services to the therapists. The only forms of accountability that the EAP provider expects, concerning the service the therapist has provided, comes from either an anonymous feedback questionnaire which the client is expected to fill in and post back after therapy has ended, or from outcome and session rating scales where clients are asked to rate their experience of the process and outcomes of treatment (see Duncan, Miller and Sparks, 2004, appendix IV, pp. 222–3). In addition, the client might receive an email or a phone call from the case manager asking for some feedback about the sessions. Much of the feedback protocols enable the client to comment on the service received without making reference to who their therapist was. The rating forms are mostly filled in at the end of the each session in the presence of the therapist. There are however difficulties with these procedures. Firstly, not all clients return the questionnaires. Secondly, clients may feel under pressure to give a good comment about the service they received when the therapist is standing in front of them. They may also not have enough time to assess the situation properly if they receive a phone call. So, despite the fact that the providers receive some account of whether or not the service is operating effectively, neither they, nor the therapist, know how therapy has helped. As a result a therapist cannot review their practices and make improvements through this manner of operating.

Quantitative research

Quantitative research enables researchers to adopt an objective stance to the studies, but in doing so may omit the individual and unique face of the therapist. Although it is generally accepted in the literature that the quality of the therapeutic alliance is the determining factor in whether therapy is successful or not, personal factors such as the therapist's thoughts, feelings or beliefs cannot be controlled for using longitudinal, or randomized controlled trials as it would be impossible to control for all confounding factors, for example: religious beliefs, cultural issues or beliefs about what the 'self' or 'the actualizing tendency' means to the therapist. This type of research does not represent a therapist's everyday work with their clients (McLeod, 2011). Despite these assertions most of the recent literature on psychotherapy and counselling has been quantitative as outcome studies, which seek definitive knowledge, and are based on objective data (Elliott, 2007; Lambert, 2013).

Process research studies on the other hand, offer more in-depth investigations into how therapy becomes effective. This type of research, which involves the observation of therapy sessions through either video or audio recordings, requires the researcher to identify the processes occurring in the sessions which indicate client progress. This includes making observations of the processes which have positive effects on outcomes. For example: do therapeutic strategies such as empathic responses or Socratic questions lead to success? Does an emotional climate such as unconditional positive regard have a positive effect on outcome? Do the claims made by the therapy theory, about the relevance of specific therapeutic interventions influence within session client processes in the assumed way? In this type of research, transcripts are made of the sessions and various methods are developed for categorizing and coding verbal events. To apply this approach, coding manuals need to be constructed, raters need to be trained (who will watch or listen to the tapes and carry out the coding procedures) and raters need to be monitored for inter-rater reliability. The observational measures of therapy process all enable researchers to glean standardized quantitative data.

Coding procedures

It would be impossible to mention all of the observational measures of psychotherapy and counselling which have been developed by researchers over the years. Here we will mention just a few of the different coding procedures which have been used by researchers in general to measure the processes involved in non-directive, as well as goal-oriented and problem focused therapies. For example: 'the non-directive classification system for therapist-client responses' (Snyder, 1945) looks at, among other things, whether non-directive therapists were really being non-directive and if the client developed insight into the understanding of their problem. The 'experiencing scale' (Klein et al., 1986) measures congruence versus incongruence by investigating depth of bodily felt experiencing in both the therapist and the client. The 'verbal response modes' (Stiles, 1992) distinguishes eight types of utterances such as interpretations, questions and reflection, and documented, among other things, differences between exploratory and prescriptive approaches.

However, studies have failed to detect much correlation between these coding and categorizing procedures and the outcome of therapy (Stiles and Shapiro, 1994; Stiles et al., 1988). Peräkylä et al. (2008) argue that 'a good therapist is assumed to be responsive to the client's specific and momentary behaviours and this responsiveness cannot be measured by a fixed coding system' (p. 11). Also coding systems, which focus on therapist behaviours, omit the fact that particular clients afford opportunities for empathy, unconditional positive regard and congruence. This is clearly so because coding systems are blunt instruments insensitive to complexities of interaction. Another weakness with these observational approaches, which produce quantitative data, is that the internal processes occurring in the therapist and the client are not taken into consideration. To deal with this problem questionnaire-based rating scales have been developed. For example the 'therapy session report' (Orlinsky and Howard, 1975) focuses on topic and concerns in the session, affective quality of the session, goal attainment and evaluation of the session. The 'working alliance inventory' (Horvath and Greenberg, 1989) focuses on goals, tasks and bonds. The 'relationship inventory' (Barrett-Lennard, 1986) focuses on congruence, level of regard and empathic understanding. The outcome and session rating scales mentioned above is filled in before the session and focuses on where the client is at in relation to their goals while the 'session rating scale' is filled in at the end of each session and focuses on how the client felt the session went for them, for example the relationship with therapist, the therapist's approach and whether the client felt heard or not (Duncan et al., 2004). Such approaches to research in psychotherapy and counselling do not provide clear and precise images of the interactions which occur in the therapy room (McLeod, 2003).

Further models have been developed which attempt to provide clearer and more detailed representations of the activities occurring. The 'interpersonal process recall' technique developed by Kagan is designed to combine the observation approach with a recall interview at the end of the session to glean information from both client and therapist about what they were experiencing at different stages on the tape (Kagan et al., 1963; Kagan, 1984). Elliott (1986) suggests that this technique enables the researcher to obtain fine-grained information and descriptions of moment-by-moment evaluations of crucial episodes occurring in the session. However, as with the questionnaire-based therapy process measure it is not possible to know if the client is recalling exactly what happened or is imposing a gloss on what they are hearing on the tape. Moreover, what the client reports is likely to be affected by other experiences in addition to what happened in the session.

Other models attempt to be more sensitive to the different tasks and developmental processes which occur between the therapist and the client. The 'assimilation model' (Stiles, 2002) seeks to track how the client's relationship with their presenting problem alters over time. For example, Stiles assume that the client's experience of their problem will develop in therapy along a sequence from 'recognizing, reformulating, understanding and eventually resolving' their difficult experiences (2002, p. 357). Also Sachse's (1990) micro-process analysis research programs provide a range of process results which explicate the importance of therapist inventions which promote self-exploration by the client. Sachse uses 'triples' to categorize sequences of speaking turns, that is, client-therapist-client and these statements are then rated on processing scales to determine the depth-inducing levels inherent in the therapist's intervention. The therapist's proposal may *deepen, maintain the level* or *flatten* the client's 'processing mode'.[1] This form of processing explicates the effect the therapist's interventions have on the client and highlights the fact that clients do not engage in much processing on their own and may be unable to deal with both content and processing of experiences simultaneously (Sachse and Elliott, 2002).

Qualitative research

Qualitative research which enables an inductive analysis to be carried out ensures that categories or pre-defined theories are not imposed upon the data (McLeod, 2011). Qualitative research seeks to respect the uniqueness of each individual case. Also, as findings need to be understood within the social, environmental, historical and cultural context, a qualitative approach enables the setting and therapeutic policies encompassing the therapeutic hour to be taken into consideration.

However, qualitative research is far more divided than quantitative methods (McLeod, 2003) as there is no coherent set of methods which would be applicable for every form of analysis from texts to talk. As qualitative researchers approach their data from the point of view that human knowledge is local and contextualized, many of the approaches used for analysing the data come from diverse traditions. For example, phenomenology and grounded theory focus on the meanings used by the participants to construct reality. Ethnomethodology eschews technical methods and tries to uncover participants' methods in constituting social interactions into what they are. The approach focuses on the way that worlds, such as the therapeutic settings are constructed though rituals and social practices (Heritage, 1984; ten Have and Psathas, 1995). Conversation, Narrative and Discourse analysis focus on how talk and language are used to construct and make sense of reality. While qualitative research of psychotherapy and counselling allows a more in-depth understanding of the knowledge of the phenomena which is short-term therapy, the approach to research must consider the researcher's philosophical stance regarding what constitutes human knowledge.

McLeod (2011) suggests that because the practice of psychotherapy and counselling is constantly changing and growing, therapists are drawn to examine their practice in various ways with a view to improving and refining that practice. The classical qualitative methods such as grounded theory (Strauss and Corbin, 1998) or the Dusquesne approach[2] which place emphasis on issues of meaning and value empowerment as both a process and a goal of research have much in common with the person-centred approach (Elliott, 2007). However, grounded theory according to McLeod (2011) causes problems for therapists who are exponents of one particular approach. For example, using grounded theory to analyse person-centred therapy will produce person-centred categories. If the therapy is more 'eclectic' or combines two major approaches, categories may be found which apply to some theoretical schools, but how the therapist combines these approaches may be ignored. Ontological issues of agency and being may also be overlooked (McLeod, 2011). The Dusquesne method employs more intuition than pure method to interpret its findings and as a result researcher influence may affect the results.

CA, on the other hand has rigorous tools and methods, such as the transcripts, the sessions and sets of terminologies which can be employed to interpret the data. By focusing on the use of language this book can investigate how therapy is made to happen in a session. A qualitative approach forces one to understand one's professional world with a sense of openness and unexpectedness concerning whatever emerges in the local and contextualized sequences of talk. One is therefore forced to account for each utterance expressed which affects how one's attempts to co-create one's practice with the client. By examining a practice using CA we encourage therapists to see their professional work as an accomplishment and to discover how the language they use affects their work.

Conversation analysis

The methodology of CA, outlined in some detail below, is robust and contains a relatively stable set of core ideas and practices which have remained for the most part intact since its inception in the early 1960s by Harvey Sacks, Emanuel Schegloff and Gail Jefferson (ten Have, 2007). CA adopts a radical approach to conventional conceptions and methods by dropping them from its agenda and instead operates as 'a detached investigation of conversational detail' (Schegloff; cf. Billig and Schegloff, 1999, p. 544). CA is focused on how individuals talk within a conversational setting and, having grown out of ethnomethodological practices, it provides researchers with tools to explicate the methods and means for the organization of talk in interaction in that setting. Ten Have notes that from the outset conversation can be seen as 'chaotic and disorderly' (1999, p. 3) yet there are also codes of conduct and pragmatic rules of thumb regarding how one communicates in specific situations. So conversation is orderly and CA can show how this orderliness is accomplished. Likewise, psychotherapy is orderly but its orderliness may go beyond everyday conversation. For example, if a client begins to ask the therapist questions about her life and how she feels about situations, this may be interpreted as projection, resistance or simply as unhelpful.

However, the methods used are not prescriptions and there are scarcely any prescriptions to be followed, if one wants to do *good* CA (ten Have, 2007). The raw material in CA consists of videos or tapes which are transcribed. 'Tape recordings and transcripts based on them can provide for highly detailed and publicly accessible representations of social interaction' (Peräkylä, 1997, p. 203). Methodological procedures should then be adequate to the materials available and the problems being addressed rather than being pre-specified. According to Sacks the methodological process in CA is inductive. The conversation as the object of inquiry is in CA presented as a completely ordered unit, constructed by the rules of conversation. The focus is on action and the aim of the research process is to describe patterns of interaction from a 'bunch of observations'.

Sacks argues that the analyst should practise 'unmotivated examination of some pieces of data' (Sacks, 1984, p. 27), rather than imposing their own categories. When we start out with a piece of data, the question of what we are going to end up with, what kind of findings it will give, should not be a consideration. We sit down with a piece of data, make a bunch of observations and see where they will go (Sacks, 1984, p. 27).

CA and sequentiality

CA examines the sequential features of talk. This means that an utterance derives its meaning from its sentential position. This emphasizes the rules of conversation, such as turn-taking and the distribution of speaking rights (ten Have, 1999, 2007). This turn-taking organization can produce long stretches of turns-at-talk that follow one another with few gaps and overlap between them. This kind of organization would be equivalent to what one would expect to find in a psychotherapy session where the sequential components are seen in CA terms as achievements. As the sequential components are linked by the elements and features of conditional relevance, for example; a question or an interpretation makes an answer relevant or expected, the participants can become engaged in a conversation when the therapist invites them to enter by asking the initial questions such as 'how can therapy help you?' or later in the session using a solution-focused approach 'tell me about the times when you did not have the problem?', or by using a series of Socratic questions in CBT: what does that mean to you?, what does that say about your beliefs about others or the world?, or by using an empathic reflecting back formulation to summarize or draw out a natural implication from what the client had said. As CA focuses on how utterances are related to both the preceding and subsequent utterances – a therapist's formulation for example, which is intrinsically tied to the client's previous utterance – means that this formulation is restricted by what was said by the client and this in turn restricts the client's response. A question is restricted by the client's topic and in turn restricts the client's response. CA can investigate the structures which organized the relations between actions occurring in a psychotherapy session and how the parties come to produce these utterances.

The materials

The policy of collecting naturally occurring data using audio and tape recorded means contrasts with the traditional methods of research within the social and behavioural sciences; that is, interviewing participants or observational studies or the tradition of using native intuitions as the basis for making analytic claims. The use of recorded material allows for a rich and vivid account of empirically occurring interactions and 'others could look at what I had studied and make of it what they could, if, for, example, they wanted to be able to disagree with me' (Sacks, 1984, p. 26). By using recording materials the limitations and shortcomings of intuition and recollection are overcome. The written transcripts which are afterwards produced (before being transcribed using Jefferson's CA transcription devices) provide the researcher with access to an extensive range of interactional trajectories which can be investigated in minute detail to produce a fine texture where recurring patterns which flow across conversational turns can be observed. The use of detailed inter-actional devices, which could be possibly overlooked by participant observational studies, can be observed by using CA. However, working with transcripts alone may cause an analyst to miss out on non-verbal communication. As a result what clients and therapists do with their body cannot be detected from transcripts alone so video-recordings may be necessary if the full extent of the interaction is to be investigated.

Elements of power

By categorizing or intuitively constructing and documenting the machinery which moves the practices of psychotherapy through its stages, elements of implicit power or control exerted by the therapist may become invisible. This is important to consider if the therapy is time-limited, as therapists may push to achieve some resolution. The asymmetrical nature of the therapeutic relationship creates the conver-sational routines which develop and it is within those routines that the institutional relations, such as the phenomena of power and control are co-constructed. These elements are intrinsic aspects of the therapeutic alliance insofar as the therapist is the expert who has a certain level of power by virtue of their knowledge of psychotherapeutic procedures and processes which the client then opts to pay for. Keys and Proctor (2007) argue that person-centred therapists need to recognize the power they hold as therapists and to be alert to the ways they could use that power. Proctor (2008b) also suggests that CBT therapists need to seri-ously consider whether or not they actually empower their clients to take control of their lives or not. Also, as therapists are members of a cultural community they need to be mindful of their own assumptions regarding cultural, religious and environmental practices to ensure that they do not attempt to impose these onto their clients. However, in attempting to create equality with their clients, therapists may minimize the aspects of power which structures in society impose on us (Proctor, 2008a). Also, in this therapy the therapist may have difficulties balancing the non-directive approach of person-centred therapy with the more directive aspects of CBT and the brief solution-focused approaches. In attempting to create a bridge between different approaches, as well as the need to use elements of confrontation in both approaches, a therapist needs to be aware of elements of power or control which may arise when approaches become intermingled. As CA adopts a bottom-up approach (ten Have, 2006) these phenomena, if they are present, will become visible in the interaction because the participants will orient to them.

The data

The data in this book comes from a corpus of 50 sessions occurring between a short-term EAP psychotherapist/counsellor and eight clients, each of whom attended between 4 and 8 sessions spread over up to 10 weeks. The therapist was first and foremost trained in the non-directive, client-centred Rogerian framework but also trained in CBT and solution-focused therapies. The clients presented with an array of typical EAP client difficulties ranging from mild depression, eating disorders, relationship problems and bereavement to interactional difficulties at work. The work was carried out with the author's own clients who agreed to take part in a project carried out as part of a study intended to promote EAP short-therapy and counselling in general. The data used in Chapter 8 consists of two role-plays engaged in by EAP trainers. As mentioned above each of the sessions was transcribed using methods based on Gail Jefferson's methods (see transcription methods). Having examined the chosen interactional devices used by the therapist in all of the sessions the analysis and conclusions were based on all of the devices found in the corpus.

Concluding comments

The question which would concern therapists is how CA can be made useful for psychotherapists in practice. Most CA studies are conducted by social scientists and not by psychologists or researchers of particular therapies. The fact that CA can make therapists more aware of their practice and what they are doing could also cause much frustration among the therapeutic community who may wish to know what the therapeutic implications are for what has been identified. Therapists need more than mere awareness producing strategies if they are to reflect on practice and pull themselves out of the bad habits they may have fallen into. Peräkylä (2004) argues that CA is not able to judge the *psychological* outcome of therapy. However, he distinguishes between internal cognitive processes and the client's behaviour. While it may be impossible to examine the neurological processes that occur for the client as they go through therapy CA does allow assessment of other sorts of outcomes, for example changes in behaviour can be detected by examining the way the client comes to talk about their difficulties and if and how they may be changing. Peräkylä et al. (2008) note, that CA could be used to 'describe the change in the pattern of interaction that may take place as the therapy progresses' (p. 25). Peräkylä (2011) found that using CA to examine his own practice has not made his practice different. CA can, however, be used as a resource for therapists to help them understand their practice and how they influence their clients to change.

CA can examine how therapists work to attempt to influence change in the client in a short space of time and thus can help to make therapists accountable for their particular style and choice of approach. The therapist then has to develop not only an enquiring mind but also an open one. This sets CA apart from other research methods such as Discourse Analysis where the work is extremely personal and the question of 'whose version is this' would be seen as another element of the discourse which would then require analysis. CA on the other hand, has some 'technical conventions and sociological considerations' (McLeod, 2002, p. 103) which would allow the researcher more scope to analyse their own work. Because CA has specific tools which enable a therapist to view their own work at a detailed level, one can achieve a level of objectivity which takes the therapeutic relationship, developed within the activities of both participants, into account. In this way therapists can use their own work to develop themselves professionally.

Therapists'/practitioners' corner

As already mentioned the methodology involves detailed examinations of transcripts of conversation paying attention to how the talk is managed on a 'turn-by-turn' basis. This involves looking at both the therapist's and the client's turns and how each participant orients to what the other has said in their previous turn. It is about recognizing structures, procedures and strategies that both the therapist and the client use so as to be able to engage with one another. For example, how the clients almost never ask questions, use formulations or continuers and how the therapist gets the client to talk at length, without telling them to do so, is particularly interesting. It is about looking at how clients learn to adjust to how therapy is conducted and may learn, for the most part, to be good clients or resistant clients as the case may be. It is about how therapists listen to extended pieces of talk and then intervene with an interpretation or a formulation. It is about recognizing that these interpretations and formulations may focus on aspects of the client's story and in doing so delete or ignore others while clients for the most part accept these procedures. Silences are particularly important aspects in therapy and are also taken seriously by CA analysts and marked and represented in the transcript in brackets. While silences can be picked up in both audio- and video-recordings, it is important to note that non-verbal aspects can only be picked up in video-recordings. In transcribing a shaking of the head, for example, a comment (client shaking head) can be added in brackets. One can add as many comments as one wishes as long as these actions have interactional significance. It needs to be emphasized again and again that a CA analysis focuses on the conversation only and the analyst needs to listen (audio-recording) or watch and listen (video-recording) over and over again, trying to clear one's mind and adopt a purely unmotivated looked approach, that is, without imposing ideas about what one thinks might be happening. Instead attention needs to be paid to what is actually happening in and between the participants. Interpretations or claims made about the in-session conversations being analysed must be supported by identifiable evidence in the conversations themselves. If it is not possible to find specific elements in the talk to support one's interpretation then one would have to be sceptical about the suggestions or interpretations being made.

This example demonstrates how important it is for therapists to avoid making assumptions based on experience or on theoretical explanations.

.hhhh in-breath (prefixed by a dot), hhhh outbreath (without a dot) 'Breathy' noises in conversation may convey something of how someone is feeling or by way of comment on what is going on in the talk. The number of 'h's' indicate the length of the breath taken.

Session 3 Jane
1. T: te- tell me what that >feeling of motivation< feels like
2. C: I think its like a dri::ve but °there's always but:° (.)
3. T: tell me what it's like without the but part

    4. C: ↑em:::::↑ hhhh (21.9) .hhh I think (1.6) (shuffling sound) °like°
           it is
    5.   ↑hard to descri:be↑ (1.0)
    6. T: o↑k:::: right ok (.) .h ahhh °when is har- you say it's hard to
           put into
    7.   wo:::rds
    8. C: yeah
    9. T: tha- that is good then isn't it↑
   10. C: ↓yeah

The therapist uses professional expertise here to manage the progress of the talk to keep it positive and solution-focused. The client attempts to move the talk towards the problem with *but* on line 3. The client finds it difficult to focus on her resources and this is indicated in the transcription on lines 4 and 5 by the rising intonations the out- and in-breaths, the long pauses (silence line 4) and the shuffling before expressing that the drive without the *but* is hard to describe. On line 6 the therapist reflects back to the client what she said by substituting her words and the client accepts this. This acceptance is then turned to into a positive by the therapist (line 9). The therapist has not actually achieved anything here except to reiterate what the client has said using another word and then got the client to accept the new word. One cannot interpret from this that the client feels understood simply because the client replied with *yeah*. It is important to be aware that the analysis must focus on the conversation as it is and no categories or theories can be superimposed onto the analysis.

5
On Active Listening in Short-Term Psychotherapy

This chapter concerns the use of 'response tokens' as listening devices in psychotherapeutic interactions where the focus is on the use of *mm* as a 'continuer', as defined by Sacks (1992) and Schegloff (1982). Such semantically empty vocalizations such as *uh huh, mm hm, mm* and *yeah* must be taken as essential components of interactional discourse if the full extent of the interactivity involved is to be revealed. Sacks focuses on the role these tokens have in storytelling in ordinary conversation and considers the interactional procedures involved in the way people listen to stories. He noted that stories in conversation are interpolated with tokens such as *uh huh, mm hm*, and so on, which indicate to story tellers that their stories are listened to as they are being told. These tokens then are 'utterances recognising that the story is yet going on' (Sacks, 1992, LC1 p. 766). Thus, in psychotherapy continuers can mark the fact that a story is underway and that the client has more to say. Sacks however, distinguished between continuers which claim listening by 'anticipating the other's intention to go on' (1992, LC2 p. 411) and continuers which can direct the speaker to say more. While the former type mark out points in the conversation 'that while the speaker is now about to pause he intends to go on' (p. 411), the latter more directive types, can be used as an 'interviewers technique (psychiatric or otherwise)' (p. 412). Here, I look at continuers as interactional devices used by a therapist to listen to the client's account in the same way as one might listen to a person's story in ordinary conversation. However, they will also be examined as therapeutic listening techniques used by the therapist to enact the business of psychotherapy. These continuers are used to practice and continually reproduce the therapeutic relationship.

Since Sacks' pioneering investigations there has been much work done on the vocal side of listening in conversation. Initial studies were somewhat inconsistent in the way the response tokens were treated and they were mostly examined as members of homogeneous groups where two or three tokens such as *yeah, mm, mm hm, uh huh* were classed together followed by an etcetera. The literature did not differentiate much between the different forms and it was difficult to say which ones were being referred to. For example Dittmann and Llewellyn grouped all response tokens together referring to them as *'mm hm, I see,* and the like' (1968, p. 79). Büblitz referred to the 'hearer signals' as 'speech acts such as agreeing, supporting, approving, doubting, inquiring etc.' (1988, p. 161). Yngve (1970) considers 'back channels' to be all utterances that are primarily displays of recipiency or listenership. This vagueness concerning recipiency, made evident through the use of 'and the like, etc.' and 'all utterances' makes it difficult to examine their usages in a specific environment. As far as their function was concerned it was claimed that they displayed listenership by indicating attention, agreement or understanding.

Studies that have differentiated between the response tokens have come from the CA tradition. Gail Jefferson (1984) focused on the differences between *yeah* and *mm hm.* Mazeland (1990) examined the usages of *yes, no* and *mhm* as acknowledgement tokens in doctor–patient interactions. Drummond and Hopper (1993b) focused on *yeah* as an acknowledgement token and Gardner (2001) distinguished between *mm* and *mm hm.* Sacks (1992) coined the term continuer for items such as *uh huh and mm hm.* Schegloff (1972) also used this term providing a wider currency for utterances such as *uh huh, mm hm* and *yeah.*

Both Gerhardt and Beyerle (1997) and Czyzewski (1995) found some distinctions between the tokens when they examined them in a specific context, that is, a psychotherapeutic setting. Gerhardt and Beyerle (1997) found an escalating affirming intensity for the tokens to which they ascribe the terms 'scale of speaker 2 alignment with speaker 1' (1997, p. 384). However, the tokens seem to be classified by dictionary definitions and not classified by examining them, as suggested by Schegloff (1993), in the local sequential context in which they are used. Muntigl and Zabala (2008) focused on the sequential environment where continuers occurred, and by focusing on the pauses surrounding continuers they found that they served as 'expansion elicitors' to get the client to say more. Peräkylä (2011) found that the use of response tokens in psychoanalysis indicated recognition and validation of the patient's experience given in their prior account. Czyzewski (1995) on the other hand, who discovered four categories of *mm hm*, found that the therapist's use of the tokens 'may involve a selective and setting-adapted use of various conversational devices, depending on theory-based work styles' (cf. ten Have and Psathas, 1995, p. xi). The distinctions found by Czyzewski between the *conversation-oriented mm hm,* designed to encourage the client to say more, and the *analytical mm hm,* which encourages the client to open up more, relate to different therapeutic approaches – the person-centred approach and psychoanalysis respectively. Czyzewski also found that the therapist tended to alter the way they used the tokens in situations containing heavy emotional content. This is an important finding as feelings are expressed in almost every therapeutic encounter.

Jefferson (2002) views these devices as 'acknowledgement tokens' which exhibit receipt of the prior turn, and suggests that they function to demonstrate an understanding of what has been said. Schegloff (1982) also suggests that these listening devices claim understanding, interest, agreement and attention rather than doing these, because such claims made by a listener are only made relevant by their positioning in the sequence and this needs to be made evident. Muntigl and Zabala (2008) suggest that the fact that the continuers are placed relatively close to the client's talk, that is, the pauses are less than one second long, indicates that the therapist may be claiming understanding of what the client has said. The idea that continuers can claim agreement with the prior talk (Schegloff, 1982) may cause difficulties for some therapies. For example, in psychoanalysis Gerhardt and Beyerle (1997) found that the therapist may use the tokens to receive the affect experienced by the client and to give expression to whatever is aroused in their experiencing of that affect. This may involve the therapist in projective identification to engage the therapist with the client's feelings or may reflect a sense of shared feelings or experiences. Müller and Frank-Ernst (1996), who investigated the use of tokens in a phone counselling encounter, found that the use of continuers indicated that the listener was taking sides by claiming agreement. In person-centred therapy claiming agreement would interfere with the non-judgemental attitude expected of the therapist. It needs to be acknowledged that some therapists[1] may disclaim the use of such devices as they may come across as judgmental, or may be seen as interfering with the transference and therefore compromise the neutral stance adopted by the therapist.

Sacks (1992, LC2, p. 10) also found that continuers can be used to listen to the progression of stories. Using this idea, one can postulate functions for these tokens other than those found by Gerhardt and Beyerle (1997) or Müller (1999). We shall see that in solution-focused therapy and CBT the continuers act as a form of management to keep the client on track until understanding is arrived at, the problem is defined and the solution emerges. In person-centred therapy one would expect that continuers would be used as listening devices to indicate that the therapist is following the client's lead as well as subtlety directing them to say more if the therapist feels the client could have more to tell. The therapeutic process is directed by what the therapist believes is the best move in the sequence. My expectation is that the location of the continuers, as well as being part of the turn taking system, reflects the therapists' support for clients as they tell their stories which can also encourage or direct the client to continue on talking rather than make an intervention. By examining their location one may learn something about where the therapists put their focus.

However there is more. Research on medical encounters has suggested that the doctor's use of continuers in the form of 'uh huh' in question sequences, does not indicate to the patient the doctor's opinion of the patient's answer (ten Have, 1991) and only functions to direct the patient to go on and provide more information. Frankel argues that these continuers do not intrude on the content of prior or subsequent talk and 'their major effect is to invite speaker continuation by signalling receipt of prior information and nothing more' (1984, p. 158). In the data collected here it was found that that prosodic features of the continuers cannot be overlooked and that focusing on the sequential features of the continuers in psychotherapy is not enough. The validity in psychotherapy of ten Have's, Frankel's and Mazeland's suggestions can be assessed by examining prosodic properties of continuers used by psychotherapists. Further to what Sacks (1992) and Schegloff (1982) suggested feelings can be inherent and expressed in the continuers.

Prosodic features

The employment of continuers as therapeutic devices can be explained both in terms of their location in the sequence and in terms of their prosody (Gardner, 2001). While some references were made to the prosodic value of an utterance in relation to continuers in the study on the preference for 'recognitionals' (Sacks and Schegloff, 1979), it seems that as far as the original CA tradition is concerned questions of intonation relate to interactional units of talk and not individual utterances (Schegloff, 1998). However, Schegloff (1998), who assigns the intonational and prosodic aspects of talk to linguists, does express his dissatisfaction with the linguistic contributions made in the field saying that 'the point of articulation between language organisation and interaction has been insufficiently explicated on the interactional side' (1996, p. 53). Where continuers in therapy are concerned, I suggest that one needs to refer to prosody in order to fully grasp the sequential environment, that is, what the continuers are doing. I agree with Voutilainen, Peräkylä and Ruusuvuori (2010) and Peräkylä (2011) that the positioning of a response token and how it is expressed says something about the level of recognition offered to the speaker. I also agree with Couper-Kuhlen and Selting (1996) who argue that prosody and verbal interaction need to take cognizance of one another.

The question then is how the interactional nature of the continuers relates to prosody. Gardner (2001) suggests that the continuers are used to manage the trajectory of the talk without displaying any emotion, attitude or feeling yet he notes that a rise-falling intonational contour on the continuers displays heightened involvement in the talk. Goodwin (1986) argues that some continuers express attitudes or emotions. Czyzewski found that in times of emotional unease or upset the therapist altered the way they used the continuers although he focused instead on the fact that therapists tolerated much longer pauses before and after the continuers. Neither Czyzewski (1995) nor Muntigl and Zabala (2008) consider the notion of low volume in the continuer as a signal of feeling which resonates with the low volume in the client's talk, or orients to the client's feelings or reflections on feelings in the surrounding talk, even though the low volume on the continuers is visible in their data[2] when the client is expressing feelings.

In fact, Schegloff noted that prosody can be employed for different tasks other than turn-taking management such as 'the display of stance, mood, uptake, or reaction, and the like' (1998, p. 243). Schegloff (1998) also noted that voice is important for telephone conversations if the stance or mood of the speaker or listener is to be fully understood. I examine whether continuers, or at least some of them, orient to expressions in the surrounding talk, where feelings are being expressed or statements are being uttered, which the therapist believes need to be marked out as therapeutically important. I expect that the relevant prosodic features of continuers such as amplitude and intonation bestow these functions on continuers in addition to those originally described by Schegloff and Sacks.

What an analysis using CA revealed

Two main types of continuers akin to those found by Sacks and Schegloff have been found in the data. As I go through the analysis I will mention whether the continuer is what has been called:

(a) The *canonical case*. These continuers function to prompt, encourage or direct the client to keep talking if the client appears to be stopping.
(b) The *bridging case*. These continuers are found when the client is in the flow of speech and occur at within-turn junctures. These types of continuers are usually followed by conjunctions, such as 'and', 'so', 'cos' which can establish links with the client's previous utterance. According to Sacks such continuers would express the respect for the client's intention to go on.

Three classes of continuers were found based on their prosodic features and they have been called:

• classical continuers
• empathic continuers
• channelling continuers

Classical continuers

As classical continuers are the main type found in ordinary conversation I will deal with them first. In the data they were used most frequently when the therapist was engaged in information-gathering but almost never when the client was engaging in emotional self- reflections or expressing troublesome inner experiences, feelings or vulnerability. They were also found when the clients talked about themselves in a positive way. Not all talk is therapeutic and one could argue that, when the therapist uses these continuers, the therapeutic aspect of the talk is suspended, at least from the therapist's point of view. They have no emotional content and their mid-volume tone indicates that they do not carry meaning other than to indicate non-finality of the speaker's turn. The turns to which they are oriented have not reached resolution regarding their topical content or their production and can therefore be deemed as incomplete as far as the therapist is concerned.

Extract (1)
A = Anna
Session 7

32. A: erm: (.) and then after the second break (.) er:m I dunno I
33.   just spoke (.) erm a girl in the group actually said that eh (.)
34.   when she met (.) her facilitator for the first time she had
35.   some (.) transference feeling that she – he reminded (.) er her
36.   of her dad? (0.2)
37. T: → ↑mm ↓hm (0.2) (((0.2)) no feeling)
38. A: so er once she that y'know she talked for a few
39.   minutes and then (.) like (.) I kind of grabbed the
40.   opportunity (.) and ( )

(( )) ... continuer duration

In the above the bridging continuer *mm hm* on line 37 fits in to prosody and functions as a listening device to acknowledge the clients intention to continue. The story, which has been projected, is hearably not complete. The rising intonation on *Dad* on line 36 indicates that the client intends continuing and the continuer functions to confirm this incompleteness. The mid-volume tone indicates neutrality except to convey to the client that the therapist is present and listening.

Extract (2)
E = Emily
Session 3

450. T: butt ehh:: (.) like .hh (.) are you sssay:::ing that °ehh° (.) >if you don't get
451.   on with them< (.) that the-there's <u>nothing</u> you can do about it. (1.1)
452. E: °I´m sayin >It makes a very< un<u>plea:sant</u> (.) environment to work in°? (.)
453.→ T: m:m::↓, (0.8) ((0.3, no feeling))
454. E: cos <u>I</u> >like to be< (.) fr- friends with everybody I suppose, (.)

The response on line 452, although syntactically complete is only a partial answer to the therapist's question. The response constitutes incipient disagreement and the client does not appear to be stopping. The mid-volume tone of the continuer indicates neutrality and ensures that the therapist remains out of the talk except to accept what the client said. The *cos* on line 454 connects the turn and indicates continuation – the client was not finished with her turn and had more to say in her response. The utterances on line 454 provide more clarity to the client's response.

Extract 3 contains another example of a classical continuer which is used when the client is providing information about a colleague who has an understanding of therapy.

Extract (3)
M = Mary
Session 2
   81. M: =>I just I just< (0.5) kno:w she's open to this
   82.→T: ↑[m::↓m:: ((0.3, no feeling))
   83. M: [kind av] area (0.5) .hhh soooo I said to her >that I
   84.   was going to do some work< related to work (0.5)
   85.   type av STUFF. (0.4)
   86.→T: ↑m::↓m (.)

Here the client provides an informative account about how others are, that is, the woman at work being *open to this* (the therapy) (line 81). These continuers (lines 82 and 86) have medium volume and resonate with the lack of feeling in the surrounding talk. They are used as supportive listening devices.

Empathic continuers

The term 'empathic' is used to describe particular types of continuers. *Empathic* continuers were found to occur when the client was revealing feelings. The volume was low, resonating with client's feelings. They do not cover all areas associated with the term empathy but describe a particular type of sensitivity or engagement with the client's feelings which one might expect from a therapist. Empathic continuers were used by the therapist when the client was revealing feelings, describing difficult emotional experiences, or personal vulnerabilities, talking about sufferings, or working through upsetting emotional insights. They are also found when the client is working through a problem and the therapist chooses to remain unobtrusive to allow the client to dialogue with self in a way a person-centred therapist would aim to do.

The client in extract 4 came to therapy to discuss problems at work where she felt she was being overly criticized. She was feeling fed up and embarrassed at work as a result.

Extract (4)
E = Emily
Session 3

615. T: soehh so ↑what does it DO:: tto ↑YOU ↓this criticism
616. E: .hhh hhh (3.4) aht (0.3) ye ↑ahh:: hh °>dunno what< it
      does° (4.4)
617.   <u>mak</u>es you look <u>incom::petent</u> (0.4)°sometimes (0.4) >it's
      to do with
618.   w<u>o</u>rk it's most to do with work< (0.5) I °get criticism↓°.
      (0.5)
619.→ T: °mm::↓°, = ((0.6, with feeling))
620. E: =em:::: (1.4) I ju- >I dunno what ever it< does it jus- makes
      you feel
621.   rea::l (.) really like (1.1) emm:: (0.6) ↓ I dunno how I can- I
      can't ↓take
622.   it (0.3) I °really ↓can't.° (0.2)

This continuer (line 619) is at the end of a turn-constructional unit,
when the client has come to a potential completion point and seems
to be stopping. The client has answered the therapist's question (line
615–618) and so could have chosen to stop here. This canonical
continuer encourages the client to say more on this topic. The client
continues after some hesitation (em + pause) (line 620) and a false
start and attempts to provide more detail about how she feels when
she is made to look incompetent. The response (line 620–622) does
not provide any extra information regarding what the criticism does
to her.

This next extract (extract 5) is an example of the therapist's use of
an empathic continuer to listen to a story containing much emotional
content.

<u>Extract (5)</u>
W = Will
Session 1
  325. W: like even when Eva's:: cousin died I still didn't really get
        <u>it</u> like you
  326.   know (1.0) you know like I obviously knew like this (0.6)
        c:ould
  327.   happen like I would have been twenty five or six bu- (0.4)
        I↓wasn't
  328.   much of a comfort to her it was kinda (.) yu know (.) I
        never said it but
  329.   your kinda thinkin well >I wonder when will she be over
        this< (0.5)

330.   ((laughs)) not ↑realizin °↓that you don't really get over it. °(.)
331.→ T: °m:m m:m:: °, (0.6) ((1.05, with feeling))
332. W: °so then I understood a lot better when mum died° (1.1)
            and we had a good chat about that actually me and Eva (.)

The continuer on line 331 comes at the end of the client's turn and fills
in the silences where the client may have been stopping and in doing so
prompts the client to say more. The low volume resonates with the low
volume on the final utterances of the turn (line 330) and also with the
low feelings expressed in the talk.

Extract 6 is an example which contains a series of empathic continuers
used to support the client as she provides an account over an extended
turn imbued with heavy emotional content. The client had been telling
the therapist that she had a miserable Christmas with her family and
spent most of Christmas day crying in her room. The therapist is trying
to examine how she actually does this crying and what brings it on.

Extract (6)
L = Liz
Session 5

253. T: when your cr::::ying >what du yu< goes through your
            mi:::nd (0.3) >↑is

254.   it like ↑my ↑life is↑terrible ↑can't see a way out::< (.0.6)↓you
            know

255.   (.) hh or is it:: (0.4) I hate my <u>father</u> or >my mothers this
            or you know i i

256.   is it< peo:::ple in your HEA::D or::::: (0.4)

257. L: ↑it's (0.5) bo::th it's I hat:::e (0.4) th them at that time (.)
            for not:: (.)

258.   even remo::tely <u>trying</u> (0.5) to ↓understand. (0.6) because
            it ↑<u>is</u> (.) I'd say

259.   a ↑lot (.) of the way I ↑am is their fau:lt °I mean ↓>and
            their not gonna

260.   understand >cos< they're in their sixties°< (0.8) and:: this
            other half is

261.   (0.6) I::'ve <u>ever::::y</u>thing like on paper but I'm I'm
            so:::↓<u>miserable.</u> (0.5)

262. T: → °°↑m↓m:°° ((0.2)) (0.2)

263. L: an I .hh (.) I w::ould love::::: (1.9) to just ↓gi:::ve this life in
            my ( )

264.   to actually (0.8) be ha::::ppy in it.=
265. T→ :=°°m↓m°°::. ((0.4)) (0.2)
266. L: like I-feel like eh >if I had one wish it would just be NOT
          to be alive?
267.   (0.3)
268. T: → °m:m::°,= ((0.2))
269. L: but I wouldn't <u>do</u> anything.=
270. T: → =°m:m::°, ((0.2)) (0.2)
271. L: it's that dar::k like. (.)
272. T: → yea::h (2.7)
273. L: it is not one thing that I can (1.0)
274. T: did you feel anything at all that you can do
275.   (to help yourself)
276. L: NOthing (0.5)
277. T: like ANYTIME when you can get ↑up and walk °down the
          stai::rs°.

The therapist listens to a problem with a very high emotional content. She sets up the structure of the sequence by pre-formulating the problem with the question on lines 253–256. The client's response to this question, which contains 4 sub-questions, is accomplished through collaboration with the therapist who uses *mm's* as cues to work through the talk. In the design of the question the therapist sets up a disjunction where the client is constrained to the possibilities of answers formulated in the question. In pre-formulating the problem the therapist uses the continuers to encourage the client to talk about the problem in a way preferred in this type of therapy, that is: tell me about the thoughts. However only two of the questions are picked up on and these are answered over an extended turn at talk. All of the above exhibit 'passive listening' or in CA terms 'passive recipiency' by the therapist. However, with the exception of line 268 these continuers (lines 262, 265, 270) are examples of canonical cases. They are placed at points, not just of syntactic completion but seemingly pragmatic completion as the falling terminal contour of the final syllable of the prior turns (lines 261, 264, 268) would signal that they are orienting to completed turns at talk (Gardner, 2001). The low volume of these continuers convey minimal encouragement to the client as well as indicating the therapist's desire to maintain low involvement as the client works through the problem. The client connects the turns with *an* on line 263 and *like* on line 266, which signal that the client is staying on topic. The continuer on line 268 is a bridging continuer. This continuer functions to mark the fact that more will come, the client intends continuing (Sacks, 1992, LC2; Schegloff, 1982), that is, the client will provide more information about her wish. The story then sounds like the expression of a list of feelings which do not indicate that a story is underway but that the questions are being answered. In therapy it would be expected that a therapist would refrain from making an intervention, interpretation or formulation until the question had been answered sufficiently. Therefore the therapist expresses a skill inherent in the way the continuers are used and designed to elicit as much detail from the client as possible.

The extremely low volume, lower than the surrounding talk, and the narrow range of the tokens resonating with the short utterances expressed by the client indicate that the continuers resonate with the client's poignant feelings. The continuers on lines 262, 265 and 268 orient to the strong feelings inherent in the final utterances in the prior turns when she expresses how *miserable* she is on line 261 and how she would give anything to be *happy* on line 264 and how she wishes she were not *alive* on line 266. These continuers are responding to dense emotional descriptions. It is the feeling in the continuers expressed through the soft response, which resonates the content and feeling in the preceding talk by the client. As the talk expresses sadness and struggle, which requires an understanding ear the therapist lowers the volume of the response to a pitch lower than the surrounding speech, which indicates the therapist's affinity with the talk as well as respect for the client.

So, even though the client seems to be stopping at relevant points at the end of her sentences in the above the therapist nudges her on to stay with the topic and the feelings. In aspects of the person-centred approach, such as focused-oriented therapy, the therapist would encourage the client to stay with their feelings until they come through the difficulty and come to a better understanding of those feelings (Mearns and Thorne, 2007). A solution- focused therapist, who would be listening out for exceptions to difficult times, may remain completely out of the problem with such high emotional content except to indicate that they are present and listening (Sharry et al., 2001). A CBT therapist would listen out for how the feelings affect behaviours, for example the therapist encouraged the client to continue until she mentioned taking action on line 273 and then the therapist intervened. Either way this therapist is allowing the client to stay alone with those feelings. However as the sequence progresses the therapist's 'passive recipiency' approach becomes more active. The therapist upgrades the continuer and the volume to a *yeah* on line 272 followed by a long pause. The client may have expected that the therapist was about to speak as the token and level of involvement had changed. The therapist may have upgraded her continuer as she had heard enough to make an intervention but the pause at the end of line 272 indicates that the therapist uses *yeah* to nudge the client to say more even though the client may have finished. The above indicates that empathic listening is a specific skill and that a therapist can use continuers to listen in specific type of ways. However, it is a specific type of style developed in this therapy where the therapist stays out of the problem until she feels the client is not going to move in the direction of a solution or something positive. The therapist takes charge of the talk by then changing its course and asking an exception question on line 274 and extended on line 277 to steer the talk towards behaviours and solutions and away from the problem.

Channelling continuers

Channelling continuers resonate with the speaker's positive expressions and indicate heightened involvement in the talk. These are loud volume continuers (relative to surrounding speech) and most of them in the data collected had high pitch levels and a rise-falling contour constituting heightened involvement.

In extract 7 the client had been talking about her difficulties at work and with the placements she had been offered.

Extract (7)
E = Emily
Session 3
456. E: and I would find it em: (1.0) I would find it ↓like ((traffic noise))
457.   >the last place I was in actually< ((background noise)) (was in
458.   Belfast) the second one I ended up I actually loved it an- was funny
459.   cos (.) it got me out for the day in work, (.)
460. →T: ↑m:↓m::,((0.5)) (heightened emotion) (.)
461. E: so i-was (.) it was GREAT that that they gave me the push you know
462. T: mm

The continuer on line 460 orients to the positive expression the client makes about her work on lines 458 and 459. The continuer encourages the speaker to continue talking in this way and the heightened emotion inherent displays an evaluative stance. This evaluation refers to the 'exceptions' (de Shazer, 1988, 1994) inherent in the prior turn which reveals a time when the problem at work did not occur and she could reveal something positive about her managers. In the above the client is expressing something positive about work. The placement of the bridging continuer, at a within-turn juncture, seems to provide reassurance to the client that she can be happy at work and it is good to work – work has positive aspects as it keeps one occupied. By using a channelling continuer here the therapist acknowledges this exception as well as supporting her intention to go on and reveal more information concerning the positive experience.

The placement of this continuer provides evidence of the focused listening skills adopted by the therapist. A solution-focused therapist would not only focus on the story but also on the signposts towards the solution – here, the insertion of a continuer on line 460 creates a therapeutic bridge within the extended turn, which acknowledges the possibility of a positive experience which the client may have overlooked in attempting to find her own solution. The client was viewing the criticism as destructive and may have overlooked her need to be pushed – *got me out for the day in work* (line 459). The continuer is inserted at a point where the client did not seem to be stopping indicated by the continuing intonation expressed on the tail of her turn. Therefore it may not seem necessary for the therapist to provide a continuer here except to acknowledge the client's intention to continue and support her talk. By using a channelling continuer with heightened emotion here the therapist marks out the positive aspect of the client's utterance as significant. The channelling continuer focuses on the positive aspects of work and how it can be good for her. Through the use of the channelling continuer on line 460 the therapist is revealing her opinion.

Here is another example of how the therapist manages to push through her beliefs using continuers. In the following extract, the therapist is directing the session by using the response tokens as interactive devices to support the client when she talks about how her life is working for her, and how she can make it better, instead of allowing her to focus on the problem. The client has said throughout the sessions that she is interested in spirituality and has engaged in reiki in order to learn about spiritual aspects of relationships. The therapist sees this admission as something positive.

Extract (8)
L = Liz
Session 8

53.	T:	↑but you see that's where you enter into the belief
54.		system (.) where you belie:::ve=
55.	L:	↑.hh >like I DO with the whole reiki thing is really
56.		that's another thing since the reiki course la::st week
57.		(0.5) I've everyday I've had to open up one of my
58.		sha::kras (.) and do (.) pra::::yers in the morning to my
59.		shakras↑=
60.	T:	=↑right ((0.4)) (.)
61.	L.	and I know it's all so::: (strange) but I really feel great
62.		and I haven't had coffee:: (.) .hh (.)WHite brea:::d (.)
63.		I've had a bit of chocolate (.) I'm not supposed to
64.		no alcohol (.) and I feel better for that alone and it's
65.		been really a fresh start >since the reiki course and
66.		every morning I've had to do it for my root shakras
67.		and<my (0.7) ↓my sou:::l and there all to look after
68.		different ↑THIngs differ[ent parts
69.	T:	→ [↑mm↓h:m ((0.3))
70.	L:	and there all about handing over, (0.2)
71.	T:	→ [↑m::↑m:↓h:m ((0.3)) (heightened emotion)
72.	L:	[your FAIth (.) to the gua::rdian angels so so in that
73.		way (0.3) it's a [bit
74.	T:	[↑but sure ↑that's the SAME thing↑ (.)

This extract reveals the sequential nature of this therapy as it unfolds in a direction which is somewhat influenced by the therapist. The continuer *right* on line 60 seems to act as a form of assessment by the therapist which contains some emotion and an attitude of approval with the reiki, that is the therapist may believe this would help her. However the therapist's stance is somewhat ambiguous and the client may have heard disapproval in the therapist's voice, indicated by the justification on line 61, *I know it's all so (strange)* followed by the *but.* Either way the client expresses how she feels great on line 61. Although it is not quite clear, the use of *right* as opposed to an *mm* continuer may relate to the therapist's strong approval but also to the fact that the prior turn has been grammatically and pragmatically completed and the therapist is coming in strongly and saying 'ok off you go now'. The client also treats this *right* as an evaluative continuer as she latches her talk to the previous turn, making her talk into one turn but upgrades it to offer more detail concerning improvements in her lifestyle and positive feelings of self. The continuers on lines 69 and 71, both of which occur in an overlap, offer a form of affirmation or acceptance of what the client has been saying and this is done discretely and without interrupting the client. The continuer on line 69 seems to project completion evidenced by the overlap on the repeating of *different* as well as claiming understanding. Pragmatic incompleteness is indicated by the conjunction *and* on line 70, which connects the turns which do not reach completion until line 73. The continuer on line 71 on the other hand, occurs at a point of grammatical, intonational and pragmatic incompletion and interrupts the talk. This continuer however, does not constitute a separate turn but instead acknowledges the client's intention to continue, as well as offering a positive evaluation of what the client is saying. This continuer is spoken with a rise-falling intonational contour which is loud, punched up and stretched on the first sound of the *mm*.

This is the final session for this client. The client indicates consistency. She engages in spiritual practice *everyday* (line 57), *every morning* (line 66). She mentions feeling great and feeling a fresh start as well as being looked after and letting go. This is confirmed by the therapist's use of channelling continuers indicating enthusiastic responses to the client's revelation that she can take control of her eating habits and therefore move more in the direction of a positive self-image. The expressions are vague for example looking after different *things* (line 68) and it's all about *handing over* (line 70) but the therapist responds with these evaluative continuers without being told that it was about faith. This indicates that the therapist is aware of some spiritual dimension and could relate to the therapist's training and philosophy of psychotherapy. The use of the continuer here reveals something about the therapist's beliefs or philosophy and about what she believes would be good for the client. The therapist may have been a bit pushy here – being more solution-forced than solution-focused in her approach.[3]

The therapist intervenes at points she believes is the best move in the sequence and in doing so directs the therapeutic process. This example shows two channelling continuers appearing in a client's extended sequence. This example shows how continuers may at times be used to lead or channel the client in a particular direction towards a resolution.

Extract 9
L = Liz
Session 1

```
415.  L:    ↓couldn't believe that ( ) I'd get to ↑u::s::e: this (.)
416.         ta::lent↑ you know outside of just my liv↑ing↑ room
417.         an[d
418. →T:     [↑m::↓m:: (0.4) ((0.3)) (heightened emotion)
419.    L:   so I took (0.9) so I started working with these
420.         producers who were really happy with my voice and
421.         (1.2) they said we`ve a- we've a song here (.) I don't
422.         know if you can write and I sa- >didn't know if I
423.         could< write either and (.) cos I hadn't actually
424.         written, (0.2)
425. →T:     [↑m:↓m::] ((0.3)) (heightened emotion)
426.    L:   [before] but- .hh (.) I just (0.6).hh °dunno>can`t
427.         remember the first:° (.) so:ng I wrote but< (.) I just
428.         started writing to a song and (0.8) tst then they said
429.         will we just make an album (1.0)
430.         and [an-
431.  T:     [↑they said that (.)
432.  L:    ↑yea::h
```

In the above the therapist attempts to keep the client talking and talking on topic. That topic contains aspects of the solution the therapist sees as significant. The therapist manages the flow of talk in the sequence by placing the continuers at apt points. The placement of the continuer (line 418) is significant here as it occurs on the overlap with the *and*. This indicates that the therapist may want to ensure that the client stays on the positive track as some doubt may have been picked up by the therapist by the *couldn't believe that* on line 415. A similar situation occurs on line 425 where the continuer responds to the expression of doubt inherent in the talk on lines 422–424 *didn't know if I could write and cos I hadn't actually written*. However, what is different here from the one on line 418 is that the turn beginning on line 419 does not seem to contain any significant doubts or negativities which need to be marked. The *so* at the beginning of the prior turn may indicate that there is a series of positive stories to come and the therapist may have felt that she had achieved something – that is, keep the talk positive by using a channelling continuer on line 425. This intervention on line 447 indicates the therapist's orientation to something new occurring – that is, the client is about to write songs – and also disregards any self-criticism which may occur as the client reflects.

The heightened emotional content of the continuers with a strong rise-fall pitch direction is an example of the therapist using an evaluative device to take control of the client's talk to direct it towards the way the therapist wants it to go. Sacks (1992, LC2) noted that in a psychiatric interview the therapist may not always consider the client's intention. In solution-focused therapy a therapist's affirming and persistent listening style would be an important indication of their belief in the client's potential and the necessity of a collaborative therapeutic alliance to move things forward (Sharry et al., 2001). As the client is expressing some past hopes, aspirations and successes the therapist needs to ensure that the client perseveres and ignores problems which may cause her to revert back to talking about her self-doubts and the problem. The therapist's interventions here uphold the positive nature of the client's turns, which end with the client revealing a time in her life when she felt really good about herself.

These channelling continuers orient to the client's speech which contains something positive and their use indicates that the therapist is engaging in solution-focused therapy. They resonate with the speaker's positive expressions in the prior turn, which express something positive about themselves – their strengths, skills or resources and/or contain positive steps or developments towards the solution. The therapist uses a loud volume continuer which can be louder or at the same volume as the surrounding speech. At times they can be quite directive in the way they channel and nudge the talk in a particular direction. These continuers have an assessment or evaluative quality and the pauses surrounding them, tend to be short or non-existent – indicating that they may be claiming understanding of the client's prior utterance as well as functioning to keep the client talking in a particular way.

Conclusions

The findings here concur with the CA findings to date that continuers firstly, display an understanding that the client shall go on talking and 'exhibit this understanding, and take this stance, precisely by passing an opportunity to produce a full turn at talk' (Schegloff, 1982, p. 81). Secondly, continuers are used to direct, prompt or nudge the client to continue even though they may be stopping (Jefferson, 1984; Sacks, 1992, LC2; Muntigl and Zabala, 2008). Also, like Czyzewski (1995) it was found that the therapist's theoretical orientation can have an effect on the way the therapist employs these continuers. In addition however, I found that the therapist managed to turn these semantically empty utterances into therapeutically important responses by reducing or increasing the amplitude and altering the intonation. By reducing the amplitude and using a falling intonation the therapist reduced her involvement in the talk. Thus, by using empathic continuers the therapist adopts an unobtrusive stance. By increasing the amplitude and using the rise-falling intonation typically found in channelling continuers the therapist increased her involvement in the talk. By remaining unobtrusive a person-centred therapist fulfils their therapeutic obligations of treating the client through non-interference to lead to his or her own experiences. By becoming overly involved in the talk using channelling continuers the therapist provided her opinion and evaluation of the problem and how it could be solved. The use of channelling continuers thus negates the principles of person-centred therapy. What I found was that the prosodic features of amplitude and intonation cannot be ignored if the full extent of the function of continuers in psychotherapy is to be explicated. I found that the continuers found were used to listen and support the client as they tell their story, to claim understanding of what the client has said, to fill pauses thus ensuring the smooth flow of conversation, to mark the client's intention to go on and at times to steer, nudge and maybe direct the client in a particular direction, for example, to speak more about a particular topic in a particular way.

The question is whether this form of listening is specific to the type of therapy in which the therapist was schooled and works. EAP short-term therapy is first and foremost Rogerian in its approach. Empathic continuers are a normative feature of this therapy as it would be expected that the therapist would first and foremost display empathic understanding when the client is revealing feelings. Empathy according to Rogers, 'involves being sensitive, moment by moment, to the changing felt meanings which flow in this other person, to the fear or rage or tenderness or confusion or whatever that he or she is experiencing' (1980, p. 142). Accurate empathy according to Miller and Rollnick, 'involves skilful reflective listening that clarifies and amplifies the person's own experiencing and meaning, without imposing the counsellor's own material' (2002, p. 7). The manner in which the therapist used continuers demonstrated the caring and helpful approach of the therapist.

As far as the literature on intonation is concerned it is generally accepted that the expression of emotion and attitude is one of its main functions (Bolinger, 1989; Cruttenden, 1997). Gardner (2001) noted that some intonational characteristics may be caused by a person's bodily processes, for example, excitement, anger, compassion and belief. In the data collected here it was found that emotion and feelings, in particular attitude, compassion and belief, had an effect on how the continuers were expressed. The channelling continuers which have high pitch and amplitude are presented as assessment tokens which 1) can align with a position or point of view adopted by the therapist, 2) can evaluate as positive those things that the client has not yet expressed a preference for, 3) can direct the client to keep talking in a way which the therapist sees as positive or good for the client. They therefore evaluate or express some attitude or statement about the therapist's affective stance. Although solution-focused therapists focus on solutions, the use of channelling continuers in this therapy may be too intrusive as far as their training is concerned. As far as Sacks (1992, LC2) and Schegloff's (1982) assessments are concerned the continuers are an exhibit by the therapist that the client's turn is still underway or that they should continue talking. The channelling continuers add something extra – the client should continue talking in a particular way.

Contrary to that suggested by Frankel (1984) and ten Have (1991) continuers can carry the practitioner's stance or opinion on what the patient/client said. In this chapter I demonstrated that in psychotherapy the placement and amplitude of continuers says a lot about the therapist's theoretical orientation. In addition, the continuers act as hidden carriers for the therapist's own feelings and emotions. Therefore a therapist's individual approach to therapy can be made visible by examining how the therapist uses continuers. It is suggested here that therapists need to be aware of how and where they use continuers as they could evaluate what the client has said by the way they use them. According to Rogers the 'tendency to react to any emotionally meaningful statement by forming an evaluation of it from our own point of view, is, I repeat the major barrier to interpersonal communication' (1995, p. 331). From Sacks's point of view listeners need to be mindful of the way they use directive continuers as with these types of continuers, if this process gets repeated, the client, would become aware that they are expected to do most of the talking and may have to learn to read what the therapist means by these continuers, for example, 'is it a matter of your thinking I intend to go on, or of your telling me to just go on until you stop me?' (LC2, p. 412). This chapter has suggested that although continuers may be small almost trivial devices used by listeners to display listening they do have some interactional power in psychotherapy. By investigating continuers and their usage one can get a clearer picture of how the therapeutic relationship is actually happening – how it develops in practice.

Therapists'/practitioner's corner

The best way for therapists to address questions they have about their work using CA is to keep in mind that it is only through reflection and practice that the necessary skills will be acquired. At the end of a session many therapists engage in note-taking, and it is during this time that therapists can begin reflecting on and jotting down utterances such as continuers that they may have used during the session. As a practitioner starts to reflect on how they use talk they will become more proficient at reflecting on the conversational structures occurring in their therapy using CA methods. It is important to become skilful at recognizing the structures which a practitioner may spontaneously produce. By becoming aware of how small details such as continuers are used in therapy one can then start to compare this with how one uses them in ordinary conversation. If a practitioner frequently uses them in mundane talk, then he or she may notice that he or she also uses them in the same way and with the same interactional effect with his or her clients and patients. On the other hand, some therapists may claim not to use them at all and if that is the case then they also need to become aware of non-verbal gestures such as head-nods or changing facial expressions. What is important about all of these devices is that they have interactional significance and can have an effect on how therapy is delivered.

6
On the Use of Formulations in Short-Term Psychotherapy

There are many ways of investigating talk to demonstrate the evolving therapeutic relationship. While Chapter 5 examined some 'active listening' devices, this chapter investigates a second listening device used by therapists in this therapy to demonstrate not just listening but also understanding. The use of formulations, more commonly known as reflecting back techniques as mentioned in the Introduction, are frequently found in short-term practices, as they are a very important tool in the three therapies examined here. Previous CA investigations of psychotherapy in general found that formulations are devices used by the therapist: 1) to express to clients their understanding of what they said but also, 2) to guide them to consider their presenting problems from therapy appropriate perspectives (Davis, 1986; Hak and de Boer, 1996; Buttny, 1996; Madill et al., 2001; Vehviläinen, 2003a; Drew, 2003; Peräkylä, 2004; Antaki et al., 2005; Hutchby, 2005; Antaki, 2003, 2008; Bercelli et al., 2008). These two uses of formulations, however, may be somewhat inconsistent with the therapists' professional understandings of what they do with formulations in therapy. A person-centred therapist, for instance, might think of formulations as empathic responses (see Rogers, 1995; Brodley, 2001; Freire, 2007; Witty, 2007). A CBT therapist may use formulations to clarify what the client said and also to lead the client to think about their problem from a different perspective (Antaki and Jahoda, 2010). In brief solution-focused therapy, formulations may likewise be thought of as empathic responses but may in addition point to problem solutions. A short-term therapist may hold that 'reflecting back' through formulations facilitates clients' internal dialogues about their problems and enables them to change through such dialogues. In any case each of the three main theoretical orientations in this therapy may claim to use the same technique but for separate reasons and with different goals in mind.

Detailed examination of psychotherapeutic talk helps us to understand what techniques such as 'active listening' (Chapter 5) and 'reflecting back' may mean in practice. Moreover, as pointed out by Peräkylä and Vehviläinen (2003), CA analysts may find that therapists do not always quite do what they say they do – a disparity which may not necessarily be obvious to themselves (Drew, 2003; Antaki, 2008; Antaki and Jahoda, 2010). In time-restricted psychotherapy, the therapist can overstep boundaries and break therapeutic maxims in rushing to get the client to resolve their difficulties. Moreover, formulations as conversational devices may require that therapists delete, select or edit in a focused way aspects of the clients' accounts. Because of this, the therapists' intention to act in a helpful way could transform into something controlling, combative or even distorted (see Antaki, 2008). If that is the case, the use of conversational devices, such as formulation, would of course go against principles of any therapeutic maxim.

CA's investigation then may help to determine both what 'reflecting back' through formulations is like in practice and whether therapists who claim to use formulations strictly as a means of 'reflecting back' indeed do just that (Peräkylä and Vehviläinen, 2003). The therapeutic relationship is also demonstrated in the way therapists use these formulations. If the reflecting back technique is carried out in a caring and helpful way, through the use of formulations, the relationship grows in a healthy direction as genuineness and empathy are practised. To investigate this matter it is important to firstly consider some professional understandings of what 'reflecting back' means.

Formulations as empathic responses in therapy

Rogers (1980, 1995) defines empathy as a way of being with another person – a whole-hearted display of their belief in *the actualizing tendency* and growth promoting potential of the client. Greenberg and Elliot (1997) define this as an attitude, that is, rather than being a tool or a technique it is a lived attitude/orientation to a client. An empathic response is a term used in person-centred therapy when a therapist communicates this way of being or attitude to the client. When a therapist uses an empathic response it is expected that they become attuned to the client's inner world of feelings and the meanings these feelings have in their current experience (Rogers, 1980, 1995; Greenberg and Elliot, 1997). When the client feels understood they begin to develop a more internal locus of evaluation with less distortions and denials of experience (Rogers, 1995). Empathic responding is a skill which has been termed in counselling psychology an 'active listening' technique but is in fact a more artful process (Rogers, 1995; Witty, 2007). If the therapist merely uses a skill of reflecting back what the client has said, by simply using the clients' words or by substituting their words, the therapist may fail to enter the client's experience fully. Also an empathic response, if used correctly by the person-centred therapist would exert very little influence or coercive power over the client (Rogers, 1995; Finke and Teusch, 2007). The approach is essentially non-directive which requires that the therapist act as a non-coercive companion. This non-directive approach is designed to facilitate choice and autonomy by the clients as they deal with their experiences (Rogers, 1951; Rice and Greenberg, 1995). In this safe environment, where the therapist maintains unconditional positive regard and a non-judgemental attitude the client would find it easier to enter into feelings and emotions which they had feared to do prior to therapy. The client then may come to relate to their internal experience differently by examining the experience afresh. The question again arises: what does being non-directive consist of in practice?

Brief solution-focused therapists focus on the clients' resilience and strong points when they tell their troubled story. The listening techniques taught in this 'can be seen as an addition to the core Rogerian counselling skills and techniques' (Sharry et al., 2001). Reflecting back assumes that the therapist will engage with the client's problematic experiences, but will focus on the client's strengths, skills and resources and will communicate these experiences back through a positive filter. Sometimes therapists use the clients words when they 'reflect back' in an attempt to highlight the client's ability to find their own solution.

CBT therapists focus on the client's maladaptive thinking and cognitive errors (Greenberger and Padesky, 1995; Neenan and Dryden, 2001) and use reflecting back techniques to firstly help the client feel understood. They are then used to help guide the client to look at their problems from different perspectives before an alternative way of thinking is elicited. Clients are taught to look at their thinking patterns, beliefs, behaviours and feelings from a CBT perspective, that is, how these negative thoughts and beliefs are making the client feel. Once this has been established formulations can be used to obtain agreement from the client about how these patterns will be addressed and treated. CBT therapists sometimes use the client's words and sometimes they use alternatives. The general question asked in conversation analytic studies of psychotherapy is: how are these techniques realized in conversational practice?

Formulations and psychotherapy – what have CA researchers found?

Work to date examines formulations as interactional devices used by the therapist to translate the client's story into a language which would define and interpret the clients' experience in a psychotherapeutic fashion (Davis, 1986; Hak and de Boer, 1996; Buttny, 1996; Madill et al., 2001; Antaki, 2003, 2008, 2010; Hutchby, 2005; Antaki et al., 2005). Davis (1986) found that this re-formulation of the client's problem is achieved by the therapist when he or she firstly psychologizes the client's problem so that it is treatable by psychotherapeutic means. Antaki et al. (2005) argued that formulations are a resource which can be used by the therapist to shape the client's talk about their problem in a focused way so that the therapist can then treat them in a way which fits in with the therapist's therapeutic beliefs or orientation. This can be achieved by deleting and editing elements from the clients' account (Antaki, 2008). Researchers also argue that therapists expect to have their formulation ratified and accepted by the recipient. Antaki et al. wrote 'it will be no surprise to see therapists work to transform the raw material of their client's talk, and get this transformation accepted by their client' (2005, p.3). In the literature on formulations in psychotherapy, the therapist is seen as the professional expert who uses formulations as a form of conversational control to get the client to view and speak about their problem in a different way – a way that fits in with the therapist's orientation.

Madill et al. (2001) looked at how the therapists attempt to bring about a transformation of the clients' problems and focus on inconsistencies and mismatches between the therapist and the client. The client is seen as a person who either complies or does not with the therapists' formulations. The process of negotiation is subject to constraints and depends on whether the client resists or takes up what the therapist said or whether or not a mismatch occurs between the two. According to Madill et al. (2001) and Buttny (1996) successful therapy may depend on the client complying with the expertise of the therapist. Antaki (2008) also sees clients' ratification of the therapists' formulations as a display of the client's co-operation. Formulations then are co-operative devices which may contain a directive element, which may not be visible to both therapist and client. Antaki sums this up by saying that formulations 'allow the therapist to suggest a tendentious reading of the client's situation and expect to have this confirmed' (2008, p. 40). This suggests that therapy serves the interest of both participants. However, this kind of engagement is not strictly consistent with the general tenets of psychotherapy.[1]

The literature coming from the CA tradition then suggests that therapists use formulations to take control and 'to manage the interactional progress of the therapeutic interview' (Antaki, 2008, p. 37).[2] The management typically has three elements. Firstly, the therapist psychologizes the client's account. Secondly, the therapist transforms the client's description of something through the linguistic art of re-phrasing, lexical substitution and extensions (Antaki, 2008; Rae, 2008) and thirdly, the therapist expects the client to accept this new version of the problem (Davis, 1986; Antaki et al., 2005; Antaki, 2008). The formulation is seen as a powerful therapeutic device as it directs the client to do something, such as to think about it from a different perspective provided by the therapist. In this kind of short-therapy, formulations could be used to 'unobtrusively lead' on to transformation or re-formulation of the whole presenting problem simply because they are a major interactional tool. By investigating an approach adopted by a therapist working for a managed care system such as an EAP short-term programme one may gain a more detailed picture of how a therapist can deviate from their orientation when 1) they combine different approaches and 2) they are restricted by time.

Formulation as a therapeutic tool

In CA formulations have been categorized as either *gists* or *upshots* (Heritage and Watson, 1979). This implies that formulations as therapeutic tools can either summarize or draw out an implication from what clients said in their previous turns. Formulations have many specific functions as therapeutic tools. The therapist may formulate statements in order to develop a point, draw out an implicit meaning, summarize utterances made by the client, explain utterances in order to obtain more clarity for the client or, as is most common in therapeutic practice, draw out a client's feelings and thoughts by either maintaining a focus or shifting a focus. Formulations can re-represent the client's utterances in a more explicit fashion by being inferentially elaborate (Heritage and Watson, 1979). This enables the therapist to focus on certain elements of the client's prior account, re-reference them and explicitly describe their relatedness to one another. Formulations re-establish the problems built into the descriptions of the experiences offered by the client and so flag them as topics for further exploration or highlight aspects of the solution which may be hidden from the client's view.

To understand the work of formulations in the therapeutic conversation it is necessary to examine how they are introduced into talk and how participants display sequentially appropriate responses to them. Sequential appropriateness refers to the way that one utterance places a restriction on the production of the next utterance, that is, a therapist expects a response to their formulation. As formulations, first and foremost, allow the therapist to air his or her understanding of the client's preceding section of talk they are deeply implicative for subsequent talk. It is this sequential nature of the adjacency pair structure that necessitates the existence of a 'formulation-decision' pair (Heritage and Watson, 1979). The decision part of this adjacency pair in everyday conversation and much institutional talk can either take the form of a confirmation or disconfirmation of the formulation (Heritage and Watson, 1979). Disconfirmations of formulations may place the sense of order and accountability of 'the talk thus far' in jeopardy (Heritage and Watson, 1979). To disagree with a formulation may serve to terminate the present topic (Heritage and Watson, 1980). Antaki suggests 'it is difficult to disagree without paying an interactional cost' (2008, p. 37). In therapy, as in most types of conversation (Heritage and Watson, 1979; Pomerantz, 1984a), there is preference for confirmation of the formulation presented by the therapist (Antaki et al., 2005; Antaki, 2008). However, unlike in everyday conversation, in psychotherapy a mere 'yes' response to a formulation may not be enough. This is so because the client needs to demonstrate that he or she is adopting the orientation to the problem indicated by the therapist and the way to do this is through an extended response (Muntigl and Zabala, 2008).[3]

I focus on how a therapist gets the client to elaborate or reflect using *gists* or *upshots*.

Checking implicit meanings are all functions of *gist* formulations while *upshot* formulations are used to channel the client to think things out in a different way. The therapist uses the formulations as reflexive devices to help create mutual understandings but also to achieve something else – to get the client to change through interactive work. I firstly examine whether or not the therapist is helping the client to come up with their own solution. Secondly, I investigate whether the therapist is helping the client to focus on their own resources to solve the problem as would be expected in EAP therapy. In doing so I examine, if, where, and how the therapist may deviate from their theoretical orientation.

What an analysis using CA revealed

In this section five examples showing typical uses of formulations found in the corpus are presented. Particular attention is paid to their placement and timing and whether they are used with a solution-focused and/or CBT spin together with how the therapist listens and gets the client to expand on the theme. As I do the analysis I also touch on discrepancies between the theories and their realization in practice.

Here are examples (extract 1 and 2) taken from the data of a *gist* formulation and an *upshot* formulation.

<u>Extract (1)</u>

In the following two extracts the client had been explaining to the therapist how she was having difficulties with her boss.

Session 2

M = Mary

44.	M:	so I've done my bes::t to kind of (0.6) make the most (.) of
45.		the humorous (.) situation and (.) the fact that he's in better
46.		form' (0.5)
47.	T:→	'o.k (.) so ah (.) you have <u>used</u> his form his better form to
48.		your advantage have you'
49.	M:	↑YEAH
50.	T:	[right]
51.	M:	[now] he↑wa:s (.) starting to kind of ((sniffing)) (0.5) befo:re
52.	em:	>on Tuesday evening he started to kind of come over and start
53.		being a bit hassley about- you know kind of- he was doing a bit of like
54.		you know the children's kind of thing of were we there yet?< (0.4)
55.	T:	mm:=
56.	M:	>using a little bit of that < an- ffffort(h)unately I was doing eh- (.)
57.	T:	↑mm: (0.4)
58.	M:	↑em:: (0.9)= but again I try to remember like>to just be in< good
59.		humour and (.) not (0.9) let that get in on top of you. (0.6)
60.	T:	right=

By providing a summary on lines 47–48 of what the client said (lines 44–45), the therapist provides the client with the security of knowing that they are being listened to. The therapist indicates through this formulation that she has heard the client's prior account and actively attempts to prove this by summarizing what the client had been saying. The formulation here is an example of a typical empathic response. Here the therapist has attuned to and focused in on the client's experience, indicated by her ability to read the client's telling correctly, before communicating back to the client what she had said. The client's confirmation of the summary on line 49 indicates that the therapist's empathic response was correct and this complies with a non-directive approach as it keeps the focus on the client's story. The solution-focused aspect is also evident and this can be seen by looking at the placement of the formulation. When the client indicates a positive strength (lines 44–45) the therapist immediately takes a turn to highlight this at the first available place.

However, even though the focus was on what the client said, the formulation deleted, selected and edited the client's telling. Firstly, the use of *ok so* to introduce the formulation on line 47 acknowledged the client's turn but also seized the topic and the client's attention so that the focus was altered. The *ok* closes the previous topic and allows the therapist to take over the floor. The *so* sets up the conditional relevance by connecting the immediately preceding client's turn with the therapist's turn to come. The formulation then restricted the topic and directed the client to elaborate on the prior utterance from a slightly different angle by glossing it. Secondly, although the use of the tag question, *have you* on line 48, invited the client to confirm or reject the summary, it compelled the client to keep talking on topic but to elaborate the utterance in a specific way. The use of the *right* on line 50 also acted as an expansion elicitor (Muntigl and Zabala, 2008) to get the client to keep talking which she did over an extended turn with the support of the therapist who displayed listening by using continuers. These continuers indicate how the therapist actively listens and keeps the client talking in a way that is appropriate to this type of therapy (Fitzgerald and Leudar, 2010).

Extract (2)

In this extract the client had been telling the therapist about how her manager's negative attitude towards his staff was causing a lot of problems in the company. However, despite the fact that the atmosphere had become much more positive recently, the client finds it difficult to accept this change.

Session 2

M = Mary

4. M: So he changed comple::tely but (0.5) in a w:a::y it doesn't matter

5.   because your kinda waitin on whether you see cos you kinda think cos

6.   you kn↑ow he can be (.) like (0.2) cos he's go↑ne through this huge

7.   phase of being like really bad once (.) for such a long ti:me that's it's left

8.   such a deep mark on peo↑ple (0.3) tha I think tha in a wa::y even though

9.   he's grand no:w your sti::::ll (0.5) in a wa::y he`s ruined it > you know

10.   what I me[an<.

11. T: [mm:m

12. M: like it's hard to come back from that cos he's ruined the mo:od.

13. →T: o.k so you you >obviously are a bitt (.) a little< bitt da↑mag↑ed by

14.   it are ye.

15. M: ↑Yeah (.) it's like we don- .hhhhh (.) personally anyway I think its

16.   nicer (.) o.k I feel a >little bit more like doin stuff >with ↓him- (.)

17.   I feel a bit bETTer about MY stuff (.) .hh you know em.m (.) but-

18.   on the other hand (2.6) (sniffs) (.) I sti:ll >don't re:::ally °feel like

19.   goin out and killin myself over it either° you know< I feel li[ke

20. T: [°yea°

In the above, the therapist enters the client's experience, which contains a lot of negative expressions concerning her boss (*really bad* line 11, *left a deep mark* line 12, *ruined it* line 13). These experiences are communicated back to the client in an empathic response on line 17–18. It is the negative expressions which are given attention as these contain the client's feelings. The formulation requires that the client explores these feelings deeper by presenting the idea that she may be damaged by the experience. The formulation indicates engagement with the client but displays the therapist's perspective on what the client is saying. It is the perspective that requires an extended response, not just agreement as such, a response is required in therapy and is consequential to the participants (Schegloff, 1972, 1991) as clients learn what is expected of them, that is elaborate on responses and not just provide yes/no answers (Muntigl and Habala, 2008). However, *damaged* seems relatively harsh for this therapy as it may be something which needs longer term therapy.

The therapist interrupts the talk with *ok* (line 17) and re-directs the topic using *so*. The client also accepts the formulation indicating that the proposal inherent in the formulation has been accepted and the therapist is given the control. This formulation interrupts the turn, links it to a previous turn and it has psychological consequences as it turns the account in lines 8–14 into a therapeutic situation. It is an *upshot* formulation as an implication has been drawn from what the client has said in the extended turn. It introduces as a topic the possibility that the client is psychologically damaged and the use of *obviously* (line 17) indicates that this implication is not debatable. The use of obviously may relate to the idea that such negative treatment by a boss will surely cause damage. The topic of the client's problem at work has been turned into a therapeutic topic as the therapist has put a direct psychological proposal to the client that she may need to explore this situation further.

The therapist's use of the formulation on lines 17–18 seems to maintain a complex connection with the client's prior utterances and this formulation presents the client with a pragmatic implication. The perspective maintained by the client (lines 8–14) is essentially an expression of opinions and feelings held towards her boss. However, in her account she avoids talking about herself directly and instead uses general terms such as *people, your, you*, throughout the turn. It is not until line 12 that the client introduces herself but at the same time continues to hold her feelings about this person and the situation at a distance. This reticence to fully engage with her feelings around the problem makes the problem definition unclear.

This lack of transparency according to Davis (1986) may make the problem untreatable in therapy. As a result the therapist uses an *upshot* formulation on lines 17–18 which isolates the problem from the context and draws the client in on a more personal level. The client does this by accepting the formulation and practising it (lines 19–23). The above *upshot* formulation alters dramatically the focus and in doing so proposes a new direction.

I will now present three more examples of this therapist's use of formulations. Some of these work as therapeutic tools and some do not.

<u>Extract (3)</u>

In this extract the client had been complaining to the therapist about how she felt trapped and hemmed in by the demands of her friends. In this third session she is beginning to realize that it was her own thoughts about the situation that were causing the problem rather than pressure being applied from the outside.

Session 3

N = Niamh

593. T: (and do you find ah like) when you're thinking (.) like (.) ho-how

594.   is this thinking (.) like affecting your life like wha- t you know-

595.   >what is it doing to you< (1.1)

596. N: well (.)

597. T: like what are you thinking about (0.5)

598. N: ↓yeah well it- (.) it's probably I think it (.) would sto::p me (.)

599.   from kind av (3.4) I feel so <u>attacked</u> by everyone you know that

600.   kind of way I start (.) you know (0.7)

601.→T: so you would in your head (.) ↑<u>battle</u> them off (.) and [kindav]

602. N: [yeah like

603.   I'll (.) ↑<u>battle</u> people off and I'm thinkin I can do this same thing

604.   now an- you know (.) this that and the other (0.3) that I've no

605.   objectivity to anything d'know what I mean like it's all very (.) the

606.   world is seen through this kind of film and- (.) ah- you know (0.4)

607.→T: so your ↑world [is like

608. N: [just kinda

609. T. it's full of people but there all in side in your [head

610. N: [yeah they're all in my

611.   hea::d an I'm just (2.1) I'm kinda the ↑same banal (.) bor::ing

612.   (.) like there's nothing profound going on there you know that sorta

613.   way it's just (.) generally just <u>banal::</u> (.) you know "if I go there

614.   now on it's Fri::day >then it's like< have I got clothes" (.) an trying

615.   to figure everything out so >everything just fits< into the kinda (.)

616.   you know rather than just kinda lettin it all just happen (1.0) which is

617.   <u>so</u> much nicer (.) you know the way=

618.→ T: =it's ↑like as °if you're kind of controlling those- trying to control the

619.   whole thing before it even° ↑[happens

620. N: [yeah °oh completely that's exactly what

621.   it's like° you know trying to fig::ure everything it will just work like

622.   clockwork an (0.6) like it's good for me in a way cos Aaron couldn't be

623.   further from that (.) if he tried can't make an arrangement he just doesn't

624.   know (.)

625. T: °mm°

626. N: that's been really good for me in a way as well

627. T: an w- an why does everything need to work like clockwork?

In this extract the therapist uses an *upshot* formulation on line 601. While the client says that she feels *attacked* (line 599) the therapist alters the perspective and proposes to the client that she defends herself, *battles them off* (line 601). The therapist also substitutes the word *everyone* on line 599 for *them* on line 601. Here the therapist hears what the client has said but offers an alternative way of expressing it. In doing so, the therapist changes the perspective- to the therapy-relevant perspective, which suggests that the client is not just a victim of attack but can also do something about this, that is fight back (what the client does matters...). This approach complies with the CBT model as aggravating thoughts would be seen as something negative and something the client can learn to control. However, as the topic refers to the client's thinking (line 597) the formulation does have a person-centred tone as it demonstrates the therapist's desire to help the client to reflect on topic. The *them* (line 601) refers to the thoughts about the people rather than the people themselves. This *upshot* formulation functions to make the client aware that it is thoughts in her head which she is battling with rather than with individuals in her life. By using this formulation the therapist draws out an implication that she has difficulties with negative thinking and in doing so psychologizes the problem. This re-formulates the client's experience for her so that as argued by Davis (1986) there is a problem definition which fits in to the therapist's way of working and can now be treated.

The client accepts the therapist's re-formulation on line (601) and goes on to elaborate this confirmation. However, she does not accept that it is only thoughts that she is battling. These thoughts correspond to real people in the client's life and her presenting problem does concern her reactions to real people in real life situations – this is how she sees her life. The therapist, on the other hand, in typical CBT fashion tries to get the client to understand that this exists as thoughts and beliefs in her head and introduces a second formulation on lines 607–609, a gist formulation, which summarizes what the client had been saying between lines 601–606. The therapist repeats that this is happening *in your head* (line 609) and then manages to get the client to agree with her formulation and then say it – *they're all in my head* (lines 610–611). The elaboration then alters from talking about people to more mundane matters such as clothes. The therapist intervenes again and offers an upshot (lines 618–619) by implying that what the client is doing is attempting to control things. She puts a spin on it by offering the word *controlling* as an explanation for the client's attempts to make everything fit. The client provides a lot of detail about what is going on in her head which the therapist chooses to ignore instead of dealing with it in a CBT manner. This is an example of deletion proposed by Antaki (2008). The client's telling provides indications of obsessive thought patterns but the therapist deletes these patterns and proposes that it is a behavioural issue instead. The therapist leads the client to think about her behaviour and suggests that she thinks it is necessary to control situations which occur in the future. The client accepts this summary completely and elaborates on the point which provides the therapist with the opportunity of asking a direct question on line 627 which directs the client to explore her behaviour further. The formulation (lines 618–619) works as it enables the therapist to explore issues at a deeper level. Elaborating on the formulation moves the client to a greater understanding of self and an acceptance of the behaviour and enables her to reflect on changes that she could make. Nevertheless, the therapist's approach to the problem demonstrates that the therapist does not entirely work from a CBT perspective.

Extract (4)

In this extract the client had been telling the therapist about how her mother's overprotective behaviour was beginning to grate on her and how she can't find a way to solve this. Her mother was becoming overly affectionate with her and smothering her somewhat. The therapist had asked her if she could discuss this with her mother but the client felt it would really hurt her if she did.

Session 4

A = Anna

73. T: ri:ght and (.) e:m (0,7) like (.) >do you think you'd really HURT
74.   her< if you said↓mum you know:: I
75. A: I rea:::lly think so yeah:: (0.5) yeah (0.3)
76. T: right=
77. A: =°she's quite sensitive° (0.7)
78.→T: ↑o.k so right one is the the affectionate thing and >the other thing
79.   is< (.) her::: (banging sound) >getting too involved in your life
80. A: ye[a::h
81. T: [eh getting too (.)
82. A: ↓yeah
83. T: concerned about you
84. A: ↑yeah (.)
85.   T right (.) ↑what is it about tha:t that bothers you (1.8)

What is noteworthy about this formulation is its placement. The therapist is attempting to understand the client's experience and sets up and completes the sequence with questions which clarify for the therapist the client's stance towards her mother. Both of the questions which frame the sequence (lines 73–74 and 85) begin with *right*. This indicates that the therapist accepts the problem. After the initial question the therapist indicates, by the *right* on line 76, that she accepts the client's assessment of her reasons for not talking to her mother about the problem. Having obtained enough information she is then in a position to produce a gist formulation, lines 78–79, thus drawing together two points which summarize what the client had been complaining about up until now. On line 75, the client not only reiterates the belief that talking to mother would hurt her; she also warrants the belief (line 77). The therapist's *ok* at the start of the formulation (line 78) acknowledges the client's assessment of her mother's likely reaction but it also, together with the following *gist* formulation, stops the client from becoming emotionally involved in her mother's sensitive feelings and towards her problem with those feelings. It does this by seizing the topic and re-directing it towards a focus on two aspects of the mother's behaviour rather than on the mother's feelings. This serves to keep the client on track of helping her to cope. Why? – the therapist is quite selective in what she picks up from the account. She ignores the revelation of the mother's sensitivities, which might be a valid point here, and instead directs the talk back to the client's experiences and feelings when confronted with the mother's behaviours. By using a formulation at this point (end of line 77), the therapist presents some sort of an understanding of the experience only after she is clear and then gets the client to agree to that understanding over a few turns. So what matters is not just the content of a formulation but when it is done, that is, not too soon and not too late.

The formulation here foregrounds and crystallizes an aspect of the problem which is that the mother aggravates the client in two areas. A third area is revealed between lines 81–83 *getting too concerned about you*. The formulation is designed around what Sacks (1992, LC2) refers to as a 'category-bound activity' for members of the category of mother. The three problematic aspects depicted in the formulation are activities which a mother would be likely to engage in. However, the problem is that these activities are overdone. The formulation then works to keep the focus on what the therapist has understood to be the problem. It works to restrict the topic and keep the client focused on her own feelings and not on those of her mother. The restriction may have been necessary in order to get the client to reflect more, and explore further what it is that bothers her. Once the client accepted the formulation with a series of *yeahs* and a final punched up *yeah* on line 84 the therapist takes up the topic (*right,* line 85) and pins it down by using a direct question which guides the client to elaborate on her problem in a particular way. However, while this *gist* formulation provides agreed grounds for topicalizing the problem at hand – what in this is the problem *for you,* there may be a loss of empathy here for the part of her that is sensitive to her mother's feelings. The question on line 85 invites the client to examine her thoughts and possible beliefs about others as a CBT therapist would aim to do. However, in doing so the sensitive aspects of the relationship between mother and daughter are being reduced to a focus on how thoughts affect feelings.

Extract (5)

In this extract this client has been explaining to the therapist that she finds criticism difficult to take. However, she has come to the conclusion that there are two types of criticism and that it is destructive criticism that she has a problem with. Here the client is giving the therapist an example of how she responds to constructive criticism.

Session 4

E = Emily

106.	E:	so that was kinda good like (.) you know I got an honour in the
107.		[end
108.	T:	[°mm°
109.	E:	which was great to hear (.) and he went through stuff (.) (with less
110.		abuse) his criticism was good (.) cos it >was very construc- tive you
111.		know
112.	T:	↑m:m (.)
113.	E:	and that's actually had a very positive >influence<↑ (.)
114.	T:	↑right=
115.	E:	=it's the way it's given you know (0.7)
116.→	T:	↑o.k so they're right ok so yu- you you do know what (.) you do
117.		know wha-what ah::: hmm (0.9) gives you that feeling of feeling
118.		more motivated to a little bit to maybe
119.	E:	↑yeah
120.→	T:	do well in the next assignment is if somebody (.)
121.	E:	yeah
122.→	T:	gives you the proper (.) criticizes you properly (.)
123.	E:	m:::m↓ well he's a counsellor↑
124.	T:	so the feeling you get is one of power ↑eh:: (1.2) power over your own
125.		motivation
126.	E:	development (0.8). I just feel that an injustice::::: has been done↓

The formulation (lines 116–122) in this extract is an example of a situation, where the formulation does not quite work. The therapist seems unsure about how to express what she wants to say and this uncertainty leads her to provide a *gist* formulation which develops over three turns at talk. After some false starts the therapist provides a summary of the client's ability to know what causes her to respond positively when she is receiving feedback. The therapist latches the positive expressions *criticism was good cos it was very constructive* on line 110 and *a very positive influence* on line 113 to a feeling of being *more motivated*. The therapist selects these positive expressions and edits them in a way which indicates their understanding of what the client needs to do on order to do well in an assignment, for example, self-motivation. The therapist deletes the reference to how the criticism was given on line 115 and instead opts to summarize the positive feelings by re-referencing them and projecting them forward in time to the next assignment. Also, in the trajectory leading up to the formulation the therapist uses 'channelling continuers' (Chapter 5) on lines 112 and 114 demonstrating how this therapist, trained in the solution-focused approach, listens out for the solution and becomes more involved in the talk when positive expressions are uttered in the client's prior turn. The therapist moves from listening to formulating when the client is moving in a more positive direction.

The use of *ok so* on line 116 indicates that the therapist is interrupting the topic and taking control of its direction. By choosing to ignore an exploration of how the boss imparted this positive influence on the client, the therapist keeps the talk focused on the client's feelings. As change in this form of therapy aims to bring about more positive feelings of self-worth, as well as an increase in awareness of a client's strengths and coping abilities, the focus will remain on the client's reactions. Other people's behaviours are only discussed when they have an impact on the client's positive sense of self. The formulation focuses on what the client inherently knows about themselves. This refers to the client's own inner skills and resources which become highlighted in the way the therapist constructs the formulation. The therapist does not use a tag here because, as the formulation occurred over three turns the client had already indicated her agreement on lines 119 and 121 with the re-formulation of the topic. However, this formulation was possibly brought in too soon. The therapist ignored the clients concerns *it's the way it is given* on line 115, and as a result failed to secure an elaboration of topic. Instead the client uses short-turns at talk (lines 119 and 121) before bringing the topic back to her boss. After the therapist attempts to use a further *upshot* formulation (line 124) the client comes in with a strong disagreement as she continues to move the topic from her own motivation to her development at work and her feeling towards her boss. This indicates that the topic was not fixed in a way that suited both parties.

Conclusions

In this analysis I hope to have shown how a therapist can deviate from their orientation. The analysis demonstrates how CA can be used to provide a detailed investigation into a therapist's use of 'reflecting back' techniques. While a more detailed picture can be obtained by adopting a comparative approach, where one could compare different therapists coming from various theoretical backgrounds, nevertheless a focus on one type of treatment made some comments and observations possible. The investigation led to the conclusion that while person-centred, brief solution-focused and CBT therapists are expected to adopt an empathic attitude and in doing so let go of their control and be purely transparent in the relationship, there is an element of internal control in how topics can be talked about using formulations. Theorists, trainers and therapists cannot overlook this. Leudar et al. (2008a) found that therapeutic orientations are not used as recipes set in stone. Instead on can use these orientations sensitively and flexibly and they may be suspended if necessary. In this therapy, where the therapist combines three therapeutic approaches and is also confined by the short-term nature of therapy, flexibility is essential. On the other hand, in person-centred therapy the therapist is supposed to work within the clients' frame of reference and act in a non-directive manner in order for therapy to be effective. While CBT and brief solution-focused therapists tend to be more directive in their approach the way formulations are offered could lead to the therapy becoming too directive for an EAP style of therapy. Rogers (1995) argued that the therapist must avoid the temptation to subtly guide their client. Nevertheless, therapists use devices such as formulations which can subtly lead the client to talk about their problem from a particular perspective. The therapist's use of formulations is an unobtrusive device for doing just that. I found that person-centred therapy (especially if this approach has other theories included) can be subtly directive as there are subtle ways of changing the way people think.

I found that there are several ways in which this is accomplished. Firstly, formulations or 'reflecting back' in therapy, do what has been suggested by Heritage and Watson (1980), and 'fix' topics, which then ensures that there is continuity of topic. When the formulation is confirmed by the client, the topic gets fixed. It is through their fixing properties that formulations can function to maintain interactional control and in doing so direct the client to think in a certain way. Instead of seeing it as a form of control it can be seen as a type of guided practice and it is this guiding and channelling makes person-centred therapy more directive than non-directive. Secondly, I agree with the literature which argues that formulations in therapy trim down a clients' definition of their problem into something treatable in therapy (Davis, 1986; Antaki et al., 2005; Leudar et al., 2008a; Antaki, 2008). Davis argues that a therapist's inferences and interpretations can be so well packaged and efficiently presented that they are difficult to resist. However, sometimes the therapist has to work at having the formulations accepted. This may require that the therapist works the formulation over several turns and then timing becomes very important. If they go on too long the therapist may come across as forceful. It cannot come in too soon or too late if the topic is to be fixed for further development.

Thirdly, I agree with Antaki (2008) who states that the therapist deletes aspects of the clients' account and selects others before offering a formulation. This analysis can appear positive or negative. On the one hand the therapist may delete or ignore aspects of the clients' account which could be crucial to the clients' understanding of their situation. On the other hand the therapist may select pieces of information which they believe need to be highlighted. I found that what is important is not the exact contents of the formulation, but how the client comes to work with the formulation through an elaboration – is the process of re-formulation positive and growth-promoting for the client? A key feature to knowing that a formulation has been successful is if the client elaborates on the topic over an extended turn. This marks the topic as being important for both parties and especially for the client who picks up some value from having been understood. It is through further development of a topic that a client may achieve insight. Further to Antaki's (2008) findings, a mere 'yes' to a formulation does not indicate that the client has become more aware as this can only be carried out by the client themselves and becomes evident when the client starts to speak about it in an elaborate way. This point is taken up in Chapter 7.

Fourthly, I found, like Heritage and Watson (1980) and Antaki (2008) that the form and function of formulations is shaped by the activities and the settings where they are used. In some settings formulations can appear more challenging. Where time restrictions occur, for example, in EAP settings, therapists may rush to get the client to see things from a different perspective resulting in a distorted form of empathy. Solution-focused therapists may also use formulations to impose the solution onto the client. CBT therapists may ignore natural feelings such as love which are not always driven by thought and cannot be reduced to a perspective. An analysis using CA can reveal if the therapist is using the formulation for the clients' benefit or to fulfil their own institutional needs – that is, nudging the client to stay with the solution.

Some of the CA literature, (for example, Davis, 1986; Antaki, 2008) which shows that therapists' use of formulations serves the therapists' interests places them in a somewhat negative light and can appear too critical of therapists. I suggest that this can happen if CA analysts overlook the therapist's theoretical orientation in their analysis. As formulations can have different meanings depending on the therapeutic approach, analysts need to respect what the therapist is attempting to do with the formulation in their practice. On the other hand therapists may idealize their practice, and if this is so, CA can make this publicly visible (Peräkylä and Vehviläinen, 2003).

The fact that formulations are deeply implicative for the development of subsequent talk (Heritage and Watson, 1979) has important ramifications for what can be said in the sessions. Formulations restrict the client to produce a decision. The therapist does not force the client to think in a certain way by offering them something to reflect on. They are free to work with the idea as they choose. Nevertheless, as the therapist can use formulations to nudge through tendentious readings of the client's account (Antaki, 2008; Antaki et al., 2005), the therapist can direct the way the talk develops in the sessions. If the therapist notices that the client feels understood the therapist is then in a position to either move the talk on to a further elaboration of the first formulation or to move the talk onto a further variant of the original topic. In other words, in addition to the interactional control held by the therapist by virtue of the asymmetrical character of the setting, the therapist can direct and so control the development of the subsequent talk through their use of formulations. CA can reveal if this control is positive or negative for the client and so can help therapists reflect on how they use them.

Roger's view of the therapeutic relationship as the main instrument for change is the ideal. What this chapter reveals, like the previous CA investigations of formulations, is that in practice that ideal can be played out differently.

Therapists'/practitioners' corner

In this corner I will explain and demonstrate the use of two specific
CA terms: 1. preferred and dispreferred; and 2. tag questions. Preferred
or dispreferred turn shapes (see Pomerantz, 1984a) are akin to agree-
ments or disagreements and refer to successful or unsuccessful actions.
For example, if one invites people to a party acceptances are normally
preferred (unless of course the person doing the inviting has another
agenda). In 'doing' reflecting back or formulations in therapy agreement
with the formulation is preferred. In addition, speakers can design their
turns as preferred (Sidnell, 2010). Therapists can use tag questions to
design a preferred turn, and they can also use pauses and short sounds. In
designing a preferred turn the therapist may express his or her opinion.
On hearing agreement the therapist may think the formulation or interpretation has been accepted. However, it is only in examining the fine
details of talk that one can determine if the formulation has really been
accepted or not.

In this example CA is used to demonstrate the difficulties that may
arise when brief solution-focused therapists try and get the client to
think about strengths they may have.

1. T: how does it feel uh (0.3) uh sort of (0.5) does it feel good to
   °exert
2.   your influence. an an have control over your partner.° (8.7)
3. C: YEAH ↑feels ↑great (.)
4. T: YEAH so then (.) you can feel ↑good with him (.)
5. C: yeah but then I wonder. °why can't I apply it to:: (0.6) ↑other
   ↑areas (0.3)
6.   with him.°

The client is given a time to reflect on the therapist's optimistic question
(line 2) and the *feels great* on line 3 aligns with the optimism posed in
the question. The therapist picks up on this and introduces a formulation on line 4. This formulation is accepted by the client (line 5) but is
then followed by a *but*. The formulation was not quite successful as the
but refers to limitations. As soon as the therapist had received a positive response to the question on line 1 she reinforced this good feeling
with a punched up *yeah*. However, the client downgrades the optimistic
content (see also extract 1 above lines 49 and 51 and extract 2 lines 19
and 21 for further examples).

Tag questions

Therapists can use tag questions to leave a topic open-ended and invite clients to continue on talking on topic. In many cases it is clear that when therapists feel sure of their formulation or question he or she may use a tag. In such cases, the function of the tag is primarily to express meaning. However, in using tags therapists can also dominate the talk by keeping a strict focus on a topic and can in doing so can delete important pieces of information.

Consider the following.

> ? indicate rising intonation at the end of a word. They do not mark questions.

1. T: o.k te- tell me about the situation in work::: as it is at the moment with this guy?
2. C: em::: well he's kinda changed (0.8) em:: somebody has even suggested that he has been
3.   affected by mood disorders em:: (0.5)
4. T: somebody SAID that did ↑they?
5. C: even the guy I work with (0.5) who is >not the most (0.5) sensitive of people< even
6.   noticed (0.3) that his mood had changed

By using the tag question on line 4 the therapist deletes references to mood disorders and the fact that the guy at work had changed and focuses the talk on the *somebody* who *said that*. One may have expected a therapist to focus on mood disorders and changes but by focusing on the *somebody* the therapist moves the client away from what she notices and instead moves the noticing onto somebody else. The client follows the therapist's lead and takes up the point about the guy she works with on line 5 although she does go back to the original observation, that the boss's mood had changed. The above seems to indicate that the neither the client nor the therapist trusts the client's observations. Tags can also be used to get clients to take up a topic and then work with a topic. This point will be further developed in the next chapter.

7
Sequencing in Short-Term Psychotherapy

This chapter investigates how therapists actively listen over several turns at talk. A third way of uncovering details about how the therapeutic relationship is produced and practised using talk, is to go beyond active listening devices and adjacency pairs. Therapy does not occur in discrete adjacent utterances but over the course of therapy, which itself has a noticeable structure. There are numerous different sequence types to be discovered and these patterns can span several turns (Peräkylä et al., 2008; Voutilainen et al., 2011). This chapter will be concerned with one such pattern obvious in this type of therapy where extended turns by a client, while being actively listened to by the therapist, alternate with therapist formulations. The previous two chapters documented the use of therapist formulations and continuers in the therapy separately from how therapists' listen actively to clients' extended turns. This chapter will analyse how the two of these, in addition, to some questions go together. It will become apparent that there is a pattern and one can track how exactly this pattern is produced. Also, this type of pattern seems to be quite specific to this kind of therapy, which expects the client to be active with the therapist supporting them. As far as CA is concerned the turn-taking system is always the same but used differently to produce different extended sequences in therapy in general. For example, some therapists who allow clients to free associate may encourage long extended sequences and may choose to remain silently in the background for extended periods while others may use many continuers, or a series of questions to pace the client through short or long sequences. For the most part, all therapists intervene at varying points with extensions, formulations, interpretations, questions or use varieties of all of the above and more. By taking a close look at these patterns, a therapist could come to identify their own unique brand of therapy, that is, how they carry out treatment.

Despite the variety and numerous patterns two very distinct sequence types were discovered in the corpus. Firstly, there is the sequence involving questions, active listening and formulations which could be called the 'enquiry sequence' and this is usually short and may contain a series of Socratic questioning. The process of this therapy normally begins with an enquiry into the presenting problem. When the therapist has expressed some understanding and clarity, usually by posing questions and then using *gist* formulations, and clients have in some way accepted this understanding, an elaboration of the client's experiences typically commences. This second sequence could then be called an 'elaboration sequence' when the client is encouraged to elaborate on certain experiences, and this sequence then gets distributed over time and talk. During this elaboration the therapist attempts to transform that experience by getting the client to change how they think and feel about their presenting issue. Sometimes these lines of action work and sometimes they do not. This chapter focuses mainly on these 'elaboration sequences' and looks at how they are created and the function they have in this therapy.

Sequencing and coherence

If one were to take a sequence and examine it as a cluster or clump of talk one will invariably find an underlying coherence. One way of examining that coherence is to investigate the topics which motivate it. Psychotherapy researchers tend to focus on the topic and theme being talked about when investigating episodes in psychotherapy and counselling (McLeod, 2011). Mental health practitioners also tend to focus on topics and themes when carrying out assessments, creating case formulations, and engaging in case discussions. In addition, supervisors tend to concentrate on recurring themes, patterns and interpretations of subject matter when working with psychotherapists. However, CA researchers have found that there is a risk involved in focusing on the topic alone as an analysis will reveal what that talk is about and may miss out on how that talk is done – essentially how participants are 'doing topic talk' (Schegloff, 1990). For example, if we listen to a therapist asking a series of Socratic questions in CBT, we will notice that the talk is 'sequentially organised in terms of more or less fixed parts, done by various of the participants in some relatively fixed order' (Sacks, 1987, p. 55). The therapist asks questions until the client begins to reflect on how their thoughts or beliefs are making them feel and behave a certain way. By examining fixed parts or clumps as sequences of action we get a picture of how a therapist gets a client to talk about a topic.

What CA researchers found out about sequences

CA studies on psychotherapy have shown that sequences of action have some form or trajectory to them and that these trajectories are organized through turns-at-talk. Investigations into sequences involving questions and responses (Muntigl and Zabala, 2008; McMartin, 2008), re-interpretations and responses (Bercelli et al., 2008), formulations and responses (Hak and de Boer, 1996; Drew, 2003; Antaki et al., 2004, 2005; Hutchby, 2005; Antaki, 2008), psychoanalytical interpretations and responses (Peräkylä, 2004, 2008; Vehviläinen, 2003a, 2008; Voutilainen et al., 2011), have found numerous different sequence types. According to Schegloff 'sequences are the vehicle for getting some activity done' (2007, p. 2) and the sequences investigated here reveal three things. Firstly, what extended sequences there are in this kind of therapy; secondly, how these are produced locally; and thirdly, what actions they do as sequences. This chapter looks at how a client would tell their troubles which would be followed by a therapist formulation which in turn would be followed by the client talking about a problem in the way proposed in the therapist's formulation, or sometimes a question. Thereafter, the therapist would encourage the client to talk further by using continuers, a further formulation, or a question, which would then be followed by the client's elaboration of what had been proposed and, more often than not, by practising a healthier way of thinking. The results clarify how therapists channel and guide clients in the hope that the client will develop new insights into their presenting problem as they talk through an extended turn.

So how does all of this work? Episodes in therapy happen in patterns. The therapist's turn is shaped by the client's prior one, which then has an effect on the client's subsequent turn (Muntigl and Zabala, 2008). In psychotherapy mere yes or no answers would be considered too minimal and an expansion on content would be deemed necessary (Muntigl and Zabala, 2008). Adequate reflection on experience can lead to change, as new insights into personal difficulties can emerge from reflective activities (Duncan et al., 2004; Muntigl and Zabala, 2008; Peräkylä, 2008). The actions within the sequences should contribute to the therapeutic work at hand and perform therapeutic activities. However, change and insight are not always the outcome of episodes found in therapy or even in full therapy sessions and some interactional problems such as misalignments, false candidate readings of the client's tellings, and client resistances can occur. I focus on these trajectories of talk and examine how the relationship can be reproduced locally and then renegotiated during an elaboration of topic. I also investigate how therapists attempt to induce changes in the way client's talk about their problems and how this occurs over extended sequences.

I found that interactional difficulties will vary depending on the content. Misalignments can be observed by investigating the client's uptake of the formulations, interpretations and questions and the therapist's decision to allow the client to continue or make an intervention. However, a therapist's attempts to make a client's experiences fit into a pattern can be met with disagreements. In psychoanalysis disagreements can be seen as resistance. In this type of therapy resistances, in the form of disagreements with the therapist's formulations, were treated as just that/at face value, as parts of the interaction and were dealt with in various ways. Sometimes the therapist pursued an agreement and in doing so asserted their institutional 'know how' taking the line that 'the therapist knows best'. At other times the therapist altered their interpretation depending on how the disagreement was expanded on by the client.

Sequences and structure

The notion of structure is central to CA (Peräkylä, 2008). While, as already mentioned, there are different sequences to be found in therapy, the structures are nevertheless created out of the same building bricks, that is: therapists listen, clients talk, therapists make interventions and clients talk some more. Some sequences typically appear in different therapy schools, for example, the 'interpretative trajectory' (Vehviläinen, 2003a) in psychoanalysis or the 'downward arrow technique' sequence in CBT (Greenberger and Padesky, 1995). In this short-term therapy, where the therapist is expected to listen, reflect back to the client what they have just heard, and then get them to say more about it, the formulation–response pair plus expansion would typically be evident in data. However, the building bricks constrain what sequences are possible. For example, the question–answer sequence, found in CBT, is a weaker expansion-elicitor than the formulation–response pair (Muntigl and Habala, 2008).

The repetition of these types of phases, right throughout the series of meetings between client and therapist indicate how both participants orient to this overall structural organization and to the constraints and restrictions which these structures impose. For example, clients come to learn that they will be expected to continue talking in an extended manner and the client may provide an expansion without being specifically asked to do so. As expansions are allowed by CA sequential rules but not dictated by them, the fact that many of these extended sequences are evident in this therapy I argue that these sequences arise from the therapist's approach to the therapy. While certain clients may 'break the norms' and continue talking themselves, for the most part, the participants themselves orient to sequence organization and use it to conduct the activity. The natural flow from one thing to another is not a contingent feature of this encounter. It is the product of the collaborative work both of the therapist and the client.

Institutional interaction and sequences

In addition to examining sequences in terms of structure and topic, a third dimension, namely the institutional character of the interaction, also needs to be taken into account. Using CA it was discovered that talk in this psychotherapy is not so much about the topic but about what the therapist and client are doing with the topic while accountably indicating a therapeutic policy. Drew and Heritage (1995) argue that the institutional character of an interaction has to be considered if the structure of the extended sequence is to be understood as separate from the topic. Investigations of institutional talk have revealed features of institutional turn-taking systems which are adapted to fit in with the constraints and restrictions of the actions they shape. As these systems affect how the participants talk to each other, they will have an impact on the sequences of action (Atkinson and Drew, 1979; Heritage and Greatbatch, 1991; Drew and Heritage, 1995; Peräkylä, 1995; Heritage and Maynard, 2006; Peräkylä et al., 2008). As far as the structure of sequences is concerned, institutional talk can contain set patterns or routines for the overall organization of conversation (Byrne and Long, 1976; Zimmerman, 1984; Drew and Heritage, 1995; Heritage and Maynard, 2006). However, while these phases are easy to distinguish in a medical encounter, for example, history taking, diagnosis, treatment plan, these are less clearly visible in psychotherapy (Peyrot, 1995). Psychotherapy is not a service point where one receives an answer, advice or recommendation. Instead the therapist uses talk to create sequences with the client which are functional and are also part of the therapist's tools or techniques. By examining the practice of psychotherapy from the point of view of functionally related sequence structure, which is typical of what one may find in psychotherapy interactions, we may come to understand stretches of psychotherapy talk better.

Introduction to the analysis

The following extracts examine how the participants align or misalign while producing 'elaboration sequences'. Having produced an account or telling, which was normally a response to a question, the therapist intervenes with either a *gist* or *upshot* formulation which was then expanded on by the client, who for the most part accepted this procedure by practising it. In this process the therapist has a double control. As mentioned in Chapter 6, the formulation itself restricts and directs the talk by deleting aspects of the client's account and focusing on others. This is also the case for questions. How the intervention is responded to is controlled by the client locally as the client is in a position to reject or accept the therapist's proposal. However, as formulations, in these sequences, require more than just yes/no answers, the acceptance or rejection is normally elaborated on by unpacking the intervention under the management of the therapist who paces the client through the process. In this way similar to what Antaki and Jahoda (2010) found, therapists allowed the sequence to develop but actually tried to keep control of the topics or agenda. In this therapy it was found that clients rarely introduce topics in the sequence except to shift topics or to explain something. In CBT where the client needs to agree on the topic or agenda to be worked on (Neenan and Dryden, 2001; Antaki and Jahoda, 2010) this may, however, be much more evident. Therapists can also draw out new topics from the client and from what they had been saying. In addition, the therapist may topicalize a theme that appeared not only in the client's prior turn but in another turn or in another session. By making links between successive utterances as well as linking to topics from another session, the therapist exercised more control over their intervention (Vehviläinen, 2003a; Peräkylä, 2004).

The following two extracts were taken from session two of this client's series of 6 sessions. In the first session the client had been explaining how her boss's behaviour ruins the mood at work as he takes his stress out on the staff. The client came to therapy to learn coping strategies and also maybe to make a decision to find a new job. In the piece, which preceded this extract the client had been telling the therapist how she had begun using good humour when dealing with the boss and tried to make the most of the humorous situation to protect herself and not allow the stressful situation ruin her day.

Extract (1)

Session 2

M = Mary

45.→ T: o.k so (0.3) e:h:: (.) >you have <u>used</u> his ↓fo:r- (.) his better
         form to your

46. →   <u>advan↑tage↓</u> have you↑ (.)
47. M: yea:h=
48. T: [right]
49. M: [now] he↑wa:s (.) starting to kind of ((sniffing)) (0.5) befo:re
50. em: >on Tuesday evening he started to kind of come over and start
51.   being a bit hassely about- you know kind of- he was doing a bit of like
52.   you know the children's kind of thing of were we there yet?< (0.4)
53. T: mm:=
54. M: >using a little bit of that < an- fffort(h)unately I was doing eh- (.)
55. T: ↑mm: (0.4)
56. M: ↑em:: (0.9)= but again I try to remember like>to just be in< good
57.   humour and (.) not (0.9) let that get in on top of you. (0.6)
58. T: right=
59. M: and try and kinda (1.5) jus- (1.5) jus- (.) eh- I ↑yeah just ↑<u>try::</u> >as best
60.   you can< of< of- <u>field</u> it ba::ck (0.4)
61. T: right (.)
62. M: and n:ot (.) let it kind of (1.8) <u>mess</u> with <u>your</u> head like (0.3)
63. T: yeah:=
64. M: and sort of (0.7) <u>int:erfere</u> ↓with the <u>com:pletion</u> of what you'r ↑<u>d:oing</u>
65.   which it can do you know (.)
66. T: ye[ah
67. M: [then] >you start thinking 'oh I can't do this',< (0.3)
68.→ T: <u>yeah</u> (0.6) ↑<u>so</u> ah (0.3) >a:r:e you saying this en-< like your <u>strategy</u> is
69. →   to kinda separate <u>yourself</u> fro:::m (0.8) <u>h:is</u> (1.0) ↑<u>attack</u> I suppose o:r
70. →   you know the stuff that he's throwing at you. =
71. M: ↑it is but this is all very light weight stuff that so >I don't know how
72.   I'd be: if it went back to being majorly bad [again]

In this extract the therapist offers a gist formulation of the client's prior talk (lines 45–46) which summarizes what the client had been saying previously. The client accepted the formulation (line 47) and proceeded to elaborate on her decision to create this extended sequence which added more information to the content provided in the formulation.

From this formulation, which focused on the client's strengths in a typical solution-focused manner, an extended sequence developed. This occurred because both participants collaboratively oriented to producing this. This sequence developed by the joint integrated use of listening and talking using active listening devices and formulations. CA can be used to help look at how the activities in therapy are organized and how therapists allow sequences to develop but also try and keep the talk focused on the agenda, clarified in the formulation. In this case the client's strengths. Firstly, the overlap which occurred (lines 48–49) indicates two things. The *right* accepts the client's response but also acts as a continuer to guide the client into providing further explanations. However, the client's use of the word *now* (line 49) seems to indicate that, while the client was agreeing with the formulation she also needed to add in this extra explanation with or without the therapist's prompting. This discourse marker *now* caused a shift which could almost be heard as the anticipation of a dispreferred response as the client goes on to provide an elaboration of how this skill, highlighted by the therapist in the formulation, depends on the boss's behaviour. The client then seems to have finished her elaboration on line 52 but is further guided by the continuers on line 53 and again 55 to keep going. When the client continues on line 54 and introduces a positive aspect, *fortunately I was doing*, the therapist becomes slightly more involved in the talk and uses a channelling continuer (see Chapter 5) on line 55 designed to channel the client to continue on talking on the topic of "I", describing what she was doing rather than what the boss was doing. The short pause on line 55, followed by the client's hesitation line 56 followed by a longer pause and then the *but* show how the client goes along with this and shifts the topic back to an elaboration of her agreement with the formulation.

During this telling the therapist could have picked up on the boss's behaviour but instead channelled the client to talk about herself and what she does through the use of continuers and silences. The result is a sequence which is performed locally, but gets extended because both parties act in a particular way. The client seemed to want to talk about the boss's behaviour, and the therapist could have followed that lead and introduced another formulation on lines 53 or 58. Instead the therapist stays with the client's preferred response to the formulation and does not get sidetracked into talking about the boss. Even though there was an indication that the client might be stopping (line 57) the therapist uses a variety of continuers to support the story and keep it going as well as channelling the client to talk about her behaviours.

The therapist then comes in with a formulation which is embedded in a question, on lines 68–70, when the client has provided a clearer definition of her problem. The boss's behaviour can affect me, so I can't do my work. This formulation again highlights the client's skill but in the form of a strategy, which elaborates on the formulation on lines 45–46. This upshot formulation (plus question) implies that the client behaves in a more constructive and healthier manner than her boss whose behaviour is destructive. The question attempts to get through a tendentious reading of the client's account (Antaki, 2008). This extended sequence provides an example of how the formulation gets extended by the therapist in order to get the client to see her problem from a different perspective. This perspective was introduced in the first formulation (lines 45–46). It is achieved by channelling the client to talk in a particular way so that the therapist guides the client towards her own resources and then reinforces this positive solution in the second formulation. In this sequence, the therapist exerts her therapeutic control by keeping the talk going in a particular direction. However, the client does downgrade the therapist's reading of the situation (line 71) *but this is all very light weight stuff.* The therapist's strategy, to use elaboration to get the client to talk differently about her problem, only partially worked here. CA helped to demonstrate not only how therapist and client develop these extended sequences but also why therapists try to keep focussed on the agenda. In short-term therapy this may be necessary.

<u>Extract (2)</u>

This is another example of how extended sequences are jointly created and how the therapist tries to steer the agenda but also gives the client the space and time to elaborate and reflect on what they said. This could not be established locally because the therapist's function as a patient and focused listener and the client's extended talk, where they have the opportunity to interact with their own thoughts and feelings over time may be overlooked.

Session 5

M = May

50. T: what does it ↑mean to yu- you that you think you are
inca:::pable

51. M: I I think I do have to remember tha- I always do get things
done so

52.   why do I ever [think
53. T: [↑ye↓ah::
54. M: oh what if I can't figure this out< (0.4) cos I always do in the end
55. T: m::hm: (0.3)
56. M: and (0.3) the only question that could ever be is speed and is probably
57.   the only reason >it's ever a question of speed cos I devote time in my
58.   head to (1.04) em:: (0.6) to worrying about not being able (laughs) to tsh
59.   figure it out yu know (.)
60. T: [↑ri↓ght
61. M: [d'junno (0.3)
62.→ T: right (0.5) ok ↑so so like >a lot of what your saying is your HEAD is
63.   → (0.5) is your best friend but °it's kinda like (.) ↓a little bit of an enemy
64.   → there too° (0.5)
65. M: ↑yeah: (0.6) ↓°yeah:::° (.) ↓definitely (0.7) ↑em::: (0.5)
66.→ T: but it sounds like your more AWARE:: of ↓that (2.6)
67. M: ↑yeah I would be more aware of it cos of the: (.) stuff I've done like
68.   em here in therapy and read [maybe (.)
69. T: [↓yeah:: (0.4)
70. M: em::: (1.1) so >I suppose that helps< at least you kinda know (1.1) plus
71.   it- its different in there you've got space to kinda em: (0.3) impro::ve in
72.   there (0.3)
73. T: °mhm::° (0.4)
74. M: whereas in the last place I was in they were constantly hounding you
75.   (1.2) like every DAY your wondering what was gonna (0.4) pop up to (.)
76.   bite you <yu know what I mean [like
77. T: [°mhm°
78. M: so it was very hard to have any space (.) and the other thing I have
79.   noticed is that (0.9) °since° I've bin in this environment that I I've I'm

80.   mo::re able to kindav ↑say (0.6) with Andrew at home like
      (.) that I'm
81.   more able kindav like e:m:: (0.7) say like he's bin partic- a
      bit kind
82.   of like >difficult or [whatever<
83. T: [mhm::::
84. M: you know the way children get tiresome as they go into
      mood kinda=
85. T: =yea:h (0.5)
86. M: they'll be a bit <u>defiant</u> or something and=
87. T: yea:h (.)
88. M: at the end [of it like you know
89.→ T: [°mhm ↓mhm° (1.1) .hh ↑but like it
90. →   sounds like May that em (0.3) eh:: (1.1) the situa:::tion that
      you in as in
91. →   the other peo::ple ( ) AROUND you (.)
92. M: ↑m:↓hm (.)
93.→ T: ah::::: can actually::::: h- have positive or negative affect on
      the way you
94.   see:: >yourself in the situation< and the way you REACT to
      the situation
95.   (2.1)
96. M: ↑yeah well it's true I mean I´ve noticed that there's a guy
      who started
97.   around >the same time as me<
98. T: uh

The therapist encourages the elaboration, responding to the client's understanding of her worrying negative thoughts with a punched up channelling continuer on line 60. The client is drawn into an elaboration of her problem by the therapist's question on line 50. The therapist's overlapping response (line 53), on hearing the word *think* (line 52), and the focus on thinking and *worrying* in the *head* (line 58) followed by the therapist's *right* (line 60) indicates that this may be CBT. It seems like the therapist is encouraging the client to continue along this line of talk until she herself is then drawn in with *d'junno* (line 61). The upshot formulation, which follows, summarizes what the client had been saying as well as implying that her thoughts oppose her. The client fully accepts the formulation *definitely* (line 65) and upon acceptance the therapist takes another turn to reinforce the formulation in an attempt to draw out the client to talk about positive changes which have occurred (line

66). This is where the therapist amalgamates two approaches of CBT and BSFT. The reinforcement of the formulation begins with the conjunction marker *but,* which develops the topic by channelling the client to focus on her improved ability to deal with this adversary by focusing on the awareness as a resource. This topic development offers an alternative to the problem. By using *but* it ties the turn to the previous turn but changes its focus. This *but* achieves a specific type of action as it is followed by an elaboration of the formulation but also adds another perspective. In this way the client is channelled into a new and different way of thinking – a way which may be appropriate to the therapy. For example, becoming aware of things would be a term used by therapists. The therapist may be psychologizing the problem here as Davis (1986) suggested. This may be apparent in therapy talk in general. As mentioned in the introduction to this book, Freud used psychological terms such as id, ego, superego, which were replaced over time in the world of psychology.

In addition, and in CA terms, the placement of the conjunction *but* develops the sequence by taking control of the expansion. This ensures that the client reflects on her improvements rather than allowing her to reflect on her problem. In CBT and BSFT therapy it is hoped that a client would become aware of their negative thinking patterns but not practice them – even in therapy. The therapist could have asked the client here to give an account of her negative thinking patterns, which only she has access to. Instead the sequence is upheld so that the client is led to expand on the topic in a particular way directed by the therapist. This is further enhanced by the use of the continuer *yeah* (line 69). The therapist again indicates that an extension of this line of talk is needed by withholding from speaking.

The client shifts topic on line 78. The topic shifts away from the client's thoughts and feelings to an account of her son's behaviour and this is supported by the continuers in a non-feeling neutral manner. Although the client introduced a topic shift, the therapist subtly keeps the talk on topic without addressing the topic itself. The therapist could have encouraged expansion of the new topic, about the son by introducing a question or formulation. However, such an intervention would have altered the sequence and the approach the therapist was adopting. The therapist maintains the agenda by staying with the topic and by indicating that she is still listening but then by offering a re-formulation of the client's tellings (lines 89–91 and 93–94). The therapist may have needed to keep control of the agenda here because of the time-limited factor in this therapy. EAP clients come to therapy to work on a specific problem outlined in the assessment stage. The re-formulation, which is almost an interpretation, introduces the client's behaviour here with the punched up *react* (line 94). The subsequent pause (line 95) signals a change in direction and the client has to take time to reflect. There is no normative disapproval by the therapist as this may be met with too much resistance from the client. One can say that therapists, who claim to be non-directive, could subtly direct the client in the way they listen and then offer formulations or questions and also interpretations. Individual therapists can choose just how subtle and unobtrusive those directions are.

<u>Extract (3)</u>

In this extract, taken from the client's second session, the client had been telling the therapist how he had been cognitively and emotionally coping with two recent bereavements. The client had been expressing how, when he became anxious or worried about things such as a thesis he was writing, he took comfort from the fact that he is still alive and the others are not. The *they* in line 154 refers to worrying thoughts. This extract provides an example of how the therapist allows the client some control. It is the final session and the client is on more of a positive track and has more control over his problem. Here the therapist is less involved in the talk and a long extended sequence develops. As it is a long sequence I have divided it into three parts to make for easier reading.

Session 6

W = Will

153.   T: wha- what eh:: >sorry wha- wha- I don't understand that<
       what stops you
154.   panicking ↑about the thesis when they come into [your
       head
155.   W: [↑the fact] that I'm (.)
156.   I'm ↑he↓re (0.4) ° you know and she° [I've gotta- (it great)
157.   T: [↑and their NOT]
158.   W: ↑YEAH °I'm doing what I wanna do° (.) an- (.) come
       summer:: >I've all
159.   sorts of <u>opportunities</u>< (.) and em:: (1.5) eh::::: hhh just
       appreciate the
160.   fact that I'm >here yu know.< (0.8)
161.→T: ok ↑so so: yu- you can take something ↑<u>positive</u> from their
       (0.4)
162.   [from

163. W: [↑yea:h
164.→ T: their death (0.4)
165. W: I suppose my point is that >I havn't been gettin much negative sstuff<
166.   (out) of it (0.6) for (0.3) a while now (.)
167. T: ↑right (0.4)

The first part of this sequence is an example of an 'enquiry sequence' as the therapist attempts to achieve clarity and understanding. The therapist's upshot formulation, lines 161–164, highlights to the client that he has the resources and strengths to deal with his losses in a positive way. The client accepts this cautiously – he produces a gist formulation (lines 165–166) as a response that he has not been *getting into negative stuff* recently. The client re-formulates positive into not negative and the therapist accepts this turn in talk using the continuer 'right' (line 167) thereby accepting a partial move towards her formulation. One could call it a 'therapeutic compromise'. This channelling continuer *right* then encourages the client to talk in accordance with his re-formulation (see below). The therapist's formulation invites him to talk in a particular way – a yes or no answer would not be enough. So this *right* warrants that kind of way of expanding the answer. The therapist also warrants with the *right* that his partial acceptance of her formulation is acceptable for now. While the response *yeah* on line 163 is a preferred, the client expands the response in his own terms to provide a clearer explanation of how he sees it. So it is a dispreferred *'I suppose my point is'*. He is not as positive as the therapist was.

168. W: em::: when your kinda living (0.4) not <u>for</u> them but the way they lived
169.   they were both very eh outgoing and (0.9) like you'd (move-) (.) they
170.   were all on about eh: (.) like mum before she died was kinda (°sayin to
171.   me°) (0.6) I'm goin die its gonna be horrible but eh (0.9) yu gotta (0.8)
172.   get ↑on an- hm (.) you'll be alive °so (0.4) like° live. (0.6)
173. T: [°mhm°
174. W: [and then Eva obviously didn't know she was gonna die but she was
175.   always very ↓much into (0.3) she went through a few deaths

176.		herself before I understood about the whole (.) I was a bit ((banging
177.		sound)) (.) useless to her >when her< .hhh grand(.) parents died (0.8) she
178.		had three deaths (.) two deaths around the same time her grandparent-
179.		(0.4) two grandparents died and then (.) a third her cousin died in a hit
180.		and run >I think I told you about it< (.)
181.	T:	mhm (0.3)
182.	W:	↑BUT EM:: (0.5) she was quite <u>upset::</u> but its all like she'd be very::
183.		↓positive herself their ↑both two well- (0.6) both two very positive
184.		people so (0.4)
185.	T:	↑mm↓hm (.)
186.	W:	em::: (0.9) but <u>since</u> (.) ↑like I HAVEN'T been <u>thinking</u> of things just
187.		during the (.) holidays (1.0) you know ↑eh:: (0.5) not necessarily
188.		>upsetting myself about it.< (0.6)
189.	T:	↑right (0.5)
190.	W:	em::: (1.7) like °jus- so eh° (1.3) so lucky I suppose it ↑helped because I
191.		<u>met</u> someone (.) °during the holidays as well (0.7) eh::: I was really
192.		sure of (0.5) we get on great an-° it just was° (1.7) like life wud eh::
193.		(1.3) uh: (0.6) >(not profound or anything)< but life would eh keep-
194.		keeps taking them (.) the older you get (0.4) and people can focus on the
195.		fact that it keeps taking them which is natural the older you get the more
196.		things happen to you obviously (.) and then (0.7) em: but it keeps givin
197.		as well yu know (0.4) and °it just keeps givin to me stuff (as) well as
198.		that°

After the therapist has accepted the client's positive talk the client's response turns into a long stretch of talk by the client which is only brought to a close by the *ok* at the beginning of the second formulation on line 199. The topic (less negative thoughts) has been negotiated by both client and therapist through re-formulations throughout the extended sequence. The therapist paced the client as he worked through the topic using a mixture of continuers.

So the therapist's formulation here was too optimistic. The *yeah* on line 163 interrupts the turn and indicates agreement with the formulation. It orients to the word *positive* (line 161) but not necessarily with death which occurs after it. The turn is then developed as an expansion of that response which provides more information about the event referred to in the formulation. There is an agenda set by the formulation and there is a movement for the client throughout the whole sequence. So throughout the elaboration the client demonstrates his less negative thinking by specifying the places where he is less negative in the form of a story. He is guided by the formulation to tell a story. Between lines 174–180 the client shifts the topic by talking about how Eva experienced deaths when she was alive and not how he is experiencing her death. So there is this shift, and with it, he produces distance. He distances himself from the suffering by talking about it through the experience of the dead person – the upset is hers: he says *I haven't been thinking of things* (line 186). However, it does not mean that this is a move towards the positive, implied in the therapist's formulation. He admits that he thinks about the deaths all the time but does not necessarily get upset about it. The positivity does not go too far as the move towards the positive does not mean he has distanced himself from the deaths.

So in this story he demonstrates the partiality of the move. What are the implications for the analysis? Firstly, it isn't enough to examine the transcript in an entirely structural way, as the content cannot be ignored altogether. This client's story is a mixture of positive and negative, and therefore the therapist does not completely focus him on positive things. The therapist warrants that his life is a mixture of positive and negative happenings, picks it up and then solidifies this type of talk through the second formulation. The result is; this second formulation is shaped by the client's account. In order to make these aspects of a practice visible on needs to look at how the topics are elaborated over extended stretches of talk.

> 199.→T: ok so so (.) eh::: (0.5) it's not like (.) it's like not all about (0.4)↓negative
> 200. things happening (0.5)
> 201. W: yeah things can happen like people eh:: (1.7) like for example (0.7) em::

202.   (1.1) like over the (0.5) over the yeah:: >holidays< (0.3) like new year
203.   (0.3) Evan (0.7) had friends over from Finland
204. T: ↑ri↓ght

On line (199–200) the therapist has picked up on the expansions and provided a formulation which aligns with what the client had been saying it's *not like it's like not all about negative things happening.* This is an example of how a sequence of interaction is collaboratively produced by both parties so that the closing formulation indicates an acceptance of the client's telling by the therapist. The sequence is an example of the therapist supporting the view that the client is the 'owner' of their experience and yet the experience became public in the therapy and is being transformed through the therapy. This extended sequence shows how the therapist allows the client more freedom when they are on a positive track and when they are moving from a problem focused place into a solution-focused one. This indicates the need for the analysis of extended sequences. There is an element of negotiation here and a compromise. Here the therapist accepts a compromise. A therapist may not accept that compromise at the beginning of therapy. The therapist supports the talk and then changes her formulation as a result of what was said by the client.

Extract (4)

This extract is an example of a mis-alignment made visible over an extended sequence between the participant's talk. This client came to therapy because of stress. A major source of stress for this client was how she deals with criticism at work. The therapist initiated the topic by engaging this client in talk, designed to channel her to reflect on whether a distinction could be made between critical self-talk and criticisms received by others. Again, I have divided this long sequence into three parts to help the reader.

Session 3

E=Emily

1154. T: but do you find eh:: difficult then to em (.) do you find it
1155.   e- ever >difficult to sort of <u>self</u>-criticise self you know self- criticism<
1156.   (2.2)
1157. E: ↑eh:::↑ hhh (0.7) ↑NO::↓(0.8) °probably not° (1.3) maybe its I I don't
1158.   >mind hearing from myself<

1159. T: right=
1160. E: ° but not from somebody else° (0.3)
1161. T: ok (0.6)
1162. E: like <u>em::</u> (.) I'm actually gonna be off now for:: a few days around
1163.   Easter so and I can't see anybody till the nineth of April (0.3)
1164. T: ↑mm↓hm
1165. E: I'm feelin rea::lly strai::ned about that (0.6) that I'm yu- >lettin
1166.   everybody down< (.)
1167. T: ↑mm:: (.)
1168. E: and eh: (.) takin the next >couple of days off next week to study< cos I
1169.   know >I <u>won't</u> have <u>time</u> [when I'm<
1170. T: [mm
1171. E: workin fulltime (0.3) .hh and I'm takin all this pressure on myself
1172.   when I shouldn't be (0.4) (traffic noise) [when
1173. T: [↑m:↓hm
1174. E: I've been told look (.) if your just too busy knock out a day:: don't see
1175.   [clients at all (0.3)
1176. T: [mm
1177. E: and ↑then (.) I feel like (.) God nineteen days before I could see
1178.   somebody (0.4) and I get ↑<u>caught</u> up (.) ↓in clients urgency (0.9)
1179. T: ↑yeah↓=
1180. E: =and eh (0.3) >I've always felt like that (probably yu know) client now
1181.   .hh (0.3) an- I'm <u>totally</u> strapped for cash an- (0.6) (traffic noise) I
1182.   haven't got a <u>penny</u> to my name and normally I get real caught up in
1183.   that (.)

This sequence was initially structured around the topic of self-criticism as the client said that she felt it easier to criticise herself (lines 1157–1158), *I don't mind hearing it from myself*, but finds it difficult to take it from others. During this extended turn, the topic changed into a problem the client might have with self-sacrifice. The problem was re-formulated during the sequence and the therapist accomplished this by channelling the client to look at her problem from a different perspective.

1184.	→ T:	yeah ↓yeah ↑ (0.5) ↑and (.) ok so >yu- yu- your (.) like< yu-your
1185.	→	<u>saying</u> yu find it <u>hard</u> to sort of put yourself ↑first (0.3)
1186.	E:	°mm: sometimes in work yeah° (0.3)
1187.	T:	↑right (.)
1188.	E:	and I feel bad about sayin it to them like oh actually I'm gonna get
1189.		more if I was like (0.5) about sayin it to her actually (0.6) or I've
1190.		squeezed round it before it (0.3) somehow (.)
1191.	T:	↑mm↓mm=
1192.	E:	=but em: (0.5) I'v said look an- I'm actually off for a few days (.)
1193.	T:	↑mm↓mm
1194.	E:	and I can't see you till then and I just feel really bad about it (.)
1195.	T:	↑mm↓mm
1196.	E:	cos I get (0.3) cos normally I don't sta- like it's only a week (.) at max
1197.		(0.3)
1198.	T:	↑yeah (.)
1199.	E:	°that I'm out from work you know° (0.3) so YEAH I suppose I do I
1200.		(0.3) °sometimes put the job before myself (0.3)
1201.	→ T:	an- what <u>prevents</u> you from puttin yourself first (0.7)
1202.	E:	let- (.) I don'- wanna let people down (1.4)
1203.	T:	↑ri↓ght
1204.	E:	because I (1.3) yu know I'm the one >well I'm the only one that
1205.		they can< (0.3) you know (0.6) >whatever they what-ever <u>I'm</u> dealin
1206.		with (if only we had) job sharing or someone else an- who could [deal with
1207.	T:	[uh: huh
1208.		em (.)
1209.	E:	your left with the job .hh (0.4) the job itself is so much (0.3) I'd
1210.		be ringing in when I'm off anyway (.)

```
1211.  T:  yeah
1212.  E:  you ring me from work (0.3) I actually say that ring me
           if there's
1213.      anything wrong >you know what I mean< (0.3) if you
           can't find a file
1214.      or whatever (.)
1215.  T:  ↑m:↓hm
1216.  E:  em (.) sometimes you know it's:: >hard to switch ↑off< (0.4)
```

However, the storytelling sequence is not closed but instead the therapist proposes a particular topic in using this *upshot* formulation (lines 1184–1185) and the nature of the topic 'putting yourself first' is expected to be within the client's experience so that the client is expected to carry the burden of the talk. The formulation works to re-formulate the client's talk so that the client's ability to engage in self-criticism becomes almost self-abusive as the client admits to putting the job and the client's work before herself in an attempt to avoid feeling she may let someone down. The question (line 1201) which presupposed the correctness of the formulation on lines 1184–1185 serves as a stage or a part of the larger sequence designed to channel the client into examining this topic in more detail to gain an insight into the behaviour. The client appeared to be stopping having provided a summary of the topic beginning on lines 1199–1200, *so yeah I suppose I do sometimes put the job before myself.* The client however offers the idea that this happens only sometimes but when pushed, the answer the client provides to the question is the same answer offered in relation to self-criticism (lines 1165–1166) above which relates to her self-sacrificial approach to clients and co-workers.

The second-pair part of the formulation, (line 1185) provides an answer to the therapist's question (lines 1154–1155). This question–answer sequence had been closed by the *ok* on line 1161. This closing of the sequence is evidenced by the fact that nothing happens after *ok* – the therapist does not continue so after a pause the client continues on the topic, giving an example of what she thinks is a self-criticism. The therapist accepts the client's problem definition, which is that she cannot take criticism from others but uses an *upshot* formulation (lines 1184–1185) which is hesitantly expressed by the therapist, indicating that the therapist is somewhat unsure if her implication will be accepted. The client then sets off an extended sequence, which provides some reflections about how the client self-criticizes by feeling that she lets people down if she does not self-sacrifice also. The therapist listens using a series of continuers which indicate that the therapist hears this story as either background information necessary for the client's telling of her story about self-criticism or as a description of a behavioural problem the client is attempting to reveal.

```
1217.→ T:   ↑ri↓ght (0.6) ok so so yu- you find it hard to kinda draw
            boundaries
1218.  →    between your own self and and the- these people that
            your working
1219.  →    with or that you have to work with (0.6)
1220.  E:   yeah but I don't bring it home like >°yu know what I
            mean that's what I
1221.       used but not- I wouldn't really say I do it now (0.3)
1222.  T:   m:↓hm: (0.3)
1223.  E:   you know I don't delve on it as as much as I do but (0.7)
            on things
1224.       about you know trying to squeeze everyone an- tryin to
            keep everybody
1225.       happy. (1.1)
1226.  T:   ↑ok
```

The therapist's re-formulation on lines 1217–1219 presents the client with the notion that her problem is not with criticism but with boundaries. The client offers a preferred answer *yeah* (lines 1220) but does not accept the therapist's formulation totally. This is then an example of a lack of common understanding of the problem on the part of the therapist who misinterprets the client's problem as being an issue with boundaries. The client reiterates that it is a problem with people pleasing.

Conclusions

The chapter looked at how formulations, active listening techniques and some questions are combined and managed, around an agenda and over extended sequences. Four important points have emerged. The first point concerns the structure of the sequence and its coherence. The therapist fixes the topic or agenda using a formulation or a question which, when positively responded to, achieves some clarity for the therapist. The therapist normally fixes this topic by relating it to the presenting problem. Thereafter, the therapist encourages the client to expand using continuers, further open-ended questions, and formulations.

Secondly, the topic cannot be altogether ignored. The sequence is structured around the topic and that topic might change if the client cannot practise the formulation. In such a case the therapist has to take charge and this is done in one of three ways: by allowing long stretches of talk with no support through continuers so that the client is left to work things out alone; by interrupting the sequence with a question so that the client is somewhat channelled to consider the topic from a different angle; or by cutting the sequence short and re-directing the talk onto another topic or tangent of the original topic. If the sequence is not working because the client is finished on that topic, or the therapist has not understood what the client had been saying prior to the onset of the sequence the therapist often intervenes to create a new sequence. Thirdly, the type of therapy being conducted determines the form and length sequences will take. For example person-centred therapists may allow longer sequences to develop than pure CBT therapists who work with more structured agendas (see Antaki and Jahoda, 2010). Brief solution-focused therapists may try and focus the talk and will allow longer sequences to occur if the solution is emerging. Fourthly, individual therapists will establish their own style as far as the length and structure of the extended sequence is concerned. As formulations are akin to empathic responses, one might expect that these types of extended sequences would be found in the talk between both participants in short-term EAP style therapy.

The therapist always introduced the formulations or questions in these sequences and these roles are practically never reversed. Also, having received a response, the therapist quickly settles into the role of listener until she decides to become speaker again and produce a new intervention. Although the therapeutic relationship is supposed to be practised collaboratively this indicates that these extended sequences in therapy are very asymmetrical and provide the therapist with most of the control over the turn-taking system. CA can be used to track whether these extended 'elaboration sequences', where the therapist has most of the interactional control, are leading the client to new insights and awareness and solutions or not.

Therapists'/practitioners' corner

If therapists look closely at their work they will notice many different types of sequences. When doing or preparing for supervision I suggest that therapists start by reflecting on the type of sequences that have been created with particular clients. They will notice that rounds of enquiry about their client's/patient's problem are continually being renewed and developed within the sessions and over the course of the sessions into long sequences where it is hoped positive changes will occur for the client. New lines of enquiry continually occur until the client/patient begins to take a different stance towards their problem. Questions such as: how these sequences were

created; how much talking the therapist had to do before they were able
to introduce a formulation or an interpretation and how the client worked
with and practised the therapist's questions over time can be considered.
It is also important to note that sequences link sessions thus creating practical historical textures to the therapy. Therapists can reflect on how the
sequences that are created link to previous sessions and pay attention to
the times when a client or patient begins to talk differently about their
problem as this often happens over an extended sequence. Also, as CBT
therapists work with agendas they might be able to track if the client or
patient is staying with the agenda or if they tend to move off track (see
Antaki and Jahoda, 2010) and with what consequences.

Consider the following.

1. T: have you have any thoughts about what we were talking
        about the last day
2. C: not ↑rea::lly I've been kind of (0.4) bus::y and (1.2) haven't
        really thought
3.   about it much
4. T: mm.mm (1.1) >is there anything specific you'd like to talk
        about today<
5. C: no I'm fine:: (0.8) ah::: I was actually driving in the car
        thinking (0.5) God
6.   what am I gonna talk about today
7. T: ((laughs)) you have to talk about somethin °[(it is your)
        per?::sonal therapy°
8. C: [Yeah (.) yea- (0.4)
9. T: o.↑k see what comes into your mind!

Here the therapist's attempts to direct the conversation towards the
formulation of a problem. In line 1 the therapist could have asked how
the client was but in typical CBT fashion she instead focuses on *thoughts*
(line 1). The client takes this up and treats the thinking about last week's
session as an activity, something she needed to work on for homework.
The therapist accepts this slowly (*mm mm* line 4) plus a pause and then
continues to press for a topic. The client in line 5 again refers to thought
but minimizes the importance of coming to therapy by indicating she is
fine but also confused, *God what am I going to talk about* (lines 5–6). The
therapist again presses for a topic before giving up. The therapist attempts
to direct the topic while the client exercises her power by not treating the
therapy as something serious – she is fine and also too busy to think about
the sessions. Here the therapist set up a link with the previous session in
an attempt to create a new line of enquiry, a new sequence.

8
Employee Assistance Programmes: A Management Tool

This chapter takes a slight twist from the previous three empirical chapters and focuses on the use of the EAP as a supportive device for managers. As the EAP provides a private, perhaps even delicate, service to its employees, managers need to conduct considerate and sensitive conversations with their employees when using the facility as a management tool. This is not always an easy task. On the one hand, managers need to carry out their duties and manage their area, while at the same time, they need to be responsive to worrying changes in their employee's behaviours and intervene where necessary (Becker, 2011). This chapter demonstrates how a CA/ethno, as well as some membership categorization devices (MCD), can be used to analyse conversations between a manager and an employee. Such an analysis can expose difficulties which may arise when managers try to combine their two roles. In MCD terms managerial roles are 'category-bound' activities (Sacks, 1992, LC1). This means that a manager's identity is recognizable by the kind of activities in which they engage. Negative assessments can be made of managers when they act in ways which may be inappropriate to their category or social identity. Managers who try to be too caring and attempt to act as counsellors may find themselves out of their depth. On the other hand, managers who believe that they are being helpful may not realize that they are using their position to achieve certain ends. The first part of this chapter will look at some recent literature on difficulties in the workplace and the use of EAPs and the latter half will introduce some analysis of role-plays between a manager and an employee when the manager attempts to use EAP as a management tool.

Concerns in the workplace

The effect of mental disorder and distress on workplace performance and absenteeism has received much attention in recent times. In Europe alone the impact of mental distress costs the economy up to 132 billion euro a year, due mainly to decreased work performance and absenteeism (Wittchen and Jacobi, 2005). A questionnaire carried out by the European foundation (INQA, 2009) for the improvement of living and working conditions showed that 28 per cent of the participants named psychological distress as the second most common work-related health problem. In the US a National Comorbidity Survey revealed that 217 million work days are lost each year due to mental disorders (Hertz and Baker, 2002). Psychological ill-health can have a major impact not only on performance but also on relationships in the workplace, as it has adverse effects on one's social role. For example, a depressed or anxious person may withdraw from teamwork or may resist giving presentations. In addition, many sufferers do not seek professional help until it is too late. In fact only about 10 per cent of sufferers actually receive therapy (Wittchen-Jacobi, 2005) and there are many reasons for this. Firstly, employees may believe they cannot be helped through professional therapy or counselling. Secondly, they may feel that getting help could expose sensitive personal information which would then be shared with a stranger. Thirdly, employees may be worried that their manager or team lead will find out personal information about them that they should not know. They may then assume that this will have a negative impact on their job. Incorrect assumptions and misunderstandings may lead an employee to think that their standing in the organization will be affected. Another possible difficulty is that an employee could be deemed a safety risk if they suffer from addictive disorders, and they may fear that they might either lose their job or be reassigned because of it. A further difficulty may be that the individual suffers from work-related stress or work-related depression. The solution then may not lie with the individual but with their work environment. In that case, the solution has to be a collaborative one involving all aspects of the organization, as therapy or counselling received at an individual level will not provide resolution.

According to the literature on psychological distress in the workplace depression and anxiety are the mental health conditions which contribute most to absenteeism or presenteeism (Stuart et al., 2003; Leidig, 2007). Presenteeism means that the individual is present at work but their normal functioning capacity is reduced due to psychological distress (Stuart et al., 2003; Leidig, 2012). Because of the taboo nature of these illnesses, sufferers may try to hide their ill-health and this may result in an increase in frequent sick days, lack of motivation, mistakes, emotional absenteeism, loss of interest, apathy and so on (INSITE

Interventions, 2009). As depression is becoming a serious world health problem (WHO, 2007) and workplace stress is on the increase (Bamber, 2011; Norbrega, 2012), it is becoming increasingly necessary for organizations to implement plans, to learn to identify early warning signs and symptoms, and to recognize workplace stress and depression as well as presenteeism before these have a major impact on workplace performance or the employee begins to suffer from burnout. A study carried out in 2008 in Germany showed that presenteeism for depressed colleagues cost the economy 9.28 billion euros (Allianz und RWI, 2011).

Stress, workplace stress, depression and burnout

Stress: Stress occurs when demands exceed one's ability to cope. However, psychological distress has many causes and its origins can frequently appear quite blurred. Many triggering factors such as family and relationships, physical ill-health, financial and legal stressors, or societal problems, such as the reduced job market or financial instability, can all have an impact on one's functioning and can test one's ability to cope. The long-term negative effects of any kind of sustained and excessive exposure to stressors can result in long-term physical and mental diseases (WHO, 2007). Illness can occur if one lacks support either in one's private life or at work, or if the work climate is unaccommodating, dismissive and possibly even punitive (Leidig, 2003), for example, sometimes employees are too readily put onto performance improvement plans.

Workplace stress: The burgeoning amount of literature on workplace stress suggests that there is now enough evidence to believe that long-term exposure to workplace stressors has a negative effect on the health and well-being of employees. Whether the stress is related to work-load pressure; unclear or unrealistic goals; environmental stressors such as noise, over-crowding or shift work; organizational changes such as layoffs or interactional difficulties resulting in poor communication, lack of support, conflicts and even bullying, it will inevitably give rise to physical, mental and emotional ill-health (Belkic et al., 2004; LaMontagne, 2008; Norbrega et al., 2010). Bamber (2011) suggests it is in the interests of both managers and employees to effectively manage the negative impact of stress on health and performance, as workplace stress is closely associated with major health problems such as heart disease, cancer, depression, and anxiety, to name but a few. Interventions need to occur at multiple levels. Firstly, managers need to become trained in recognizing stress symptoms and to learn how to support individual employees in developing healthier coping mechanisms. Secondly, employers can seek to improve psychosocial conditions such as communication, transparency, control or workload reviews. Thirdly, interventions can occur at an organizational level where management policies involve not only the implementation of work-related tasks but also the execution of a 'duty of care' policy. Such a policy bestows two roles on the manager. Firstly, managers are required to complete their job specific tasks and adhere to deadlines and timelines. Secondly, it is imperative that they look after the health and well-being of their employees. Research suggests that organizations need to make their employees' well-being a priority and adjust their policies accordingly (West et al., 2012; Bamber, 2012).

Workplace depression: While much research has been done on workplace depression, there are not many accounts of how the workplace affects depression or contributes to depressive-like symptoms in employees (LaMontagne et al., 2007). Much of the work carried out on this topic has focused on an individual's symptoms and how to treat them, rather than on the workplace itself which may be causing the depression (West and Poynton, 2012). While CBT is becoming the preferred treatment for depression (Lambert, 2013), little collaborative work has been done on the specifics of how the work context contributes to individual depression. Could CBT treatments be effective in addressing workplace depression? In treating depression the therapist focuses on reducing helplessness and resourcing the client to cope in his or her social environment. However, in many organizations the management of the problem tends to be taken away from the workplace (West and Poynton, 2012). In terms of medical treatment, the symptoms are addressed and the worker returns to the same context. I agree with those studies which suggest that workplace policies need to focus on preventative measures, with a focus on the events and processes which precede the employees' efforts to seek help.

Burnout: This term was originally coined by psychoanalyst Herbert Freudenberger in 1974, who observed common symptoms in sufferers working mainly in the helping professions (Behrends-Krahnen, 2011). It is a psychological term used to describe long-term exhaustion and diminished motivation and interest. In this state a person's ability to recover is severely impaired and natural recovery times are not possible (www.insite-interventions.com). Currently, everyday and workplace stress, changes in the workplace that focus on increased performance, the expectation that one is continually reachable though the digital media, as well as the expectation that everyone can multitask, all mean that the diagnosis of burnout is becoming more and more visible in a variety of professions. Symptoms of total exhaustion have even been reported among the unemployed and student populations (Tenzer, 2011). Burnout results in withdrawal symptoms and behaviours in sufferers and this inevitably leads to absenteeism, which can be up to a year long. This results in high costs for organizations (Rosentiel and Nerdinger, 2011). Increasing costs as well as the fear of losing high-quality personnel have led many companies to look to external managed care systems to help cope with and manage these problems. This chapter looks at how systems such as EAPs are being used by managers as tools to implement a 'duty of care' policy for all employees. CA is used to analyse role-played conversations between managers and employees to demonstrate what managers need to be aware of when using EAP as a tool.

Employee assistant programs

The EAP system acts as an external support system for organizations to assist employees in dealing with workplace stress and other psychosocial difficulties. While changes in workplace practices have led to an increase in psychological and physical pressure and strain, difficulties in one's personal life cannot always be left at the doorway when one arrives at work (Haberleitner et al., 2007). Whether one develops stress-related illnesses, depression, workplace depression, or burnout, depends on the individual and his or her own personal coping strategies. What is a stressful situation for one person may be regarded as an opportunity by another. Leidig (2011) argues that those who suffer from general anxiety disorders or depressive tendencies will invariably find it difficult to cope with high levels of workplace stress. These factors then play a major role in the emergence of stress-related illnesses (Riechert, 2011). Nevertheless, organizations can create atmospheres at work which contribute to or inhibit workplace anxieties and depressions. Policies on workplace stresses need to take the personal factors of the employees into consideration. This means that employers must always take a collaborative approach in dealing with psychological stress at work (West et al., 2012) – that is, the context needs to be conducive to workplace health and well-being. This means that managers need to become astute at recognizing behavioural changes in their employees and need to take these changes seriously.

When organizations have committed themselves to the importance of healthy workers and have purchased managed care systems such as an EAP programme, it would seem natural, that a 'duty of care' policy would become part of the management structure and culture of the organization. However, this requires that managers themselves receive coaching in the use of such systems and this would necessitate that they learn how to conduct particular types of conversations with employees when a behavioural change becomes evident. Firstly, they would need to learn how to recognize the changes and thereafter learn how to approach and talk to an employee. This would require that managers learn a particular type of speak –one could call it a 'health speak', as opposed to a managerial or expert type of conversation. For example, EAP consultants could train managers in how to speak to employees in a caring manner. This may require that managers firstly reflect on how they normally engage with employees to achieve organizational goals. As managers are experts in their own fields they may tend to deal with stress-related or personal problems in the same way, that is: find the cause, come up with an appropriate solution or treatment, and offer this solution to the affected parties (see healthy leading approaches www.insite-interventions.de). However, this manner of talking may be disadvantageous when dealing with personal, psychological, or stress-related difficulties among employees (Becker, 2009, 2011). Managers do not need to know the causes and they do not need to find solutions. What they need to do, according to Becker (2009, 2011), is to hand over the problem to specialists, such as EAP counsellors or health experts, who have experience and training in dealing with people with such difficulties. In order to manage employees from this perspective managers would however, need to: 1. learn how the workplace and/or a person's workload can affect their health, for example, too much multi-tasking is an assault on the body (Becker, 2009, 2011); 2. become sensitive to their own and their employees' changing behaviours and emotions; 3. intervene in a genuine and helpful manner before handing it over. Any intervention seems to be better than no intervention as waiting too long may result in long-term presenteeism or, at worst, long-term absenteeism (Rosentiel und Nerdinger, 2011).

Research has shown that EAP counselling or therapy has positive effects on absenteeism, performance, and general contentment at work (Van der Klinik et al., 2001; Masi and Jacobson, 2003; Csiernik, 2005; Selvik et al., 2004; Rost, Fortney and Coyne, 2005; LaSasso, Rost and Beck, 2006; Hargrave, Hiatt and Shaffer, 2007; McLeod, 2010; Leidig, 2010). These findings are true not only for those who presented with work-related problems but also for those with private difficulties. The research suggests that short-term EAP counselling or therapy brings about an improvement in a person's psychological well-being for the majority of those who use it, and this also means a return on investment for organizations (Dickerson et al., 2012).

Nevertheless, despite limitations to these findings, which were carried out using questionnaires, interviews and rating scales, there are still some impediments at an organizational level to the full integration of a managed care system into the culture of the establishment. In addition to learning how to detect behavioural changes in employees and how to recognize stress symptoms, managers also need to acquire an awareness of psychological distress and its negative effects (Leidig, 2011). This would necessitate that solution strategies would be developed as management tools at all hierarchical levels. Organizations could then define themselves as healthy social systems where it is accepted that psychological distress reduces workplace productivity and performance and this would be recognized in leadership and management circles (Badura et al., 2003). As already pointed out, as there is an alarming increase in psychological distress in the workplace, prevention can only occur if organizations make counselling and therapy the norm rather than something that is perceived to be engaged in only by those who are weak, inadequate or unwell (Leidig, 2011).

EAPs are robust associates of occupational health and serve their managers and employees in numerous ways (Norbrega, 2010). This support can range from working with individuals to coaching managers in how to deal with difficult and problematic situations with their employees and teams. Healthy communication is necessary in order for an EAP programme to become fully integrated into the culture of the organization. If it is seen as a service only to be used in support of individual employees, it will always remain on the fringes of the organization (West et al., 2012). On the other hand, it can be integrated into the culture if psychological health and well-being in the workplace are promoted and encouraged. Through healthy communicative measures, managers can ensure that there is transparency around the need to have an EAP programme and can reduce potential inhibitions which may arise. However, talking to employees about personal matters is not an easy and straightforward activity; there are advantages as well as pitfalls to be observed. The following section looks at a simulated conversation between a manager and two employees. This conversation at first glance may seem straightforward. However, using CA and some MCD a number of detailed and interesting observations are revealed.

Analysis of conversations

The following two extracts (split into six parts), are role-play conversations between a manager and an employee. In both instances the manager noticed perturbing changes in the employee's behaviour and arranged a meeting to talk about the matter.

Extract (1)

Roleplay 1. Part (1).

M = manager

E = employee

1. M: yeah ah (1.0) hello mrs müller
2. E: good↑day↓
3. M: nice that you found the time
4. E: ↑yeah
5. M: em (0.5) i was saying to you yesterday and that i ↑would ↓like to speak to you
6.   today
7. E: ↑mm ↓hm
8. M: hh firstly i would like em to say (0.8) that I really value you that i really ↑value
9.   your work↑ (0.5)
10. E: ↑thank you ↓very much=
11. M: eh in the last few months you did really good work (2.3) eh::: th: the project
12.   went very well and today's conversation is (0.5) em::: not about your work i am
13.   very happy with your work
14. E: oh a[ch super thanks
15. M: [and also with your performance .hhhhhhh eh it has occured to me that (1.5)
16.   in the last few weeks (4.5) you are becoming increasingly (0.8) irritated .hhh
17.   (2.5) and (1.5)
18. E: °ah ↑so° (1.0)
19. M: and react in an irritated manner (0.7) .hh that was especially noticeable to me in
20.   the weekly ↑team ↑meetings
21. E: °↑mm ↓hm°
22. M: and also in the individual conversations with colleagues when you were
23.   speaking to (0.5) colleagues (1.5) that you eh:::::: ah reacted in a very aggressive
24.   manner (1.5) and i don't ↑know you like this at [all↑

25. E: [°yeah
26. M: I know you as friendly and even tempered
27. E: ↓[yeah
28. M: [°>↓i would say< (0.5)↑yeah and now (0.8) i am worried
         ↑(1.5)
29. E: ye[ah::
30. M: [eh what is up with you and >that is why i am speaking
         with you today<

The pauses occurring mark a dispreferred – the manager finds it unpleasant to speak in this manner. In terms of MCD this type of conversation is unpleasant as it is more personal and lies somewhere between a counsellor's role and a manager's role. The manager represents the problem episodically – it happened recently at team meetings, over the last few weeks. He downgrades the problem to avoid presenting it as something typical of the employee as a person. What has occurred to him (lines, 15 and 19) and what he has noticed is not in doubt. However, there is also no room for discussion as to whether the employee was really acting in that manner or whether it was appropriate to act in such a manner because of another employee's negative behaviour. Instead, the behaviour is formulated as inappropriate. The manager creates the space for the explanation but actually does not allow the explanation to occur because he immediately moves to a description of his own experience of the employee *I don't know you like this* (line 24) and *I know you as even tempered* (line 26). In denying the fact that the employee is not an irritable person he seems to introduce the possibility that she might very well be – it is just that 'I don't know this'.

Part (2)
This extract continues on from extract 1 and sees the employee doing exactly what was expected of them.

31. E: yeah mm yeah i don't know i (0.5) yeah i have a few prob-
         lems (0.6) at home and
32.   so my child is sick and my husband is eh hhhhh always
         ↑away and so on and
33.   (0.5) I am not sleeping well and .hhhh I am a bit under
         stress and have a lot to
34.   do at home perhaps=
35. M: °mm°
36. E: yeah but >you don't need to worry (0.5) everything will be
         fine (0.8)

37. M: yeah I↑am worried >that is why i am speaking to you< und
        firstly of all eh eh
38.   thanks for your trust that you so openly spoke about it .hh
        em: (3.3) well for me
39.   it is important tha↓em that you feel well >also her at work
        and< (1.0) yeah (0.5)
40.   I need to ask the question if there is anything I can do ↓for
        you at the moment
41.   in my capacity as manager↓ (1.1)
42. E: NO::: i don't think so that it so eh:: yeah as soon as every-
        thing is ↑stable at
43.   home it then everthing will be fine
44. M: ↓mm
45. E: i think it is::: only a bit of stress at the moment [in
46. M: [mm

Here the employee does what is expected of her. She co-operates with the
manager and gives an explanation for her behaviour in some detail. The
manager is now in the listening role and allows the client to tell her story.
He also accepts the employee's explanation there is *a lot to do at home*
(lines 33–34). The employee downgrades the problem everything will
be fine (line 36). However, the manager disagrees and says *I am worried*
(line 37). The manager takes control of the conversation by steering
the problem back to his concerns. He does not ask for an explanation
and does not listen for too long to the employee's story but glosses it as
speaking openly, *you so openly spoke about it* (line 38). Having thanked the
employee for her trust he again steers the conversation to how he feels, *for
me it is important* (line 38–39), *I need to ask the question if there is anything I
can do* (line 40). By expressing his feelings the manager demonstrates that
he cares about the employee and her work. However, he also tried to keep
the agenda. This way of conversing is similar to what Antaki and Jahoda
(2010) talk about when referring to CBT where the therapist tries to move
the client back on track when the client goes off topic. Here the manager's
agenda is his own problem as a manager and this problem will go away
if the employee solves it. The employee does give an account that it will
be solved (line 43) and that is just a matter of time *as soon as everything is
stable at home* (line 42–43) and *stress at the moment* (line 45).

Part (3)

47. E: it will work out itself i will take care of it that eh tha i will
        take care
48. M: ah↑

49. E: when dealing with my [colleagues
50. M: [ah super ↑yeah ok .hhhhhhhh (0.5)
         em i also would
51.   like to inform you eh:: (0.5) very independently (1.3) you
         (0.8) maybe it can
52.   help or not yeah i want to inform you about the opportu-
         nities↑ we have in the
53.   company (1.0)
54. E: ↑mm ↓hm (0.5)
55. M: for example (1.0) well you can confidentially contact the
         company doctor if
56.   you want to speak to something about it .hh (0.4) the other
         possibility is that
57.   we have an external counselling service (0.5) which you
         can confidentially use
58.   they are available 24/7 and they are professionals and eh:: (0.5)
59. E: [yeah
60. M: [if you have difficulties with children (1.5) or family prob-
         lems that you can
61.   receive some counselling if you ↑wish::: i just wanted to
         tell:::::: you about it
62. E: mm hm

The employee again assures the manager that she will solve the problem
with her colleagues (line 47). The manager expresses real satisfaction with
this *super yeah* (line 50) and once he is certain that his problem is solved,
he talks about helpful ways the employee could solve hers. The manager's
problem has been solved (line 50) and the problem is now for the employee
to solve. The manager was responsive to the employee's expressed concerns
and she also reassures him she would solve them in time. The manager
accepts the solution but provides for other possibilities – the company
doctor and the EAP service can be used. The problem of other employees
or the management of the team in general was not addressed. The problem
here was kept at the individual and personal level. The manager could
however, have allowed the client some space and it may have been appropriate here to arrange another meeting before introducing the EAP service.

Extract (2)

Part (1)

In this extract the manager has invited the employee to a meeting as he
had detected a smell of alcohol and wishes to discuss his concern further.

M = manager

E = employee

1. M: Yeah::::: .hhhhh Hello Mrs Hartmann
2. E: Hello
3. M: yeah thank you that, eh::::: (1.5) that we are able to have this
4.   conversa↑tion(0.5) I ↑men↓tioned to you yesterday=
5. E: yeah:::
6. M: that i wanted to spe↑ak sometime with you (2.5) >I want to say< that I em::
7.   ↑value you as an employee (0.8)
8. E: yeah↑ (0.5)
9. M: that your performance in the last few months em:: (0.8) was very ↑good (0.5)
10.   >you did good work<=
11. E: yeah↑ (.)
12. M: and I would also like to thank you (1.0) em::: beforehand I would like to say
13.   eh::: (1.5) that it is not about your work em: (.) I am very pleased with your
14.   wo↓rk
15. E: ah so↑
16. M: the conversation em:: (1.2) is a bit unpleasant (1.2) for me but anyway (0.7) i
17.   just wanted to say to you °>because you are an important employee<° yeah::
18.   that it has occurred to me (1.5) that you::::: (2.0) >smell of alcohol here at work
19.   < (0.7)
20. E: EH? .hhh
21. M: °mm° hm ° (0.5)
22. E: AH (0.5) who said that↑ (noise of paper) (0.3)
23. M: that was me eh:: I smelt alcohol from you
24. E: WHAT
25. M: °mm°

In terms of membership categorization analysis – in the opening lines of this part of the extract there is an asymmetry reflective of a boss talking to an employee; yet on line 3 the manager thanks the employee for the meeting as if the employee could have refused. So the manager/employee interaction is locally managed into some-thing democratic; the employee can make choices but in terms of turn-taking, the asymmetry is there. The manager is not identified indicating that this conversation is about the employee, who has been summoned to a meeting. The manager's intention to conduct a conversation is also indicated by the rising intonation on the word *conversation,* on line 4, *mentioned* on line 4, and *speak* on line 6. The employee settles into the role as listener and immediately accepts the asymmetry – she does not interrupt and ask questions. However, the extract is divided into two parts. The assessment of the employee as a valued member of staff comes first, so that the problem discussed will not be seen as a performance or a discipline problem. The employee remains upbeat, indicated by her consistent listening style before changing this style on line 20. The manager's extended turn looks like it has been planned in advance, and it is something typical of an approach one might find in a manual; build the person up before you introduce the problem. He does not see the need to answer Mrs Hartmann's minimal questions on lines 20 and 22. This seems to be because the manager is delivering a message not actually having a conversation. The delivery of the message on line 18 is a dispreferred, and is uncomfortable for the manager. The pauses, the long stretch on *you*, and the quick delivery *you smell of alcohol,* contrasts greatly with the first part of the message. However, the first part did not work. The employee immediately downgrades the problem as something malicious (line 22) and probably a false accusation.

Part (2)

This part of the extract seems more like a conversation than the one above when the talk shifts to the problem.

26. M: yeah I noticed that you smelt of alcohol and as a result
     eh::: em:: I am worried
27.   about you and your ↑health
28. E: did you ↑think that I was DRUNK
29. M: it smelt of alcohol em: eh::::
30. E: .hhhhhh ah::: [hhhh ah
31. M: [and you know em: the ↑smell eh::: ↓em::
     (1.5) i ca- I can
32.   detect and i could smell eh:.> that you had drank alcohol<
33.   em: eh ah hhhhhh when was ↑that so sometimes i drink a
     glass of wine in the
34.   evening but i am not an alcoholic well eh:: i drink very
     little eh:::: i don't

35.   know what it could have ↑been
36.   M: yeah em: i noticed eh:: (1.5) eh:: ↑yesterday (0.5) eh::: that you smelt of
37.   alcohol yesterday morning and eh last Friday i noticed it and because of the
38.   time of day and the ↑smell eh em:: i was worried about you and em::: as a
39.   result I wanted to >speak to you here today↑< (0.5)
40.   E: .hhhhh ah I do- I don't know I don't know what that could be eh:: >i do not
41.   drink alcohol in the morning therefore it could not be alcohol< but (.) yeah at
42.   the moment I am taking cough bottle and maybe it had something to do with
43.   that but it is not alcohol (0.8) yea- (2.5)
44.   M: ah:: mm ja it did not smell of ↑cough bottle it was clear to me that it smelt of
45.   alcohol em i am concerned about your ↑health em you are an important
46.   employee i want you as an employee (0.5) eh::: i NEED you as an employee in
47.   the ↑team here [↓yeah
48.   E: [yeah but you are JUDGING me tha-that i eh:: alcohol drink
49.   alot of alcohol=
50.   M: °eh:°=

In the above the manager keeps the topic on Mrs Hartmann's problem but situates it within his own observations, and in doing so becomes part owner of the problem. His observations, for example, *I noticed* and *I am worried about you* (line 26–27) brings the manager straight into the problem. The problem is not formulated from the position of manager as somebody who can discipline employees; instead it is from a position of a manager who cares about the employee personally – a point which is then seized on by the employee. On line 28 the employee attempts to take control of the conversation by asking a direct question about the manager's opinion *did you think I was drunk*. The manager is invited to accept or reject this but instead he avoids answering and continues to share the problem by focusing on his observations *it smelt of alcohol* (line 29). However, the manager loses the control somewhat and seems confused on line 31 indicated by the false starts and hesitations. Instead of staying with his opinion, the manager starts to defend his point of view *I can detect and I could smell* (lines 31 and 32). It seems as if he was pulled into this confusion by the employee's probable own sense, genuine or otherwise, of confusion, *I don't know what it could have been* (lines 34 and 35). When the employee interprets the problem as implying that she is an alcoholic she immediately denies it (line 34). The manager then upgrades the problem by bringing in the element of time and suggesting that this did not just happen once. This is again denied, but in a different way now, by bringing in the cough medicine (line 42). Because the problem is formulated as a personal problem it seems that the membership categorization of both parties is corresponding – both parties have problems. The employee tried to take control and tell the manager exactly what he was doing wrong, *you are judging me* (line 48). So, the consequence of dealing with the problem informally might be that the employee rejects and challenges the manager's right to discuss the problem. It seems the manager pushed himself into the corner by trying to set aside his power as a manager and stressing that he is happy with her work.

Part (3)

This extract demonstrates how the employee takes control and it is only when the manager is able to bring in a management tool, for example, the EAP system, that the manager is able to assert dominance again.

51. E: and ↑yea->what i know of alcohol< is that yes when one drinks and eh em: one
52.   drinks right through the night that one stinks of alcohol the next day (0.5) but
53.   (0.7) i don't do ↑that ↓h
54. M: °mm°
55. E: yeah: : em::
56. M: °mm°
57. E: i find that terrible (0.5)
58. M: °mm° [°mm°
59. E :   [yeah Mr Carroll tha- tha- eh that you are saying this to me (0.5) em:: eh
60.   ↓when i i take cough bottle when i i don't feel well then (0.6) that does not
61.   mean that i am an ↑alcoholic
62. M: ↑mm::::↓mm

63. M: em .hh eh of course the conversation can be unpleasant
          for you eh::: em you

64.   are ↑important to me and that is why i am speaking to you
          (0.5) em the

65.   conversation is also not ↑pleasant for me (.) I noticed that
          you smelt of alcohol

66.   and >I am now worried about you< (6.0) .hh em: (1.5) of
          course I am asking

67.   myself if there is anyway i eh:: could ↑support you in my
          position as manager

68.   em:: (.) yeah em: (0.6) now that you have said to me em::
          that you have taken

69.   cough mixture i would suggest em:: that em:: i will watch
          em: and i will

70.   continue to observe you >not keep an eye on you< but eh::
          be aware of the

71.   smell and em that we could >sit down again together
          sometime< em:: i eh

72.   know it could be unpleasant for employees to speak to
          managers about these

73.   things that there are things with managers it is better (1–5)
          better not to speak

74.   about

75. E: ↑yeah

76. M: therefore i would like to give you some information which
          you can use (1.7) eh::

77.   confidentially if you need help (1.5) .hhhhh as I say you
          are important to me

78.   (1.5) and your health is important and therefore I want to
          give you some

79.   imformation

80. E: Yeah

81. M: ↓yeah

82. E: °yeah°

Part (3) begins with the employee attempting to convince the manager that he is mistaken. She asserts her dominance by producing an extended turn at talk moving from lines 52–62. The manger here adopts a very unobtrusive listening role indicated by the use of empathic continuers (Chapter 5) (lines 55, 57 and 59). The fact that the manager now receives an identity also indicates that the roles have shifted and the employee's strong opinion *I find that terrible* (line 58) is not only an attempt to control the conversation but also the topic, that is, the manager is now the one with the problem. The manager accepts this (line 59) but the way he listens has now changed. He now upgrades his continuer to more of a channelling one (line 63) possibly indicating disagreement and also that he now about to take the floor. What follows is an uninterrupted turn at talk where the manager reclaims his dominance through the use of his opinions, feelings and observations, *you are important to me* (lines 64–65), *not pleasant for me, I noticed* (line 66), *I am now worried about you* (67), *I am asking myself* (line 67–68), *it could be unpleasant for employees* (line 73), before going on to introduce the topic of the EAP system. The manager is able to assert his full dominance by having a tool to use.

In this extract the manager never accused the employee of being an alcoholic. The employee upgraded smelling alcohol into being an alcoholic and challenged this categorization. The manager sticks with the smelling of alcohol – that is what he will monitor not her being an alcoholic. It is when he establishes his membership position, as manager (lines 64–75), from which he is having this unpleasant conversation, he is able to hand over some EAP leaflets and the employee does not intervene further.

Concluding comments

The question is: can a manager enact these two roles? The analysis above demonstrates that in terms of membership categorization it will invariably be difficult to switch categories without this being perceived. While long-term resolution may not be realized at an individual level, the service which is provided by EAPs should help managers to address the problems, if the concern about appearing too harsh or overly caring remains. On the other hand, if EAPs are used as collaborative tools involving all aspects of the organization, as suggested by West et al. (2012), the individual may attempt to bring the manager and the organization at large into the problem, and thus the individual problem may become lost in the process. In extract (1) the employee forfeits certain rights and obligations while the manager uses his rights and obligations to accomplish the outcome, that is, the employee does what is expected. She provides an account of her behaviour. In extract (2), the membership categories seem to be equivalent for a time, before the manager then needed to assert his position to get the employee to accept the problem. While managers need to become astute at recognizing behavioural changes in their employees, and need to take these changes seriously,

I am arguing that they do not need to consult textbooks before having caring conversations with employees, because managers cannot become counsellors. Managers can, however, improve how they converse with employees to enable them to help themselves. Who precisely has the problem can only be ascertained if organizations remain aware of the particular norms and cultures that have developed and are being developed in the workplace. I then suggest that instead of talking in terms of 'cultures' one could talk in terms of CA and MCDs; this is because MCDs are designed and run by the people themselves, and the categories are talked into being and are observable through the structures of conversation. As mentioned many times in this book Rogers (1951, 1995) emphasizes the therapeutic relationship as being the vehicle for change. Relationships between managers and their employees can also be therapeutic, but the talk cannot be the same as that between therapists and clients. Instead, managers need to become aware of whether they are being genuine, congruent and non-judgmental when having these personal conversations with employees. If employees experience this genuine non-judgmental approach it will make it easier for them to choose to accept helping relationships offered by EAPs, if extra help is needed. In analysing conversations an analyst needs to demonstrate: 1. if the MCD is at work; and 2. if the manager is genuine. One does not need to learn how to converse, that is, learn what is a right or a wrong way to talk. One knows how to converse based the tools of conversation developed in mundane social practices.

Manager's corner

This corner provides an example of how one might engage with an employee or team member who is experiencing some personal difficulties which need to be addressed. Managers can create favourable conditions so that employees make their own decisions.

Firstly, it is important to prepare oneself for this conversation.

- A private meeting place needs to be arranged, preferably in a closed office. Do not discuss something in passing.
- Plenty of time needs to be allowed for this conversation.
- Make sure you are not disturbed. Managers should turn off phones, iPads and so on.
- The meeting should take place fairly quickly after it has been arranged, preferably on the same day. This is to prevent the employee from unnecessary worry.

- Introductory small talk should be avoided or at least kept to a minimum. This is a serious conversation.

Secondly, managers need to follow some basic guidelines:

- A manager needs to communicate his or her observations without causing resistance. This can be achieved when the manager focuses the talk on his or her own observations by using 'I' statements. For example, 'I have noticed', 'I am concerned' is better that 'you are not doing so well'.
- Employees need to feel comfortable and reassured. Managers should reassure them that he or she does not need to know details. This level of reassurance is important if the difficulty is personal.
- Mangers should remain objective and hand over some information about the support systems in place. Handing over something allows the employee the time to reflect and make up his or her own mind.
- If in doubt, or if the employee becomes upset or resistant, arrange a follow-up meeting for a few days time if possible.
- Do not press them for an answer.
- Repeat your message.
- A follow-up meeting needs to be scheduled.

9
Conclusions and Implications

In producing this book, I was interested in how it was that I, as a therapist, could claim to change a person in a short space of time using talk as my only tool. I was inspired by Freud's remark 'by words one person can make another blissfully happy or drive him to despair' (Freud, 1916–1917, p. 17; cf. de Shazer, 1994, p. 3) because in ways I felt the conversational tools I was using as a psychotherapist were merely an extension of what was available to me in ordinary conversation. I thus became interested in looking at how the 'the talking cure' works, the efficacy debate and if it really works, and the research methods used by training schools to support the view that therapy or their type of therapy works. Feeling disillusioned with the effectiveness debates, which have proved inconclusive, I became interested in how individual therapists could go about investigating the talk in their own practice with a view to developing it, because the 'talking cure', simply put, is just another form of human interaction. Therapists use ordinary structures of conversation to enact their business. However, training courses, offering qualifications in psychotherapy or supervision, tend to overlook the therapist's use of language and focus instead on topics and themes and what the therapist is doing with the theory informing the practice. After many years working as an EAP therapist I became interested in how the organizations were actually integrating the service into their management structure. As 'duty of care' policies in organizations began to develop I wanted to investigate some of the practices involved yet in another form of human interaction, that is, caring and helpful conversations between managers and employees, when managers notice that an employee may be suffering from some psychological distress. As both helpful therapeutic conversations and helpful management conversations use talk to enact their business, I wanted to see if EAP providers could train managers to use talk in a more caring and thera-peutic manner. Organizations would come to integrate therapy/coun-selling as a natural and normal feature of any health and safety policies in the workplace rather than something which sits on the fringes as a service to be used only when necessary.

However, psychotherapy is not just talk. It is also more than just 'a bunch of talk' (de Shazer, 1994, p. 3) and also involves more than Freud's description 'an interchange of words...the patient talks...the doctor listens' (1915–1917, vol. 15, p. 17). Psychotherapists understand their work and view their practice and how they act through their 'ther-apeutic policies'. These policies resource the talk and are inscribed in the practice but are rather specific to different therapeutic orientations as well as to the setting. I found that we need to look at therapy in two ways. Firstly, we have to examine different therapeutic approaches in order to decide which things are generic to the practice of psycho-therapy, for example, formulations, questions, continuers, interpreta-tions. Secondly, we need to focus on the sequential structures to see how such devices are used by the therapist as tools to conduct the business of therapy. Thirdly, we need to look at these devices to see if they work to bring about change and how.

Growth in the number of psychotherapy schools of thought has led to an increase in competition in the therapeutic market and while research has shown that certain therapies are effective with specific disorders and complaints no single theory has been able to corner and dominate the market on utility. While certain CBT or psychoanalytical practitioners rely exclusively on their theoretical orientation there seems to be an increasing awareness in the field that no single approach is clinically sufficient for all clients and situations (Norcross and Garfield, 2005; Lambert, 2013). I tried to find a research method which would allow me to investigate the therapy *in situ* as I felt I was not learning enough from the outcome-rating scales and setting rating scales used by some EAP providers (see Duncan et al., 2004). I was also not interested in finding out if my practice was following the model set by the theory or if I was working counterproductively to my theoretical orientation because I felt I was working 'eclectically'. I felt that supervision, which helped me to reflect on my practice, was also not enough as it was based only on what I recalled during my work with clients. I was interested in Roger's approach to research where he taped the sessions but I was also concerned about the fact that, when these recordings were exam-ined by therapists during group supervision, therapists tended to catego-rize what other therapists were doing in accordance with the theory of person-centred therapy, CBT and/or brief solution-focused therapies. It seemed to me that therapists would try to fit clients into psychological theories. I did not find this satisfactory as there were subtle aspects and finer details being overlooked and dismissed as possible unnecessary and trivial details. Finally, I felt that I was making general idealizations when I talked about how I conducted therapy but I knew there were some gaps between the ideals and the goals I had for my work and what I was doing in practice.

Overview of the findings

The therapist's theoretical orientation is never a focal issue for the participants. This orientation is instead presupposed and remains in the background. In other words the therapist is not trying to treat the client with some theory which will make them feel better. CA can, however, show how therapists' orientations are introduced into the talk and become consequential. While much of the CA literature found that talk in therapy differs from talk in ordinary conversation, in addition I found that talk in therapy can differ from orientation to orientation and even from therapist to therapist. Psychotherapy is characterized by an imbalance in turn-size, for example, formulations are relatively brief by comparison with 'elaboration sequences' provided by the client and continuers are even briefer. Heritage and Greatbatch (1991) found that in news interviews continuers are withheld by the interviewer which provides the interview pattern with a different sequential structure from ordinary conversation. One would also not expect to find formulations in an interview setting, at least the kinds described by Heritage and Watson (1979), where the speaker wishes to state or restate the topic of concern for the participants. This therapy assumes an interview pattern but formulations are one of the therapist's main interactional devices. This also contrasts with psychoanalysis where interpretations are the analyst's main tool. Also one would rarely find the types of formulations, that is, empathic responses, found in this therapy in ordinary conversation. Continuers on the other hand can be used in ordinary conversation.

However in therapy, one would expect more empathic listening, that is more unobtrusive empathic continuers than found in ordinary conversation. Managers, engaging in 'health speak' tend to use more empathic listening devices than found in ordinary conversation and less than one would find in therapy. However, while the therapist here uses continuers as a listening device, other therapists claim not to use them at all and therapists from different orientations can also differ in the way they use them (Czyzewski, 1995). Managers on the other hand, used much the same devices when engaging in 'health speak' except there was an notable absence of formulations, the turn-size was much smaller and managers turns at talk were much longer than what one would find in EAP therapy. Managers could, however, be taught to use formulations, to develop elaboration sequences and also to allow the client to have more speaking time.

Although therapists from similar orientations will use similar conversational tools and interactional devices with their clients, not all therapists coming from the same orientation use these devices in the exact same way all of the time. How the devices are used, for example, the points where the therapist makes interventions using devices such as formulations, questions or continuers can vary from therapist to therapist. It was important therefore for me to look at my own work if I really wanted to develop my practice, make improvements where necessary and afford myself the opportunity of confronting bad habits. CA can make evident habits and routines of which therapists are not explicitly aware. CA can then falsify or correct practitioner versions which do not correspond with what actually happens in the talk (Peräkylä and Vehviläinen, 2003). If this EAP therapy is being carried out according to its theories, changes should occur naturally from and for the client while being facilitated by the therapist.

The non-directive therapist Proctor (2002) warns against the dangers of therapists exerting power and argues that therapists can be oblivious to how much power they actually possess as well as use. This is also important for managers to take on board when they attempt to engage in helping relationships with their employees. CA can be used to help therapists and managers look at how each of the participants contributes to the trajectories of talk. The therapeutic activities may be norms within practices but much may also be overlooked by the participants – good as well as bad habits may go unnoticed and that is the same for managers speaking to employees. These roles get talked into being by the therapist or manager assuming the role of questioner, formulator or interpreter and by the client or employee assuming the role of answerer and explainer; CA can be used to demonstrate whether these roles produce positive or negative results.

What I found

This book looked at the relationship between the client and therapist as the most salient issue. As the 'talking cure' is language based, investigations of the interactive processes, within which the therapeutic relationship evolves, occurred. The processes consist of the joint partici-pation of two social actors operating as speakers and listeners engaged in orderly dialogue. Within and through these structures the therapeutic relationship is produced, reproduced and developed. CA cannot help a person to understand the therapeutic relationship. However, it can help a person understand how people talk to each other. While much of rela-tionship is obvious and demonstrated, other less obvious aspects can be understood by examining how it is produced in and through the talk because it is through the devices used, that the relationship is managed and practised. I suggest that much of the relationship becomes visible by looking at an ongoing accrual of sequences of talk. In addition, instead of looking at the theory and how it translated into practice I looked at how the theoretical dictums I learned in training modulate my practice. Person-centred therapy is first and foremost non-directive. Rogers (1951) argued that the therapist must avoid the temptation to subtly guide their client. By using CA research I found that therapists use interactional devices – namely continuers and formulations – which can subtly direct or lead the client to talk about their problem from a particular perspec-tive. I found that person-centred therapy (especially if this approach has other more direction theories such as CBT or BSFT included) can be subtly directive as there are subtle ways of changing the way people think. The most unobtrusive of these devices is the continuer and the second most unobtrusive is the therapist's use of formulations.

The therapist's use of continuers

Based on informal talks with colleagues, practitioners agree that contin-uers must be doing something very important. Research to date on the practice of psychotherapy has failed, for the most part, to take these tokens seriously and as a result they are not given much, if any, atten-tion in psychotherapy training courses. My findings support Czyzewski (1995) in that the use of continuers is an individual matter but that does not mean they are not doing anything except to display a therapist's listening style as well as a type of listening associated with a specific theoretical orientation. My research found that individual therapists need to take these devices seriously as they have a lot more interactional power than research to date has shown. I found that continuers are first and foremost used by therapists to convey to the client that they are present and listening and involved in the story. Under-involvement is as real a hazard as over-involvement with the client as it implies a lack of empathy (Rogers, 1995). I found that they are used to support the talk in a sort of public way which supports the client and keeps the client talking in a way which is appropriate to the therapy. In addition, they were also found to act as devices to subtly nudge or direct the client to keep talking in a particular way. Contrary to what Frankel (1984) and ten Have (1991) found, continuers can carry the therapist's opinion or evaluation of what the speaker has said.

The therapist's use of formulations

Antaki (2008) argues that formulations are seldom found in ordinary conversation so I examined them as practical interactional tools used by the therapist to help the client reflect on their thoughts and feelings by re-representing what they had expressed in the prior turn. In the same way as the literature suggests, the therapist prefers to have their formulation accepted (Antaki et al., 2005; Antaki, 2008). While the therapist sometimes has to work at having the formulation accepted, I found that a key feature to knowing that a formulation has been successful is if the client takes up the topic and works through it. A mere 'yes' to a formulation does not indicate that the technique of 'reflecting back' is helping the client to reflect. Also, the client may feel under pressure to say 'yes' and it is only by encouraging the client to practice the formulation that the therapist can see if it helps stimulate the client to explore a topic further or not.

I found that formulations are subtle devices for checking understanding and for getting the client to explore the topic further. The therapist could ask the client outright what they meant by something or ask them outright to look at their situation from a different perspective. I agree with Antaki (2008) who states that the therapist deletes aspects of the client's account and selects others before offering a formulation. I did find that the therapist focuses on aspects of the client's problem, problematic feelings or difficult behaviours and picks out aspects which the therapist feels the client needs to work on. In addition the therapist can also pick up bits of progress and use a formulation to build a positive solution. However, I found that some of the literature (Davis, 1986; Antaki, 2008) which shows that therapists' use of formulations serves the therapists' interests and places them in a somewhat negative light and can appear too critical of therapists. I suggest that this can happen if CA analysts overlook the therapist's theoretical orientation in their analysis.

Rogerian dictums stress how the therapist must relinquish control. However, in this type of therapy, which is affected by time constraints, some level of control will become evident. But what is more important is how this control is exercised. I do not force the client to think in a certain way by offering them something to reflect on. They are free to work with the idea as they choose. While I agree with the CA literature that therapists may try to get clients to see things from their perspective, that perspective is offered, not forced, on the client. Also, the perspective must firstly be understood in terms of the therapeutic polices. Once these are taken into consideration CA can then determine if the therapist is working outside of these and attempting to force their perspective onto the client.

Sequencing

The main finding that emerged from my data is that a fine-grained analysis of psychotherapy sessions, using CA, cannot focus on local adjacent utterances alone. I found that empathy, unconditional positive regard and congruence is being lived by the therapist over extended sequences and these are imparted to the client through devices such as formulations and continuers, and questions which support the client as they tell their story. I observed what the therapist is doing by examining the synergy between these devices over extended sequences. In ordinary conversation one can look at extended sequences such as storytelling and I looked at these sequences here as client's tellings in the form of stories. I found that the story isn't any particular problem but it is the whole extended sequence and it gets extended because it is taken in that way and because people act in a particular way. I found that empathic responses and the therapist's listening style work together in concert in these extended sequences.

I found that formulations are devices used to get the client to think around the issue. The issue can be the problem which needs defining or which needs to be worked through or it can be the solution which needs highlighting. Either way the therapist expects the client to work on the formulations by practising an elaboration sequence. If the client is not offering the elaboration themselves, they may be prompted by the therapist to do so which would require them to do some work. In addition, there is a call for confirmation or disconfirmation of the therapist's understanding of the client's talk and this is sometimes carried out by using a 'tag' question. The therapist then uses a continuer plus pause which communicates to the client that elaboration is needed. The elaboration sequences allow the client to practice what the therapist's formulation or question indicates. It was found that these sequences allow guided practice rather than imposing a viewpoint.

This contrasted with how managers dealt with the employee's story in Chapter 8. If managers could begin to use formulations they may firstly, demonstrate more empathy and secondly, may come across as genuine as they would be restricted from imposing their own, or the organization's point of view. As they would be re-formulating the employee's perspective they would also be less inclined to come across as judgmental. On the other hand, I found that managers cannot be counsellors and if this therapeutic device is to be utilized it needs to be used with caution, at least until the employees come to learn that 'health speak' means being encouraged to elaborate. On the other hand, managers do not need to know the client's personal details in order to address the issue of EAPs with employees.

Methodological implications

In order to examine an individual's practice, research must go beyond focusing on what both therapist and client say about their experiences. It must also go beyond categorizing activities and events occurring in the sessions. It cannot also rely on controlled trials or questionnaires filled in by clients at the end of therapy. One can instead, roll up one's sleeves and get one's hands dirty by confronting the fine-grained procedures used by a therapist to influence change in the client.

However, more research needs to be done to examine how therapists of different orientations use formulations and listen to clients in a similar way as well as how individual therapists of varying orientations develop their own style. While it may be unlikely that the conversational devices will differ between therapists of the same orientation, how often and where these devices are used by individual therapists will indeed vary. Some training programmes now insist that trainees provide transcripts of audio-taped samples of their work with clients as part of their clinical training. Conversation Analysis could be used as a method to examine these transcripts to determine if the trainee is applying their approach correctly and sufficiently but knowledge of the practice is necessary if the full extent of a therapist's practice is to be properly understood.

Therapeutic Implications

This book examined talk in psychotherapy as not just a series of words or a chain of utterances but as a pattern of utterances and actions joined together by a network of understandings and responses. While these patterns form aspects of interaction from where workings of a therapist's practice can be made visible they are still a subspecies of a larger category. That category comprises firstly the entire session from which they are taken and then the even larger series of between 4–8 sessions. In order for funders of therapy to understand how a client is being helped with their problem in the larger session or series of sessions it is not enough for managed care companies to base improvements on statistical evidence based on outcome-rating scales. Therapists may see measurement and rating of sessions as extra to their work and something which chiefly benefits referral agencies and third-party funders (Duncan et al., 2004). These rating scales simply become another new tool, in the same way as continuing professional development programmes teach new tools and techniques and impart new ideas to help therapists improve their work with clients.

I found that if a therapist really wants to improve their approach and style of working they need to start from where they are at and not simply integrate more and more ideas into their basic therapeutic orientation. I suggest that therapists need to start with themselves, go back to basics, and focus on the therapeutic relationship and explore how it is woven into the talk. Some therapists will need to rid themselves of habits which are negative or no longer beneficial before they add on new techniques by attending continuing professional programmes. In other words, therapists need to examine themselves and not just develop themselves professionally. I found that by examining and reflecting on my work my practice was enhanced. I was forced to re-examine my attitude as a therapist and as a result I became more open to the fact that I do not have the answer to what makes humans function psychologically.

This book is a documentation of aspects of a practice. I made certain aspects explicit and looked at the methods I could use to do just that. The findings show that non-directive therapy can be subtly directive. However, the findings here show that the relationship for the most part is experienced in and through language techniques which are used in a systematic way at particular moments. Therapists who claim to be use the person-centred approach cannot fully justify the relationship and yet ignore the techniques of language used. Finally, while many areas of therapist activity in this short-term practice, which combine person-centred, CBT and brief solution-focused methods have been investigated in this book, it is clear much remains to be explored and discovered in this field. This is also true for managers who wish to use EAP short-term therapy as an instrument to encourage psychological health and well-being among employees.

Notes

1 Introduction

1. The 'organismic valuing process' is a fluid, ongoing process whereby a person's experiences are accurately symbolized and valued to provide optimal enhancement of the organism and the self (Rogers, 1959).
2. Epictetus, Discourses, I,1, 4.
3. See Chessick (1977, p. 32).
4. Plato, *Apology of Socrates*, 29d–e.
5. End of God of Socrates, cited in Foucault (1988, p. 45).
6. Foucault (1988, p. 48).
7. See Foucault (1985). The chapter on the 'Birth of the Asylum', which describes the methods of cure and the experience of madness.
8. Ellenberger's cites Psychiatrists such as Moebius and Bleuler as part of this developmental phase. Sexual psycho-pathology was also being developed.
9. Psychotherapists in Ireland and in the UK do not need to have a psychological or medical background to practice.
10. See, Bergin, A.E. (1970) 'The Deterioration Effect: A Reply to Braucht', *Journal of Abnormal Psychology*, 75: 300–2; Luborsky, L. (1954) 'A Note on Eysenck's Article, "The Effect of Psychotherapy: An Evaluation"', *British Journal of Psychology*, 45: 129–31; Luborsky, L., Singer. B. and Luborsky, L. (1975) 'Is it True That "Everyone has Won and All Must have Prizes?"', *Archives of General Psychiatry*, 32: 995–1008; Smith, M.L. and Glass, G.V. (1977) 'Meta-analysis of Psychotherapy Outcome Studies', *American Psychologist*, 32: 752–60; Smith, M.L., Glass, G.V. and Miller, T.I. (1980) *The Benefits of Psychotherapy*. Baltimore: The John Hopkins University Press; Shapiro, D.A. and Shapiro, D. (1982) 'Meta-analysis of Comparative Therapy Outcome Studies: A Replication and Refinement', *Psychological Bulletin*, 92: 581–604.
11. See, also Kendall, P.C. (1998) 'Empirically Supported Psychological Therapies', *Journal of Consulting and Clinical Psychology*, 66, 3–10; Holmes, J. (2002) 'All You Need is Cognitive Behaviour Therapy?' *British Medical Journal*, 324 (7332): 288–90.
12. Research carried out on the effect of CBT on bulimia nervosa found a mean reduction on binge eating and purging: Mitchell, J.E., Pyle, R.L., Eckert, E.D., Hatsukami, D. (1990) 'A Comparison Study of Antidepressants and Structured Intensive Group Psychotherapy in the Treatment of Bulimia Nervosa', *Archives of General Psychiatry*, 47 (2): 149–57; Craighead, L.W. and Agras, S.W. (1991) 'Mechanisms of Action in Cognitive-behavioural and Pharmacological Interventions for Obesity and Bulimia Nervosa', *Journal of Consulting and Clinical Psychology,* 59: 115–25; Wilson, G.T. and Fairburn, C.G. (1993) 'Cognitive Treatments for Eating Disorders', *Journal of Consulting and Clinical Psychology*, 61, 261–9.

13. I have sometimes used Brief solution-focused therapy and sometimes BSFT.
14. Client processing refers to the client's self-explorative behaviour or intra-personal explorations (Sachse, 1990). See also Chapter 4. Processing is a general term used in research into person-centred therapy to describe how the client processes information cognitively.

2   Interaction Issues in Short-Term Psychotherapy

1. Each school of psychotherapy is bound by a Code of Ethics such as the one adopted by The British Psychological Society, The British Association of Counsellors and Psychotherapists .
2. Moral here refers to the ethnomethodical usage of the term where participants orient to normative matters such as the question–answer adjacency pair (Drew, 1990).

3   Conversation Analysis and Psychotherapy

1. The exceptions are if the therapist engages in self-disclosure (Antaki et al., 2005).
2. Of course, despite theoretical differences, the therapists may follow similar conversational strategies.
3. According to the Wikipedia 'The therapeutic relationship, also called the helping alliance, the therapeutic alliance, and the working alliance, refers to the relationship between a mental health professional and a patient. It is the means by which the professional hopes to engage with, and effect change in, a patient'.

4   A Note on Methodology

1. It is assumed that the essential goal of person-centred therapy involves the explication of the client's internal frame of reference in regard to his or her relevant problems (Cooper et al., 2007). The essential aspects of the internal frame of reference are considered as 'personal relevant meaning structures or schemata' (Sachse, 1989) which contain evaluations or emotions which activate feelings or felt meanings. The clarification process requires a client to face the relevant parts of his meaning structures through relevant questions. These questions aim to clarify the client's feelings and the felt meanings determined by aspects of the problem with a view to explicating the problem-determined meaning structures (Sachse, 1986, 1988). These questions, are described as the client's processing modes.
2. See Giorgi (1970), Constance Fisher (1984), Fred Wertz (1984), and Chris Aanstoos (1984) cf. McLeod (2002).

5   On Active Listening in Short-Term Psychotherapy

Chapter 5 was originally published in 2010 as: 'On Listening in Person-centred, Solution-focused Psychotherapy', *Journal of Pragmatics*, 42: 3188–98.

1. These comments were obtained informally by asking colleagues about their use of response tokens in therapy. When listening to tape-recordings in supervision of sessions carried out by supervisees they were surprised and sometimes shocked at the amount and variation of the tokens which they themselves used in therapy.
2. See Czyzewski (1995, extract 9, p. 87; extract 5, p. 83; extract 3, p. 78). Muntigl and Zabala (2008, extract 13, p. 207; extract 15, p. 10).
3. Based on informal conversations with colleagues, some therapists believe that solution-focused therapist can often try and force a solution onto the client.

6   On the Use of Formulations in Short-Term Psychotherapy

Chapter 6 was originally published in 2012 as: 'On the Use of Formulations in Person-centred, Solution-focused psychotherapy', *Communication and Medicine*, 9 (1): 13–22.

1. See *On Becoming a Person* (1995) Chapters 2 and 3.
2. Antaki (2008) suggested that the therapist's use of formulations can be quite manipulative. This suggests that the therapist is serving the clients' needs but in a directive way their own needs by attempting to control the client's point of view. This would be seen as a total abuse of professional power (Masson, 1992; Proctor, 2008).
3. There are, of course, other devices a therapist can use to encourage the client to say more, such as questions, continuers, re-interpretations, extensions and so on.

References

Allianz Deutschland AG und RWI. (2011) Depression – Wie die Krankheit unsere Seele belastet, Allianz Deutschland AG und RWI, http://www.rwi-essen.de/media/content/pages/others/Allianz-Report-Depression.pdf.

Anderson, H. and Goolishan, H. (1992) 'The Client is the Expert', in S. McNamee and K.J. Gergen (eds) *Therapy as a Social Construction* (London: Sage).

Antaki, C. (2003) 'It's not Mills and Boon, Is It?: Interviewers' Use of Idiomatic Expressions in Mental-health Consultations', (reprinted) *Journal of Pragmatics* (2007) 39 (3), March: 527–41.

Antaki, C. (2008) 'Formulations in Psychotherapy', in A. Peräkylä, C. Antaki, S. Vehviläinen and I. Leudar (eds) *Conversation Analysis of Psychotherapy* (Cambridge England: Cambridge University Press).

Antaki, C. (2011) 'Six Kinds of Applied Conversation Analysis', in A. Antaki (ed.) *Applied Conversation Analysis: Intervention and Change in Institutional Talk* (London: Palgrave Macmillan).

Antaki, C., Barnes, R. and Leudar, I. (2005a) 'Diagnostic Formulations in Psychotherapy', *Discourse Studies*, 7 (6): (Sage London CA and New Delhi).

Antaki, C., Barnes, R. and Leudar, I. (2005b) 'Self-disclosure as a Situated Interactional Practice', *British Journal of Social Psychology*, 44: 181–99.

Antaki, C. and Jahoda, A. (2010) 'Psychotherapists' Ppractices in Keeping a Session "On-track" in the Face of Clients's "Off-track" Talk', *Communication and Medicine*, 7 (1): 11–21.

Antaki, C., Leudar, I. and Barnes, R. (2004) 'Trouble in Agreeing on a Client's Problem in a Cognitive-Behavioural Therapy Session', *Rivista di Psicolinguistica Applicata*, 4: 127–38.

Arminen, I. (2000) 'On the Context Sensitivity of Institutional Interaction', *Discourse & Society*, 1 October, 11 (4): 435–58.

Atkinson, J.M. and Drew, P. (1979) *Order in Court: The Organization of Verbal Interaction in Judicial Settings* (London: Macmillan).

Atkinson, J.M. and Heritage, J. (eds) (1984) *Structures of Social Action: Studies in Conversational Analysis* (Cambridge: Cambridge University Press).

Badura, B., Schnellschmidt, H. and Vetter, C. (2003) 'Gesünder älter werden – Betriebliche Personal- und Gesundheitspolitik in Zeiten demografischen Wandels', in Badura, B. Schnellschmidt, H. and Vetter, C. (eds) *Fehlzeiten-Report* (Berlin: Springer).

Balint, M. and Balint, E. (1961) *Psychotherapeutic Techniques in Medicine* (London: Tavistock Publications).

Bamber, M.R. (2011) *Overcoming Your Workplace Stress: A CBT-Based Self Help Guide* (London: Routledge).

Barrett-Lennard, G.T. (1986) 'The Relationship Inventory Now: Issues and Advances in Theory, Method and Use', in L.S. Greenberg and W.M. Pinsof (eds) *The Psychotherapeutic Process: A Research Handbook* (New York: Guilford Press).

Barrett-Lennard, G.T. (2007) 'Origins and Unfolding of the Person-centred Innovation', in Mick Cooper, Maureen O'Hara, Peter F. Schmid and Gill Watt (eds) *The Handbook of Person-Centred Psychotherapy and Counselling* (New York: Palgrave Macmillan).

Becker, H. (2009) 'Value for Money – EAPs rechnen sich für Ihr Unternehmen'. Verfügbar unter http://www.insite-interventions.com/ de/aktuell/Publikationen.

Becker, H. (2011) EAP von INSITE. Fragen, Antworten und Hintergründe. Frankfurt. Verfügbar unter http://www.insite-interventions.com/de/aktuell/ Publikationen.

Behrends-Krahnen, E. (2011) 'Burnout – eine Herausforderung im Coaching', *Organisationsberatung, Supervision, Coaching,* Band 18, Nummer 3: 333–41.

Belkic, B.E., Landbergis, P.A., Schnall, P.L. and Baker, D. (2004) 'Is Job Strain a Major Source of Cardiovascular Disease Risk?' *Scandanavian Journal of Work, Environment and Health*, 30 (2): 85–128.

Bercelli, F., Rossano, F. and Viaro, M. (2008) 'Clients' Responses to Therapists' Reinterpretations', in A. Peräkylä, C. Antaki, S. Vehviläinen and I. Leudar (eds) *Conversation Analysis of Psychotherapy* (Cambridge, England: Cambridge University Press).

Bergin, A.E. (1970) 'The Deterioration Effect: A Reply to Braucht', *Journal of Abnormal Psychology*, 75: 300–2.

Bergmann, J.R. (1992) 'Veiled Morality: Notes on Discretion in Psychiatry', in P. Drew and J. Heritage (eds) *Talk at Work* (Cambridge: Cambridge University Press).

Bertram, P., Karon, B.P. and Widener, A.J. (1995) 'Psychodynamic Therapies in Historical Perspective: "Nothing Human Do I Consider Alien to Me"', in B. Bongar and L. Beutler (eds) *Comprehensive Textbook of Psychotherapy: Theory and Practice* (Oxford University Press).

Billig, M. and Schegloff, E.A. (1999) 'Critical Discourse Analysis and Conversation Analysis: An Exchange between Michael Billig and Emanuel Schegloff', *Discourse & Society*, 10 (4): 543–82.

Bolinger, D. (1989) *Intonation and Its Uses* (London: Edward Arnold).

Bongar, B. and Beutler, L. (1995) *Comprehensive Textbook of Psychotherapy: Theory and Practice* (Oxford University Press).

Borkovec, T.D. and Ruscio, A.M. (2001) 'Psychotherapy for Generalized Anxiety Disorder', *Journal of Clinical Psychiatry*, 62 (11): 37–42.

Büblitz, W. (1988) *Supportive Fellow Speakers and Cooperative Conversations* (Amsterdam and Philadelphia: Benjamins).

Buttny, R. (1996) 'Clients' and Therapist's Joint Construction of the Clients' Problems', *Research on Language and Social Interaction*, 29 (2): 125–53.

Byrne, P.S. and Long, B.E.L. (1976) *Doctors talking to Patients: A Study of the Verbal Behaviours of Doctors in the Consultation* (London: HMSO).

Chambles, D.L., Sanderson, W.C., Shoham, V., Johnson, S.B., Pyne, J. and Pope, K.S. (1996) 'An Update on Empirically Validated Therapies', *Clinical Psychologist*, 49: 5–18.

Chambless, D.L. and Gillis, M.M. (1993) 'Cognitive Therapy of Anxiety Disorders', *Journal of Consulting and Clinical Psychology*, 61: 248–60.

Chessick, R. (1977) *Great Ideas in Psychotherapy* (Northvale, New Jersey: Jason Aronson, Inc.)

Comer, J.S. and Kendall, P.C. (2013) 'Methodolgy, Design and Evaluation in Psychotherapy Research', in M.J. Lambert, A.E. Bergin and S.L. Garfield (eds) *Handbook of Psychotherapy and Behavior Change* (6th edn, New York: Wiley).

Constantine, M. and Kwong-Liem, K. (2003) 'Cross-Cultural Considerations of Therapist Self-Disclosure', *Journal of Clinical Psychology*, 59 (5): 581–8.

Corey, G. (1996) *Case Approach to Counselling and Psychotherapy* (4th edn, Brooks/Cole Publishing Company).

Couper-Kuhlen, L. and Selting, M. (1996) (eds) *Prosody in Conversation: Interactional Studies* (Cambridge: Cambridge University Press).

Craighead, L.W. and Agras, S.W. (1991) 'Mechanisms of Action in Cognitive-behavioural and Pharmacological Interventions for Obesity and Bulimia Nervosa', *Journal of Consulting and Clinical Psychology*, 59: 115–25.

Craske, M. (2010) *Cognitive-Behavioral Therapy* (New York, NY: APA Books).

Cruttenden, A. (1997) *Intonation* (Cambridge: Cambridge University Press).

Csiernik, R. (2005) *Wellness and Work: Employee Assistance Programming in Canada* (Toronto: Canadian Scholars Press).

Cushman, P (1995) 'Psychotherapy to 1992: A Historically Situated Interpretation', in D.K. Freedheim *A History of Psychotherapy: A Century of Change* (Washington D.C.: American Psychological Association).

Czyzewski, M. (1995) 'Mm Hm Tokens as Interactional Devices in the Psychotherapeutic In-take Interview', in P. ten Have and G. Psathas (eds) *Situated Order: Studies in the Social Organization of Talk and Embodied Activities* (Washington, D.C.: University Press of America).

Davis, K. (1986) 'The Process of Problem Re(formulation) in Psychotherapy', *Sociology of Health and Illness*, 8: 44–74.

De Shazer, S. (1988) *Investigating Solutions in Brief Therapy* (New York: Norton).

De Shazer, S. (1994) *Words Were Originally Magic* (New York: Norton).

Dickerson, S.J., Murphy, M.W. and Clavelle, P.R. (2012) 'Work Adjustment and General Level of Functioning Pre and Post-EAP Counselling', *Journal of Workplace Behavioural Health*, 27: 217–26.

Dittmann, A. and Llewellyn, L. (1968) 'Relationship between Vocalizations and Head Nods as Listener Responses', *Journal of Personality and Social Psychology*, 9 (2): 79–84.

Dobson, K.S. (1989) 'A Meta-analysis of the Efficacy of Cognitive Therapy for Depression', *Journal of Consulting and Clinical Psychology*, 57: 414–419.

Dobson, K.S. and Pusch, D. (1993) 'Towards a Definition of the Conceptual and Empirical Boundaries of Cognitive Therapy', *Australian Psychologist*, 28: 117–34.

Dobson, K.S. and Shaw, B.F. (1995) 'Cognitive Therapies in Practice', in B. Bongar and L. Beutler (eds) *Comprehensive Textbook of Psychotherapy: Theory and Practice* (Oxford: Oxford University Press).

Dodds, E.R. (1965) *Pagan and Christian in an Age of Anxiety* (New York: Norton).

Dreier, O. (2008) *Psychotherapy in Everyday Life: Learning in Doing, Social Cognitve and Computational Perspectives* (Cambridge: Cambridge University Press).

Drew, P. (1991) 'Asymmetries of Knowledge in Conversational Interactions', in I. Markova and K. Foppa (eds) *Asymmetries in Dialogue* (Herfordshire: Harvester Wheatsheaf).

Drew, P. (2003) 'Comparative Analysis of Talk-in-interaction in Different Institutional Settings: A Sketch', in P.J. Glenn, C.D. LeBaron and J. Mandelbaum (eds) *Studies in Language and Social Interaction: In Honor of Robert Hopper* (Mahwah, NJ: Erlbaum).

Drew, P. and Heritage, J. (1992) *Talk at Work* (Cambridge University Press).

Drummond, K. and Hopper, R. (1993b) 'Some Uses of Yeah', *Research on Language and Social Interaction*, 26 (2): 203–12.

Duncan, B., Miller, S. and Sparks, J. (2004) *The Heroic Client: A Revolutionary Way to Improve Effectiveness through Client-directed, Outcome-informed Therapy* (John Wiley & Sons, Inc.).

Duncan, B., Miller. S., Sparks. J., Claud, D., Reynolds, L., Brown. J. and Johnson, L. (2003) 'The Session Rating Scale: Preliminary Psychometric Properties of a "Working Alliance" Measure', *Journal of Brief Therapy*, 3 (1), Fall/Winter.

Ehrenwald, J. (1976) *The History of Psychotherapy: From Healing Magic to Encounter* (Jason Aronson, Inc.).

Ellenberger, H.F. (1970) *The Discovery of the Unconscious: The History and Revolution of Dynamic Psychiatry* (London: Allen Lane, The Penguin Press).

Elliott, R. (1986) 'Interpersonal Process Recall (IPR) as a Psychotherapy Process Research Method', in L.S. Greenberg and W.M. Pinsof (eds) *The Psychotherapeutic Process: A Research Handbook* (New York: Guilford Press).

Elliott, R. (1996) 'Are Client-centered-experiential Therapists Effective? A Meta-analysis of Outcome Research', in U. Esser, H. Pabst and G.W. Speierer (eds) *The Power of the Person-centered Approach: New Challenges, Perspectives, Answers* (Koln, Germany: GwG Verlag).

Elliott, R. (2001) 'Research on the Effectiveness of Humanistic Therapies: A Meta-analysis', in D. J. Cain and J. Seeman (eds) *Humanistic Psychotherapies: Handbook of Research and Practice* (Washington, D.C.: American Psychological Association).

Elliott, R. (2007) 'Person-centred Approaches to Research', in M. Cooper, M. O'Hara, P.F. Schmid and G. Watt (eds) *The Handbook of Person-Centred Psychotherapy and Counselling* (New York: Palgrave Macmillan).

Elliott, R., Greenberg, L.S. and Lietaer, G. (2004) 'Research on Experiential Psychotherapies', in M.J. Lambert, A.E. Bergin and S.L. Garfield (eds) *Handbook of Psychotherapy and Behavior Change* (5th edn, New York: Wiley).

Elliott, R., Greenberg, L.S., Watson, J., Timulak, L. and Freire, E. (2013) 'Research on Experiential Psychotherapies', in M.J. Lambert, A.E. Bergin and S.L. Garfield (eds) *Handbook of Psychotherapy and Behavior Change* (6th edn, New York: Wiley).

Elliott, R. and Shapiro, D.A. (1988) 'Brief Structured Recall: A More Efficient Method for Identifying and Describing Significant Therapy Events', *British Journal of Medical Psychology*, 61: 141–53.

Emmelkamp, P.M.G. (2013) 'Behaviour Therapy with Adults', in M.J. Lambert, A.E. Bergin and S.L. Garfield (eds) *Handbook of Psychotherapy and Behaviour change* (6th edn, New York: Wiley).

Eysenck, H.J. (1952) 'The Effects of Psychotherapy: An Evaluation', *Journal of Consulting Psychology*, 16: 319–24.

Farber, B. (2003) *Patient Self-Disclosure: A Review of the Research* (Wiley Periodicals).

Farber, B. (2006) *Self-Disclosure in Psychotherapy* (New York: Guilford Publishing).

Finke, J. and Teusch, L. (2007) 'Using a Person-centred Approach within a Medical Framework', in M. Cooper, M. O'Hara, P.F. Schmid and G. Watt, *The Handbook of Person-Centred Psychotherapy and Counselling* (New York: Palgrave Macmillan).

Fitzgerald, P.E and Leudar, I. (2010) 'On Listening in Person-centred, Solution-focused Psychotherapy', *Journal of Pragmatics*, 42: 3188–98.

Foppa, K. (1995) 'On Mutual Understanding and Agreement in Dialogues', in I. Markova, C. Graumann and K. Foppa (eds) *Mutualities in Dialogue* (Cambridge University Press).

Foucault, M. (1980) *The History of Sexuality: Vol 1 An Introduction* (New York: Random House).
Foucault, M. (1985) *Madness and Civilisation: A History of Insanity in the Age of Reason* (Great Britain: Tavistock Publications Ltd).
Foucault, M. (1988) *The History of Sexuality: Vol. 3* (New York: Random House).
Foucault, M. (1991) *Discipline and Punishment: The Birth of the Prison* (London: Penguin Books).
Frankel, R.M. (1984) 'From Sentence to Sequence: Understanding the Medical Encounter through Micro-interactional Analysis', *Discourse Processes*, 7: 135–70.
Freud, S. (1916–1917) *Introductory Lectures on Psychoanalysis* (London: Hogarth Press, 1963).
Freud, S. and Breuer, J. (1991) 'Fräulein Anna O', in S. Freud (ed.) *Studies on Hysteria* (pp. 73–102) (London: Penguin [Original work published 1895]).
Gains, R. (2003) 'Therapist Self-Disclosure with Children, Adolescents and their Parents', *Journal of Clinical Psychology*, 59: 569–80.
Gale, J.E. and Newfield, N. (1992) 'A Conversation Analysis of a Solution-Focused Marital Therapy Session', *Journal of Marital and Family Therapy*, 18: 153–65.
Garafanga, J. and Britten, N. (2004) 'Formulation in General Practice Consultations', *Text*, 24 (2): 147–70.
Gardner, R. (2001) *When Listeners Talk: Response Tokens and Listener Stance*. Pragmatics and Beyond Series (Amsterdam: Benjamins).
Gerhardt, J. and Beyerle, S. (1997) 'What if Socrates Had Been a Woman? The Therapist's Use of Acknowledgement Tokens (*mm-hm, yeah, sure, right*) as a Non-reflective Means of Intersubjective Involvement', *Contemporary Psychoanalysis*, 33 (3): 367–410.
Gill, V.T. and Roberts, F. (2013) 'Conversation Analysis in Medicine', in J. Sidnell and T. Stivers (eds) *Handbook of Conversation Analysis* (Oxford: Wiley-Blackwell).
Gloaguen, V., Cottraux, J., Cucherat, M. and Blackburn, I. (1998) 'A Metal-analysis of the Effects of Cognitive Therapy in Depressed Patients', *Journal of Affective Disorders*, 49 (1): 59–72.
Goldfried, M., Burckell, L. and Eubanks-Carter, C. (2003) 'Therapist Self-Disclosure in Cognitive-Behaviour Therapy', *Journal of Clinical Psychology*, 59 (5): 555–68.
Goldman, R. N., Greenberg, L. S. and Angus, L. (2006) 'The Effects of Adding Emotion-focused Interventions to the Client-centered Relationship Conditions in the Treatment of Depressions', *Psychotherapy Research*, 16: 537–49.
Goodwin, C. (1986) 'Between and within: Alternative Sequential Treatments of Continuers and Assessments', *Human Studies*, 9: 205–17.
Greenberg, L. and Elliott, R. (1997) 'Varieties of Emotional Expression', in A. Bohart and L. Greenberg (eds) *Empathy Reconsidered: New Directions in Theory Research & Practice* (Washington, D.C.: APA Press).
Greenberg, L., Elliott, R. and Lietaer, G. (1994) 'Research on Humanistic and Experiential Psychotherapies', in A. Bergin and S.L. Garfield (eds) *Handbook of Psychotherapy and Behavior Change* (4th edn, New York: Wiley).
Greenberger, L. and Padesky, C. (1995) *Mind over Mood* (New York: The Guilford Press).
Haberleitner, E., Deistler, E., Ungvari, R. (2007) *Führen, Fördern, Coachen. So entwickeln Sie die Potentiale Ihrer Mitarbeiter*, 2 (Aktualisierte Auflage, Heidelberg).

Hak, T. and de Boer, F (1996) 'Formulations in First Encounters', *Journal of Pragmatics*, 25: 83–99.

Halgin, R.P. and Murphy, R.A. (1995) 'Issues in the Training of Psychotherapists', in B. Bongar and L. Beutler (eds) *Comprehensive Textbook of Psychotherapy: Theory and Practice* (Oxford University Press).

Halonen, M. (2008) 'Person Reference as a Device for Constructing Experiences as Typical in Group Therapy', in Peräkylä, A., Antaki, C., Vehvilänen, S. and Leudar, I. (eds) *Conversation Analysis and Psychotherapy* (Cambridge: Cambridge University Press).

Hargrave, G.E., Hiatt, D. and Shaffer, I.A. (2007) 'The Impact of Mental Health Disorders on Work Productivity', *EAP Digest*, 27 (3): 34–5.

Heritage, J. (1984a) 'A Change of State Token and Aspects of its Sequential Placement', in J.M. Atkinson and J. Heritage (eds) *Structures of Social Action: Studies in Conversation Analysis* (Cambridge: Cambridge University Press).

Heritage, J. (1984b) *Garfinkel and Ethnomethodology* (Polity Press: Cambridge).

Heritage, J. (1997) 'Conversation Analysis and Institutional Talk: Analysing Data', in D. Silverman (ed) *Qualitative Research: Theory, Method and Practice* (London: Sage).

Heritage, J. and Greatbatch, D. (1991) 'On the Institutional Character of Institutional Talk: The Case of News Interviews', in D. Boden and D. Zimmerman (eds) *Talk and Social Structure* (Cambridge: Polity Press).

Heritage, J. and Maynard, D. (2006) *Communitcation in Medical Care: Interactions between Primary Care Physicians and Patients* (Cambridge: Cambridge University Press).

Heritage, J. and Robinson, J.D. (2011) '"Some" versus "Any" Medical Issues: Encouraging Patients to Reveal Their Unmet Concerns', in A. Antaki (ed) *Applied Conversation Analysis: Intervention and Change in Institutional Talk* (Hampshire: Palgrave Macmillan).

Heritage, J. and Watson, D.R. (1979) 'Formulations as Conversational Objects', in G. Psathas (ed.) *Everyday Language: Studies in Ethnomethodology* (New York: Irvington).

Heritage, J. and Watson, D.R. (1980) 'Aspects of the Properties of Formulations in Natural Conversations: Some Instances Analysed', *Semiotica*, 30 (3/4).

Hertz, R.P. and Baker, C. L. (2002) *The Impact of Mental Disorders on Work* (Groton, CN: Pfizer Pharmaceuticals Group).

Hoffman, S.G. and Smits, J.A. (2008) 'Cognitive-behavioral Therapy for Adult Anxiety Disorders: A Metaanalysis of Randomized Placebo-controlled Trials', *Journal of Clinical Psychiatry*, 69, 621–32.

Hollon, S.D. and Beck, A.T. (2005) 'Cognitive and Cognitive-behavioural Therapies', in A.E. Bergin and S.L. Garfield (eds) *Handbook of Psychotherapy and Behaviour Change* (4th edn, New York: Wiley).

Hollon, S.D. and Beck, A.T. (2013) 'Cognitive and Cognitive-behavioural Therapies', in M.J. Lambert, A.E. Bergin and S.L. Garfield (eds) *Handbook of Psychotherapy and Behaviour Change* (6th edn, New York: Wiley).

Hollon, S.D., Shelton, R.C. and Davis, D.D. (1993) 'Cognitve Behaviour Therapy for Depression: Conceptual Issues and Clinical Efficacy', *Journal of Consulting and Clinical Psychology*, 61: 270–75.

Holmes, J. (2002) 'All You Need is Cognitive Behavioural Therapy', *British Medical Journal*, 324 (7332): 288–90.

Hopko, D.R. and Johanson, L.C. (2010) 'The Impact of Cognitive Interventions in Treating Depressed Breast Cancer Patients', *Journal of Cognitive Psychotherapy*, 24, 314–28.

Horvath, A.O. and Greenberg, L.S. (1989) 'Development and Validation of the Working Alliance Inventory', *Journal of Counseling Psychology*, 36: 223–233.

Hubble, M.A., Duncan, B.L. and Miller, S.D. (1999) 'Directing Attention to What Works', in M.A. Hubble, B.L. Duncan and S.D. Miller (eds) *The Heart and Soul of Change* (Washington, D.C.: APA Press).

Hutchby, I. (2005) 'Active Listening: Formulations and the Elicitation of Feelings-talk in Child Counselling', *Research on Language and Social Interaction*, 38 (3): 303–29.

INQA (2009) Gesunde Arbeit trotz Zeitdruck, Arbeitsverdichtung und Stress. http://www.inqa.de/Inqa/Navigation/Themen/stress,did=252374

James, W. (1902) *The Varieties of Religious Experience: A Study in Human Nature* (London: Longmans, Green and Co.).

Jefferson, G. (1984) 'Notes on a Systematic Deployment of Acknowledgement Tokens "yeah" and "Mm hm"', *Papers in Linguistics*, 17 (2): 197–216.

Kagan, N. (1984) 'Interpersonal Process Recall: Basic Methods and Recent Research', in D. Larsen (ed.) *Teaching Psychological Skills* (Monterey, CA: Brooks/Cole).

Kagan, N., Krathwohl, D. R. and Miller, R. (1963) 'Stimulated Recall in Therapy using Videotape: A Case Study', *Journal of Counseling Psychology*, 10: 237–43.

Kalmthout, M. (2007) 'The Process of Person-centred Therapy', in M. Cooper, M. O'Hara, P.F. Schmid and G. Watt (eds) *The Handbook of Person-Centred Psychotherapy and Counselling* (New York: Palgrave Macmillan).

Käsermann, M.L. (1991) 'Obstruction and Dominance: Uncooperative Moves and Their Effect on the Course of Conversation', in I. Markova and K. Foppa (eds) *Asymmetries in Dialogue* (Herfordshire: Harvester Wheatsheaf).

Kendall, P.C. (1998) 'Empirically Supported Psychological Therapies', *Journal of Consulting and Clinical Psychology*, 66: 3–10.

Keys, S. and Proctor, G. (2007) 'Ethics in Practice in Person-centred Therapy', in M. Cooper, M. O'Hara, P. F. Schmid and G. Watt (eds) *The Handbook of Person-Centred Psychotherapy and Counselling* (New York: Palgrave Macmillan).

Kirschenbaum, H. and Henderson, V. L. (1989) (eds) *The Carl Rogers Reader* (Boston: Houghton Mifflin Company).

Klein, M.H.. Mathieu-Coughlan, P. and Kiesler, D.J. (1986) 'The Experiencing Scales', in L.S. Greenberg and W.M. Pinsof (eds) *The Psychotherapeutic Process: A Research Handbook* (New York: Guildford Press).

Lambert, M.J. (2005) 'Introduction and Historical Overview', in M. J. Lambert (ed.) *Bergin and Garfield's Handbook of Psychotherapy and Behavior Change* (5th edn, New York: John Wiley), 3–15.

Lambert, M.J. (2013) 'Introduction and Historical Overview', in M.J. Lambert, A.E. Bergin and S.L. Garfield (eds) *Handbook of Psychotherapy and Behaviour change* (6th edn, New York: Wiley).

Lambert, M.J. and Bergin, A.E. (1994) 'The Effectiveness of Psychotherapy', in A.E. Bergin and S.L. Garfield (eds) *Handbook of Psychotherapy and Behavior Change* (4th edn, New York: Wiley).

LaMontagne, A.D., Keegel, T., Louie, A.M., Ostry, A. and Landsbergis, P.A. (2007) 'A Systematic Review of the Job Stress Intervention Evaluation Literature:

1990–2005', *International Journal of Occupational & Environmental Health*, 13 (3): 268–80.

LaSasso, A.T., Rost, K. and Beck, A. (2006) 'Modelling the Impact of Enhanced Depression Treatment on Workplace Functioning and Costs: A Cost-benefit Approach', *Official Journal of the Medical Care Section*, 44 (4): 352–58.

Leahy, R. (2003) *Cognitive Therapy Techniques: A Practitioner's Guide* (New York: The Guilford Press).

Leahy, R. (2010) *Anxiety Free: Unravel Your Fears before They Unravel You* (Hay House UK, Ltd).

Leidig, S. (2003) *Arbeitsbedingungen und psychische Störungen* (Lengerich: Pabst Science Publishers).

Leidig, S. (2007) 'Psychische Störungen und Stress in der Arbeitswelt: Ansätze für eine zeitgemäße Gesundheitsförderung', *Personalführung*, 1: 20–31.

Leidig, S. (2011) 'Employee Assistance Programme (EAP) in Deutschland', in E. Bamberg et al., (Hrsg.): *Gesundheitsförderung und Gesundheitsmanagement in der Arbeitswelt* (Ein Handbuch, Göttingen, S. 393–411).

Leudar I., Antaki C. and Barnes R. (2006) 'When Psychotherapists Disclose Personal Information about Themselves to Clients', *Communication and Medicine*, 3 (1): 27–41.

Leudar, I. and Thomas, P. (2000) *Voices of Reason, Voices of Insanity: Studies of Verbal Hallucinations* (London: Routledge).

Leudar, I., Sharrock, W., Hayes, J. and Truckle, S. (2008a) 'Therapy as a "Structured Immediacy"', *Journal of Pragmatics*, 40: 863–85.

Leudar, I., Sharrock, W., Truckle, S., Colombino, T., Hayes, J. and Booth, K. (2008b) 'Conversation of Emotions: On Transforming Play into Psychoanalytic Psychotherapy', in A. Peräkylä, C. Antaki, S. Vehviläinen and I. Leudar (eds) *Conversation Analysis of Psychotherapy* (Cambridge, England: Cambridge University Press).

Lietaer, G. (1984) 'Unconditional Positive Regard: A Controversial Basic Attitude in Client-centred Therapy', in R.F. Levant and J.M. Shlien (eds) *Client-centred Therapy and the Person-centred Approach* (New York: Praeger).

Luborsky, L. (1954) 'A Note on Eysenck's Article, "The Effect of Psychotherapy: An Evaluation"' *British Journal of Psychology*, 45: 129–31.

Luborsky, L., Crits-Christoph, P., McLellan, A.T., Woody, G., Piper, W., Liberman, B., Imber, S. and Pilkonis, P. (1986) 'Do Therapists Vary Much in their Success? Findings from Four Outcome Studies', *American Journal of Orthopsychiatry*, 56: 501–12.

Luborsky, L., Rosenthal, R., Diguer, L., Andrusyna, T.P., Berman, J.S., Levitt, J.T.,Seligman, D.A., Krause, E.D. (2002) 'The Dodo Bird Verdict is Alive and Well – Mostly', *Clinical Psychology: Science and Practice*, 9: 2–12.

Luborsky, L., Singer. B. and Luborsky, L. (1975) 'Is it True That "Everyone has Won and All Must Have Prizes"'? *Archives of General Psychiatry*, 32: 995–1008.

Madill, A., Widdicombe, S. and Barkham, M. (2001) 'The Potential of Conversation Analysis for Psychotherapy Research', *The Counselling Psychologist*, 29: 413–34.

Mahoney, M.J. (1995) 'The Modern Psychotherapist and the Future of Psychotherapy', in B. Bongar and L. Beutler (eds) *Comprehensive Textbook of Psychotherapy: Theory and Practice* (Oxford University Press).

Maione, P.V. and Chenail, R.J. (1999) 'Qualitative Inquiry in Psychotherapy: Research on the Common Factors', in M.A. Hubble, B.L. Duncan and S.D.

Miller (eds) *The Heart and Soul of Change: What Works in Therapy* (Washington, D.C: American Psychological Association).

Masi, D. and Jacobson, J. M. (2003) 'Outcome Measurements of an Integrated Employees Assistance and Work-Life Program', *Research on Social Work Practice*, 13 (4): 451–67.

Masson, J. (1992) *Against Therapy* (London: HarperCollins).

Mazeland, H. (1990) '"Yes", "no", and "mhm": Variations in Acknowledgment Choices', in B. Conein, M. de Fornel and L. Quéré (eds) *Les formes de la conversation. Issy les Moulineaux, Réseaux, Communication – Technologie – Société*, 8 (1): 251–82.

McLeod, J. (1998) *An Introduction to Counselling* (2nd edn, Berkshire: Open University Press).

McLeod, J. (2002) *Qualitative Research in Counselling and Psychotherapy* (London: Sage).

McLeod, J. (2003) *Doing Counselling Research* (London: Sage).

McLeod, J. (2010) 'The Effectiveness of Workplace Counselling: A Systematic Review', *Counselling and Psychotherapy Research: Linking Research with Practice*, 10 (4): 238–48.

McLeod, J. (2011) *Qualitative Research in Counselling and Psychotherapy* (2nd edn, London: Sage).

McMartin, C. (2008) 'Resisting Optimistic Questions in Narrative and Solution-focused Therapy', in A. Peräkylä, C. Antaki, S. Vehviläinen and I Leudar (eds) *Conversation Analysis of Psychotherapy* (Cambridge England: Cambridge University Press).

McNamee, S. and Gergen, K.J. (1994) *Therapy as Social Construction* (Sage Publications Ltd).

Meares, R., Stevenson, J. and D'angelo, R. (2002) 'Eysenck's Challenge to Psychotherapy: A View of the Effects 50 years On', *Australian and New Zealand Journal of Psychiatry*, 36 (6): 812–15.

Mearns, D. (1996) 'Working at Relational Depth with Clients in Person-centred Counselling', *Counselling*, 7 (4): 306–11.

Mearns, D. and Thorne, B. (2007) *Person-Centred Counselling in Action* (3rd edn, London: Sage).

Meichenbaum, D. (1995) 'Cognitive-Behavioural Therapy in Historical Perspective', in B. Bongar and L. Beutler (eds) *Comprehensive Textbook of Psychotherapy: Theory and Practice* (Oxford University Press).

Mellinger, W. M. (1995) 'Talk, Power and Professionals: Partial Repeats as Challenges in the Psychiatric Interview', in J. Siegfried (ed.) *Therapeutic and Everyday Discourse as Behavior Change: Toward aMicroanalysis in Psychotherapy Process Research* (Norwood, NJ: Ablex).

Messer, S.B. (2001) 'Empirically Supported Treatments: What's a Nonbehaviourist to Do?' In B.D. Slife, D. Brent, R.N. Williams and S.H. Barlow (eds) *Critical Issues in Psychotherapy: Translating New Ideas intoPpractice* (Thousand Oaks, C.A: Sage).

Metcalf, L. and Thomas, F. (1994) 'Client and Therapist Perceptions of Solution Focused Brief Therapy: A Qualitative Analysis', *Journal of Family Psychotherapy*, 5 (4): 49–66.

Metcalf, L., Thomas, F., Duncan, B., Miller, S. and Hubble, M. (1996) 'What Works in Solution Focused Brief Therapy: A Qualitative Analysis of Client and Therapist Perceptions', in S.D. Miller, M.A. Hubble and B.L. Duncan (eds) *Handbook of Solution Focused Brief Therapy* (San Francisco: Jossey-Bass).

Meyer, A., Richter, R., Grawe, K., Schulenberg, J. and Schulte, B. (1991) *Forschungsgutachten zu Fragen eines Psychotherapeutengesetzes* (Hamburg: Universitätskrankenhaus).

Miell, D. (1997) 'The Self and the Social World', in I. Roth (ed.) *Introduction to Psychology* (Milton Keynes: Open University Press).

Miell, D. and Croghan, R. (1998) 'Examining the Wider Context of Social Relationships', in D. Miell and R. Dallos (eds) *Social Interaction and Personal Relationships* (Milton Keynes: Open University Press).

Miller, W.R. and Rollnick, S. (2002) *Motivational Interviewing* (New York: The Guilford Press).

Mitchell, J. E., Pyle, R. L., Eckert, E. D. and Hatsukami, D. (1990) 'A Comparison Study of Antidepressants and Structured Intensive Group Psychotherapy in the Treatment of Bulimia Nervosa', *Archives of General Psychiatry*, 47 (2): 149–57.

Muntigl, P. and Zabala, L.H. (2008) 'Expandable Responses: How Clients get Prompted to Say More During Psychotherapy', *Research on Language & Social Interaction*, 41 (2): 187–226.

Neenan, M. and Dryden, W. (2000) *Essential Cognitive Therapy* (London: Whurr).

Norbrega, S., Champagne, N.J., Azaroff, L.S., Shetty, K. and Punnett, L. (2010) 'Barriers to Workplace Stress Interventions in Employee Assistance Practice: EAP Perspectives', *Journal of Workplace Behavioural Health*, 25: 282–95.

Norcross, J. (ed.) (2002) *Psychotherapy Relationships That Work: Therapists Contributions and Responsiveness to Patients* (Oxford University Press).

Norcross, J. C. and Goldfried, M. R. (2005) *Handbook of Psychotherapy Integration* (2nd edn, New York: Oxford University Press).

Norcross, J. and Prochaska, J. (1983) 'Psychotherapists in Independent Practice: Some Findings and Issues', *Professional Psychology: Research and Practice*, 14: 869–81.

Norton, P.J. and Price, E.C. (2007) 'A Meta-analytic Review of Adult Cognitive-behavioral Treatment Outcome across the Anxiety Disorders', *Journal of Nervous and Mental Disease*, 195: 521–31.

Orlinsky, D.E. and Howard, K.I. (1975) *Varieties of Psychotherapeutic Experience: Multivariate Analyses of Patients and Therapists Reports* (New York: Teachers' College Press).

Orlinsky, D.E. and Howard, K.I. (1995) 'Unity and Diversity among Psychotherapies: A Comparative Perspective', in B. Bongar and L. Beutler (eds)*Comprehensive Textbook of Psychotherapy: Theory and Practice* (Oxford University Press).

Peräkylä, A. (1995) *AIDS Counselling: Institutionalinteraction and Clinical Practice* (Cambridge: Cambridge University Press).

Peräkylä, A. (1997) 'Conversation Analysis: A New Model of Research in Doctor-Patient Communication', *Journal of the Royal Society of Medicine*, 90: 205–08.

Peräkylä, A. (2004) 'Making Links in Psychoanalytic Interpretations: A Conversation Analytic View', *Psychotherapy Research*, 14 (3): 289–307.

Peräkylä, A. (2005) 'Patients' Responses to Interpretations: A Dialogue between Conversation Analysis and Psychoanalytic Theory', *Communication & Medicine*, 2 (2): 163–76.

Peräkylä, A. (2011) 'A Psychoanalyst's Reflection on Conversation Analysis's Contribution to His Own Therapeutic Talk', in A. Antaki (ed.) *Applied*

Conversation Analysis: Intervention and Change in Institutional Talk (Hampshire: Palgrave Macmillan).

Peräkylä, A. (2013) 'Conversation Analysis in Psychotherapy', in J. Sidnell and T. Stivers (eds) *Handbook of Conversation Analysis* (Oxford: Wiley-Blackwell).

Peräkylä, A., Antaki, C., Vehviläinen, S. and Leudar, I.(2008) 'Analysing Psychotherapy in Practice', in A. Peräkylä, C. Antaki, S.Vehviläinen and I. Leudar (eds) *Conversation Analysis and Psychotherapy* (Cambridge: Cambridge University Press).

Peräkylä, A. and Silverman, D. (1991) 'Owning Experience: Describing the Experience of Other Persons', *Text*, 11 (3): 441–80.

Peräkylä, A. and Vehviläinen, S. (2003) 'Conversation Analysis and the Professional Stocks of Interactional Knowledge', *Discourse & Society*, 14 (6): 727–50.

Peyrot, M. (1987) 'Circumspection in Psychotherapy: Structures and Strategies of Counselor-client Interaction', *Semiotica*, 65 (3/4): 249–68.

Peyrot, M. (1995) 'Therapeutic Preliminaries: Conversational Context and Process in Psychotherapy', *Qualitative Sociology*, 18 (3), Springer Netherlands.

Pomerantz, A. (1980) 'Telling My Side: "Limited Access" as a Fishing Device', *Sociological Inquiry* 50: 186–98.

Pomerantz, A. (1984a) 'Agreeing and Disagreeing with Assessments: Some Features of Preferred/Dispreferred Turn Shapes', in J.M. Atkinson and J. Heritage (eds) *Structures of Social Action: Studies in Conversational Analysis* (Cambridge University Press).

Pomerantz, A (1986) 'Extreme Case Formulations: A Way of Legitimizing Claims', *Human Studies*, 9: 219–29.

Pomerantz, A. (1998) 'Multiple Interpretations of Context: How Are They Useful?' *Research on Language and Social Interaction*, 31.

Prince, R. (1975) 'Symbols and Psychotherapy: The Example of Yoruba Sacrificial Ritual', *Journal of American Academic Psychoanalysis*, 3: 321–38.

Prochaska, J. O. (1999) 'How do People Change and How Can We Change to Help Many More People', in M.A. Hubble, B.L. Duncan and S.D. Miller (eds) *The Heart and Soul of Change: What Works in Therapy* (Washington, D.C: American Psychological Association).

Proctor, G. (2008a) *The Dynamics of Power in Counselling and Psychotherapy: Ethics, Politics and Practice* (Ross-on Wye: PCCS Books).

Proctor, G. (2008b) 'CBT: The Obscuring of Power in the Name of Science', *European Journal of Psychotherapy, Counselling and Health*, 10 (3): 231–45.

Psathas, G. (1995) *Conversation Analysis: The Study of Talk-in-interaction* (Thousand Oaks, California: Sage).

Rae, J. (2008) 'Lexical Substitution as a Therapeutic Resource', in A. Peräkylä, C. Antaki, S. Vehviläinen and I. Leudar (eds) *Conversation Analysis and Psychotherapy* (Cambridge: Cambridge University Press).

Rice, L.N. and Greenberg, L.S. (1995) 'Humanistic Approaches to Psychotherapy', in D.K. Freedheim (ed.) *A History of Psychotherapy: A Century of Change* (Washington D.C: American Psychological Association).

Riechert, I. (2011) *Psychische Störungen bei Mitarbeitern. Ein Leitfaden für Führungskräfte und Personalverantwortliche – von der Prävention bis zur Wiedereingliederung* (Heidelberg: Springer).

Robinson, L.A., Berman, J.S. and Neimeyer, R.A. (1990) 'Psychotherapy for the Treatment of Depression: A Comprehensive Review of Controlled Outcome Research', *Psychological Bulletin*, 108: 30–49.

Rogers, C.R. (1942) *Counseling and Psychotherapy* (Boston: Mifflin).

Rogers, C.R. (1951) *Client-Centered Therapy: Its Current Practice, Implications, and Theory* (Boston: Houghton Mifflin).

Rogers, C.R. (1957) 'The Necessary and Sufficient Conditions of Therapeutic Personality Change', *Journal of Consulting Psychology*, 21: 95–103. Re-published in H. Kirschenbaum and V.L. Henderson (eds) *The Carl Rogers Reader* (1989) (London: Constable).

Rogers, C.R. (1959) 'A Theory of Therapy, Personality and Interpersonal Relationship', in S. Koch (ed.) *Psychology: A Study of a Science*, 184–256 (New York: McGraw).

Rogers, C.R. (1980) *A Way of Being* (Houghton: Mifflin).

Rogers, C.R. (1995) *On Becoming a Person: A Therapist's View of Psychotherapy* (London: Constable & Company Ltd).

Rogers, C.R. and Dymond, R.F. (eds) (1954) *Psychotherapy and Personality Change: Coordinated Research Studies in the Client-Centered Approach* (Chicago: University of Chicago Press).

Rost, K., Fortney, J. and Coyne, J. (2005) 'The Relationship of Depression Treatment Quality Indicators to Employee Absenteeism', *Mental Health Services Research*, 7 (3):161–9.

Roth, A. and Fonagy, P. (2005) *What Works for Whom?: A Critical Review of Psychotherapy Research* (2nd edn, New York: Guildford Press).

Rush, A.J., Beck, A.T., Kovacs, M. and Hollon, S.D. (1977) 'Comparative Efficacy of Cognitive Therapy and Imipramine in the Treatment of Depressed Patients', *Cognitive Therapy and Research*, 1: 17–37.

Sachse, R. (1990) 'Concrete Interventions are Crucial: The Influence of the Therapist's Processing Proposals on the Client's Intrapersonal Exploration', in G. Lietaer, J. Rombauts and R. van Balen (eds) *Client-Centered and Experiential Psychotherapy in the Nineties* (Leuven: University Press).

Sachse, R. (1992) 'Improving Client Processes by Understanding and Intervening: Theoretical and Practical Advances in Client-centered Therapy Based on Psychological Concepts', *Berichte aus der Arbeitseinheit Klinische Psychologie, Fakultät für Psychologie* (Ruhr-Universität Bochum), 81.

Sachse, R. and Elliott, R. (2002) 'Process-outcome Research in Client-centred and Experiential Therapies', in D. Cain and J Seeman (eds) *Humanistic Psychotherapies: Handbook of Research and Practice* (Washington, D.C.: APA).

Sacks, H. (1984) 'Notes on Methodology', in J. Maxwell Atkinson and John Heritage (eds) *Structures of Social Action: Studies in Emotion and Social Interaction* (Cambridge: Cambridge University Press).

Sacks, H. (1987) 'On the Preference for Agreement and Continuity in Sequences in Conversation', in G. Button and J.R.E. Lee (eds) *Talk and Social Organization* (Clevedon: Multilingual Matters).

Sacks, H. (1992) *Lectures on Conversation Vol 1 and 11* (Oxford and Cambridge: Blackwell).

Sacks, H. and Schlegoff, E.A. (1979) 'Two Preferences in the Organisation of Reference to Persons and their Interaction', in G. Psathas (ed.) *Everyday Language: Studies in Ethnomethodology* (New York: Irvington Publishers).

Sanders, P. (2007) 'Introduction to the Theory of Person-centred Therapy', in M. Cooper, M. O'Hara, P. F. Schmid and G. Watt (eds) *The Handbook of Person-Centred Psychotherapy and Counselling* (New York: Palgrave Macmillan).

Schlegoff, E.A. (1963) 'Toward a Reading of Psychiatric Theory', *Berkeley Journal of Sociology*, 8: 61–91.

Schlegoff, E.A. (1968) 'Sequencing in Conversational Openings', *American Anthropologist*, 70 (6): 1075–95.

Schlegoff, E.A. (1972) 'Notes on a Conversational Practice: Formulating Place', in D.N. Sudnow (ed.) *Studies in Social Interaction* (New York: Free Press).

Schegloff, E.A. (1982) 'Discourse as an Interactional Achievement: Some Uses of "uh huh" and Other Things that Come between Sentences', in D.Tannen (ed.) Georgetown University Roundtable on Language and Linguistics, *Analyzing Discourse: Text and Talk* (Washington D.C.: Georgetown University Press).

Schlegoff, E.A., (1988) 'Discourse as an Interactional Achievement II: An Exercise in Conversation Analysis', in D.Tannen (ed.) *Linguistics in Context: Connecting Observation and Understanding, Lectures from the 1985 LSA/TESOL and HEH Institutes* (Norwood, NJ: Ablex).

Schlegoff, E.A. (1990) 'The Organization of Sequences as a Source of Coherence in Talk-in-Interaction', in B. Dorval (ed.) *Conversational Organization and its Development* (Norwood, N.J.: Ablex).

Schlegoff, E.A. (1991) 'Reflections on Talk and Social Structure', in D. Boden and D. Zimmerman (eds) *Talk and Social Structure* (Cambridge: Polity Press).

Schlegoff, E.A. (1993) 'Reflections on Quantification in the Study of Conversation', *Research on Language and Social Interaction*, 26 (1): 99–128.

Schegloff, E. A. (1997) 'Whose text? Whose context?' *Discourse & Society* 8 (2): 165–87.

Schegloff, E.A. (1998) 'Reflections on Studying Prosody in Talk-in-Interaction', *Language and Speech*, 41 (3/4): 235–63.

Schegloff, E.A. (2007) *Sequence Organization in Interaction: A Primer in Conversation Analysis,* vol. 1 (Cambridge: Cambridge University Press).

Schutz, A. (1967) *The Phenomenology of the Social World* (Evanston. IL: Northwestern University Press).

Selvik, R., Stephenson, D., Plaza, C. and Sugden, B. (2004) 'EAP Impact on Work, Relationship, and Health Outcomes', *Journal of Employee Assistance*, 34 (2): 18–22.

Shapiro, D.A. and Shapiro, D. (1982) 'Meta-analysis of Comparative Therapy Outcome Studies: A Replication and Refinement', *Psychological Bulletin*, 92: 581–604.

Sharry, J., Madden, B. and Darmody, M. (2001) *Becoming a Solution Detective: A Strength- based Guide to Brief Therapy* (London: BT Press).

Shiang, J. and Bongar, B. (1995) 'Brief and Crisis Psychotherapy in Theory and Practice', in B. Bongar and L. Beutler (eds) *Comprehensive Textbook of Psychotherapy: Theory and Practice* (Oxford: Oxford University Press).

Smith, M.L. and Glass, G.V. (1977) 'Meta-analysis of Psychotherapy Outcome Studies', *American Psychologist*, 32: 752–60.

Smith, M.L., Glass, G.V. and Miller, T.I. (1980) *The Benefits of Psychotherapy* (Baltimore: The John Hopkins University Press).

Snyder, W.U. (1945) 'An Investigation of the Nature of Non-directive Psychotherapy', *Journal of General Psychology*, 33: 193–223.

Spence, D. (1984) *Narrative Truth and Historical Truth: Meaning and Interpretation in Psychoanalysis* (New York: Norton).

Stewart, R.E. and Chambless, D.L. (2009) 'Cognitive-behavioral Therapy for Adult Anxiety Disorders in Clinical Practice: A Meta-analysis of Effectiveness Studies', *Journal of Consultant Clinical Psychology*, 77: 595–606.

Stiles, W.B. (1992) *Describing Talk: A Taxonomy of Verbal Response Modes* (Newbury Park, CA: Sage).

Stiles, W.B. (2002) 'Assimilation of Problematic Experiences', in J.C. Norcross (ed.) *Psychotherapy Relationships that Work: Therapist Contributions and Responsiveness to Patients* (New York: Oxford University Press).

Stiles, W.B. (2008) 'Forward, Filling the Gaps', in A. Peräkylä, C. Antaki, S.Vehviläinen and I. Leudar (eds) *Conversation Analysis and Psychotherapy* (Cambridge: Cambridge University Press).

Stiles, W.B. and Shapiro, D.A. (1994) 'Disabuse of the Drug Metaphor: Psychotherapy Process-outcome Correlations', *Journal of Consulting and Clinical Psychology*, 62: 942–48.

Stiles, W.B. and Shapiro, D.A. and Firth-Cozens, J.A. (1988) 'Verbal Response Mode Use in Contrasting Psychotherapies: A within Subjects Comparison', *Journal of Consulting and Clinical Psychology*, 56: 727–33.

Strauss, A. and Corbin, J. (1998) *Basics of Qualitative Research: Techniques and Procedures for Developing Grounded Theory* (2nd edn, Thousand Oaks, CA: Sage).

Streeck, U. (2004) *Auf den ersten Blick: Psychotherapeutische Beziehungen unter dem Mikroskop.* (Stuttgart: Klee-Cotta).

Streeck, U. (2008) 'A Psychotherapist's View of Conversation Analysis', in A. Peräkylä, C. Antaki, S. Vehviläinen and I. Leudar (eds) *Conversation Analysis and Psychotherapy* (Cambridge: Cambridge University Press).

Strupp, H. (1978) 'Psychotherapy Research and Practice: An Overview', in S.L. Garfield and A.E. Bergin (eds) *Handbook of Psychotherapy and Behavior Change* (2nd edn, New York: Wiley).

Taylor, D. (2008) 'Psychoanalytic and Psychodynamic Therapies for Depression: The Evidence Base', *Advances in Psychiatric Treatment*, 14: 401–43.

Ten Have, P. (1999) *Doing Conversational Analysis: A Practical Guide* (London: Sage).

Ten Have, P. (2001) 'Applied Conversation Analysis', in A. McHoul and M. Rapley (eds) *How to Analyse Talk in Institutional Settings* (London and New York: Continuum).

Ten Have, P. (2006) 'Conversation Analysis Versus Other Approaches to Discourse', *Special Issue: FOS Reviews IV- Thematic Issues* 7 (2).

Ten Have, P. (2007) *Doing Conversation Analysis: A Practical Guide* (2nd edn, London: Sage).

Ten Have, P. and Psathas, G. (1995) *Situated Order: Studies in the Social Organisation of Talk and Embodied Activities* (Washington D.C.: University Press of America, Inc.).

Tenzer, E. (2011) 'Burnout ist eine Form der Depression', in *Psychologie Heute*, Heft 12 (Weinheim), 30–3.

Teusch, L., Böhme, H. and Gastpar, M. (1997) 'The Benefit of an Insight Oriented and Experiential Approach on Panic and Agoraphobia Symptoms: Results of a Controlled Comparison of Client-centered Therapy and a Combination with Behavioural Exposure', *Psychotherapy and Psychosomatics*, 66: 293–301.

Teusch, L., Finke, J. and Böhme, H. (1995) 'Grundlagen eines Manuals für die gesprächspsychotherapeutische Behandlung von Panik und Agoraphobie'

(Fundamental principles of a manual for client-centered therapy of panic and agoraphobia), *Psychotherapeut*, 40: 88–95.

Vandenbos, G. R., Cummings, N.A. and DeLeon, P.H. (1995) 'A Century of Psychotherapy: Economic and Environmental Influences', in D.K. Freedheim (ed.) *History of Psychotherapy: A Century of Change* (Washington D.C.: American Psychological Association).

Vehviläinen, S. (2003a) 'Preparing and Delivering Interpretations in Psycho-analytic Interaction', *Text* 23: 573–606.

Vehviläinen, S. (2003b) 'Avoiding Providing Solutions: Orienting to the Ideal of Students' Self-Directedness in Counselling Interaction', *Discourse Studies*, 5 (3): 389–414.

Vehviläinen, S. (2008) 'Identifying and Managing Resistance in Psychoanalytic Interaction', in A. Peräkylä, C.Antaki, S.Vehviläinen and I. Leudar (eds) *Conversation Analysis and Psychotherapy* (Cambridge: Cambridge University Press).

Von Rosenstiel, L. and Nerdinger, F.W. (2011) *Grundlagen der Organisationspsychologie. Basiswissen und Anwendungshinweise* (Stuttgart: Auflage).

Voutilainen, L., Peräkylä, A. and Ruusuvuori, J.E. (2010) 'Therapeutic Change in Interaction: Conversation Analysis of a Transforming Sequence', *Psychotherapy Research*, 21 (3): 348–65.

Wampold, B. E. (2001) *The Great Psychotherapy Debate: Models, Methods, and Findings* (Lawerence Erlbaum Associates, Inc.)

Watson, J.C. and Greenberg, L.S. (1996) 'Pathways to Change in the Psychotherapy of Depression: Relating Process to Session Change and Outcome', *Psychotherapy*, 33: 262–74.

Weber, M. (1963) *The Sociology of Religion* (Boston: Beacon Press).

Wessely, S. (2001) 'Randomised Controlled Trials: The Gold Standard?' In C. Mace, S. Moorey and B. Roberts (eds) *Evidence in the Psychological Therapies* (London: Brunner-Routledge).

West, L., Lee, A. and Poynton, C. (2012) 'Becoming Depressed at Work: A Study of Worker Narratives', *Journal of Workplace Behavioural Health*, 27: 196–212.

Wetherell, M. (1998) 'Positioning and Intepretative Repetoires: Conversation Analysis and Post-Structuralism in dialogue', *Discourse and Society*, 9 (3): 387–412.

Wilson, G.T. and Fairburn, C.G. (1993) 'Cognitive Treatments for Eating Disorders', *Journal of Consulting and Clinical Psychology*, 61: 261–69.

Wittchen H.U. and Jacobi, F. (2005) 'Size and Burden of Mental Disorders in Europe – A Critical Review and Appraisal of 27 Studies', *European Neuropsychopharmacology*, 15 (4): 357–76.

Witty, M.C. (2007) 'Client-Centered Therapy', in N. Kazantzis, L. L'Abate and F. Gerard (eds) *Handbook of Homework Assignments in Psychotherapy: Research, Practice and Prevention* (New York: Springer).

World Health Organization (2007) 'Ten Statistical Highlights in Global Public Health', Retrieved from www.who.int/whosis/whostat.

Yngve, V. (1970) 'On Getting a Work in Edgewise', *Papers from the 6th Regional Meeting, Chicago Linguistics Society*, 16–18 April (Chicago: Chicago Linguistics Society).

Zimmerman, D.H. (1984) 'Talk and its Occasion: The Case of Calling the Police', in D. Schriffin (ed.) *Meaning, Form, and Use in Context: Linguistic Applications* (Washington, D.C.: Georgetown University Press).

Index

hypnosis, 9, 15
hysteria, 1

incongruence, 69
institutional interaction, 32–4,
    64–5, 126
institutional power, 49
interaction issues, 29–43, 167–8
  asymmetrical relationships, 35–9
  doctor-patient interactions, 34, 36,
    44–5
  institutional interaction, 32–4,
    64–5, 126
  interactional models of
    psychotherapy, 29–31
interpersonal process recall, 70
interpretative trajectory, 51–2
interruptions, 41–3
intonation, 97–8
introspection, 8

James, W., 14
Jefferson, G., 72, 80, 81
Jung, C., 14

Kasermann, M.L., 37
Kleinian therapists, 1–2

Lambert, M.J., 18
Leudar, I., 35, 56
libido, 1
listening, 4
  reflective, 6
local, 26
Logos, 10

Madill, A., 103
magical cures, 9, 15, 16
maladaptive thinking, 3
managed care, 2, 19
managers, 145, 149–67, 171
Mazeland, H., 80, 82
McLeod, J., 71
McMartin, C., 55
medical model, 29
medicine men, 8–9
Mellinger, W.M., 45
membership categorization devices
    (MCDs), 145

mental distress, impact of, in the
    workplace, 145–7
mesmerism, 9, 15
Middle Ages, 9
Miller, W.R., 97
miracle question, 29, 56
misalignments, 125, 138–9
Mooerman, M., 35
Müller, F.E., 81, 82
Muntigl, P., 81

New Testament, 9
non-directive techniques, 21
note-taking, 99

oblique proposals, 38–9
occupational health, 151
Oedipus complex, 13, 14
optimistic questions, 55, 56
overlapping talk, 41–3

panic disorder, 20
passive recipiency, 90
Pavlov, I., 14
Peräkylä, A., 7, 33, 36, 40, 51, 56, 61,
    76, 80, 101
person-centred therapy, 4–5, 12, 30,
    31, 37, 40, 57–8
  efficacy of, 20–4
  empathic approach, 101–2
  goal of, 174n1
  role of therapist in, 48–9, 51, 74–5
Peyrot, M., 38
phenomenology, 71
philosophy, 11
Pinel, P., 12
positive questioning devices, 38
power/powerlessness, 35, 37, 39, 45,
    49–50, 74–5
preferred, 120
problem definition, 57
processing mode, 70
process research, 24–5
Proctor, G., 37, 167
prosody, 82–3
psychiatry, 14
psychoanalysis, 13, 30, 52–3
psychoanalytical theory, 15
psychodynamic therapy, 4, 52

Printed and bound in the United States of America